Tom Bradley

J Gregory Payne

Scott Ratzan

TOM BRADLEY
THE IMPOSSIBLE
DREAM

Tom Bradley proudly waves the Olympic flag at Opening Day Ceremonies of the 1984 Los Angeles Olympic Games. (Courtesy of Long Photography)

TOM BRADLEY
THE IMPOSSIBLE
DREAM

A Biography

by

J. Gregory Payne

and

Scott C. Ratzan

ROUNDTABLE PUBLISHING INC.
SANTA MONICA   CALIFORNIA

First printing, 1986

Library of Congress Catalog Card Number—85-052373

Photos by Rick Browne, page 132, copyright © 1973; pages 172, 228, 244 and 272, copyright © 1982; page 294, copyright © 1983; page 344, copyright © 1986; page 344, copyright © 1982. Reprinted by permission.

Photo by Jonathan Selig/LPI, page ii, copyright © 1984.

Cartoon by Paul Conrad for the Los Angeles Times, page 272, copyright © 1986, Los Angeles Times Syndicate. Reprinted by permission.

PRINTED IN THE UNITED STATES OF AMERICA

To   **Frances, Dawne, Jerry, Tami,
Zulene, Jim, and Janice
for their faith, support and love,**

**and to Crenner. . . . and mothers everywhere
who dare their children to dream.**

Acknowledgements

Tracing the roots and chronicling Tom Bradley's dream was a cooperative effort made possible through the assistance of hundreds of people in government, business, labor, politics, education, and the arts, as well as the countless friends and colleagues throughout the world who were unselfishly eager to share particular stories, personal letters, and accounts of a man they often refer to as "Tom." The one consistent trait most commonly associated with Tom Bradley during the hundreds of hours of interviews with friend and foe alike, was "honesty"—a rare association for today's public servant.

While space does not allow us to properly thank all of those who contributed to this publication, we do want to personally acknowledge Tom Bradley and his family for all the interviews, photographs, and untiring cooperation which made the project possible. Colleagues at City Hall provided invaluable assistance with names and addresses of those who might offer pertinent information of Bradley's life. The result was an intricate web—a career of contacts in California, America, and throughout the world.

In addition to the Bradleys, there are others who deserve special recognition for their assistance and concern: Richard Alatorre, Ken Anderson, John Argue, Robert A. Baukus, Jessie Mae Beavers, Leroy Berry, Lloyd Bitzer, Sissila Bok, Bishop H. H. Brookins, Edmund G. "Pat" Brown, Anton Calleia, Connie Chappell, Ruth Anne Clark, Larry Connor, Ken Crannell, Raye Cunningham, Ed Davis, Grace Montanez Davis, Phil Depoian, Claudia Deske, Edwin Diamond, Steve Doran, Mary Jane England, Tommy Ford, Betty Frailey, Carol Franco, Duane Garrett, Walter Gerken, Jean Gibson, Meg Gilbert, Alex Haley, Sara Hankins, Harold Harder, Georgia Hill, Michael Hird, Ted Hollingworth, Michael Horton, Bob Kholos and his unpublished manuscript, *The Life and Times of A Jewish Press Secretary,* George Davis Kieffer, Maureen Kindel, Mike Kittross, Win Knowlton, John Knox, Allen E. Koenig, Fran La Shoto, Bee Canterbury Lavery, Jackie Liebergott, Martin Linsky, Walt Littlefield, Ray Locke, Nancy Altman-Lupu, Linda Lyke, Jack MacKenzie, Bernadette MacPherson, John Marlier, Eileen Matthews, Carl McBain, Kathy Meany, Dodo Meyer, Marie Nichols, Ron Niles, Gary Orren, Omar Paxson, Jules Radcliff, Andy Rancer, Stephen Reinhardt, Ira Reiner, Ray Remy, Julius Richmond, Nelson Rising, Bill Robertson, Fred Schnell, Charlotte Shaw, Sanford Sigoloff, Vito Silvestri, Norman Smith, Tom Sullivan, Jack Tenner, John Tunney, Rick Tuttle, Ali Webb, Maury Weiner, Chris Weir, Jerry Weintraub, Sam Williams, David Wolper, Sam Yorty, and John Zacharis.

A special thanks to Irving Stone and Ken McCormick who believed in the project, and to our New York editor Beth Rashbaum for her valuable assistance in the development of the book. In addition, Rick Allen, John Andrews, Chris Barboza, Maya Bohsali, David Cohen, Lynn Disbrow, Ervin Fang, Chris Francese, Tricia Goodnow, Keith Krobeth, David Loftus, Peter Loge, Rich McGuire, Jim Meehan, Tami Ratzan, Marc Reisler, Lorna Schmidt, Christi Schutts, Craig Vachon, Gina Yarbrough, among others helped in the compilation of sources, phone calls, and transcription of over two hundred interviews.

Finally, our gratitude to the Emerson College community, to Michel Fattah, our publisher, and to Shirley Pescia and Linda Carwin of Roundtable. A special thanks to Jim Neyland for his invaluable critical eye in final editing. All have helped translate our faith in a book into a reality.

J. Gregory Payne and Scott C. Ratzan

April 1986, Boston

Contents

Foreword

by Alex Haley

When one ventures to comment upon a current biography, and particularly if a black person is the book's subject, as is the case with *Tom Bradley, the Impossible Dream,* the reader definitely should keep in mind that, to a considerable extent, our society has improved in racial aspects since that person's childhood.

Tom Bradley, the boy, the youth, and the young man, competed within a racially far more difficult society than similarly ambitious young black people would tend to encounter these days. So the successive ordeals he confronted—and coped with—deserve to be multiplied or magnified at least ten times in comparison with what similar young men would be faced with today.

In the time and social setting when Tom Bradley was growing up, it was no small achievement for a black person to acquire even a high school diploma, not to mention a college degree, and it would have been extremely foolish for that person to consider it possible to become the mayor of Los Angeles.

My own presumption in accepting an invitation to provide the foreword to this book is that I have known Tom Bradley for over a decade. We were introduced by my manager Louis Blau, who earlier had expressed his belief that it was important for Los Angeles to elect Bradley as mayor. We did attend Bradley's mayoral victory party within a few weeks. Subsequently, I have come to know the mayor on a more personal basis, and I have heard him discussed at length by others who know him as boss or friend, as political colleague or ally or adversary, or as foe or fan. From my experience and knowledge of the man, I feel that the authors of this book have captured the essence of Tom Bradley, of his struggles to rise as a scholarly and ambitious young man, as a policeman, and as a young politician who has since become a veteran.

Certainly one cornerstone that underlies Tom Bradley's escalating political success was the impact of his early experiences with racism, not only against blacks but against other minorities as well. It was these experiences that instilled distaste for any form of ethnic polarization, regardless of the source or the target, and helped to develop his career trademark of serving not some but all of the people. As a mayor, he has clearly and definitely displayed, particularly to younger politicians, the wisdom, indeed the necessity, of developing and coalescing a broad-based constituency.

Another of the Tom Bradley cornerstones—a tradition that is frequent among a widely diverse range of black achievers—is that his early life was rooted strongly within the church. Significantly, the family church was where he and Ethel met and were married. Ethel was a beautician with a drive similar to Tom's to get up and go and achieve something of herself. He was drawn to Ethel, not simply because she was pretty, but also because her strong desire for success approximated his own.

Finally, the hardworking mother of Tom Bradley supplied his anchor, with her constant encouragement, even when his dreams seemed ridiculously unattainable.

The young athlete Tom Bradley symbolized the using of sports ability to increase opportunities beyond what he would have had otherwise, another black tradition both then and today. If you visit any American city's black communities around sundown, every playground will contain scores of youthful basketballers getting in the loving last shots and agile body moves of that day, each and all of them fantasizing themselves to be some superstar or other such as Kareem or Moses or Magic or Dr. J. But unfortunately few among the local playgrounds' stars realize that the higher odds for success depend upon applying comparable energy to academic pursuit, as young Tom Bradley seemed to know instinctively. As a policeman walking a beat, he talked himself hoarse trying to drum this into the heads of young blacks on the Los Angeles streets—even as his private dream was one day to be the first black mayor of that city.

It is as a fellow author that I am able to see the major problem that the authors of this book faced and have dealt with as best they could. The authors ultimately found that not only is Tom Bradley characteristically the stoic and impassive politician, but that also has become his inherent style in almost any public interfacings. Politically this has proved to be a distinct positive, for time and again all those who know how Tom Bradley functions as a mayor are most aware that beneath his stoic surface there is a granite determination to accomplish his intended objectives. Even those who oppose and detract Tom Bradley, for political or personal reasons, still fully respect that he is a tough administrator who makes tough decisions and then makes them stick.

But from an author's point of view, an inherently impassive stoic can easily prove to be a difficult subject to write about—as this book sometimes reflects. For the biography, like its subject, tends to be impassive in its account of a man's life with no storms, rarely a squall, and just a few ripples of emotion. This is due largely to the fact that Tom Bradley does not relish discussing his emotions.

Nevertheless, the authors, being trained specialists, researched widely and ably, finally obtaining a mass of raw data, which they have kept categorized and focused to give the readers fresh insights into Mayor Tom Bradley. The authors' discipline has kept this book from being just another volume of puffery or praises for its subject.

For the story of Tom Bradley is told with an omnipresent critical examination of the famous and popular mayor, who is— and should be—one of the most important and studied political figures of our time. It candidly addresses how he met his challenges and his failures, and how he coped with his failures, usually managing ultimately to achieve what he had wanted.

Overall, I am unaware of any other book that can afford a reader a better look at how a young black from a small southern town realizes the vital importance of gaining an education, and then—dreaming to achieve the seeming impossible—in his calm, stoic way, he incredibly does actually achieve much more than he previously had dared to dream.

Young Tom Bradley (circled) poses with his Somerton Grammar School Class. (Courtesy Yuma Daily Sun, Yuma, AZ)

A young man, Tom enjoys an outing in the San Bernardino Mountains. (Bradley Family Collection)

1

The Birth of the Dream

"When you set out for Ithaka, pray that your road's a long one, full of adventure, full of discovery. . . . Arriving there is what you're destined for. But don't hurry the journey at all."

—C. P. Cavafy

The Coliseum was silent when Juan Antonio Samaranch passed the white flag emblazoned with the black, green, red, blue, and yellow circles to the Mayor of Los Angeles. Across the world, two-and-a-half billion people, the largest audience in the history of mankind, watched as Mayor Tom Bradley officially welcomed 140 countries to the opening ceremonies of the Twenty-third Olympiad. To Bradley, this was the culmination of a ten-year struggle to bring the Games once again to the City of Angels. As his eyes fell on the flag's five Olympic rings, symbolizing the union of the five continents, which had sent 7,800 athletes to Los Angeles, he looked back on his own long journey and its Olympian struggles.

Like so many of those who would be competing in the Games, Bradley had overcome tremendous odds to reach this point. He had been told throughout his life that some goals were impossible to attain. Now, Bradley remembered the words of a speech he had planned to make just two years before, on election night in 1982. The speech was a public reaffirmation of his belief in California as a very special place, a frontier land where the old-fashioned values of hard work and faith still had meaning, where the Olympic motto *"Citius, Altius, Fortius"*—"Swifter, Higher, Stronger"—could still serve as practical advice to its young people.

The opportunity to deliver that speech had eluded Bradley in his first try to become Governor of California. But now the torch that Jesse Owens' granddaughter carried into the Coliseum with the Olympic flame did more than just officially open the 1984 Games. It rekindled Tom Bradley's determination to build upon his already distinguished career, to rededicate himself to the values embodied in that as yet undelivered speech. The flare of the Coliseum's Olympic torch bathed the grandson of slaves in a light seen around the world. It marked a special moment in what some would call Tom Bradley's "impossible dream."

During the Reconstruction period, the move from the Carolinas to Texas promised the hope for a better life, a chance to be independent and to make an honest living. The prospect of sharecropping—leasing land and putting out one's own crop—was the motivation for thousands to make the trek westward from the plantations of the Old South and the Deep South.

Among the hopeful who made the trip to Texas in the 1880s were the parents of Lee Bradley, bringing their young children with them. Surveying the broad plains, they decided this was where they would make good on the promise of their recently gained freedom. Calvert, Texas, located between Waco and Houston, would become their home. Its wide open spaces seemed welcoming; here was the land of opportunity they had longed for.

Calvert blossomed into one of Texas' most promising towns by the early nineteenth century. Cotton was the common currency of the area, and for awhile Calvert could boast of the world's largest cotton gin, which treated the cotton crops harvested by the Brazos riverbottom farmers. In the 1870s, in the wake of the Civil War, the Houston and Texas Central Railroad had brought over 30,000 refugees to Central Texas by way of Calvert, which was now the state's fourth largest city. For a time, due to King Cotton's promise, it appeared that Calvert might even rival Houston or Dallas, but its promise quickly faded. A yellow fever epidemic combined with tornados, floods, and devastating fires, took a toll on the town's population. But even in bad times, Calvert looked good to former slaves.

The Bradley family had heard that Texas was big, but they had not realized it would be quite so vast and open. Why, on the outskirts of Calvert—which was just a town for seed, supplies, and selling crops—one couldn't even see a hill or, for that matter, anything else for miles around. Nothing except the disciplined straight rows of cotton, planted as far as the eye could see, the rows stretching like roads, so far that they seemed to just disappear in the crystal blue skies. Yes, Texas was different from the Carolinas. Here there was neither a mountain nor a master to keep one's hopes hemmed in.

Leasing the flat land in Central Texas offered the Bradleys and thousands like them the opportunity to plant, harvest, and sell their crops, to put in a good day's work in exchange for what they hoped would be a good day's pay. Here families like theirs could be free and independent.

They hoped that sharecropping could be the means of making a decent living and offering a brighter future for the young ones. There was the dream that, one day, their children or at least their grandchildren could go to school. They could get an education that might really make the difference. They might be able to control their own lives.

No longer would the families be mere chattels—broken up, shipped away, and passed on like human machines from one generation to the next, under the old southern rules. Instead, sharecropping seemed like a chance for a real partnership with the Texas soil. Gone would be the days of clearing and ploughing the land, of preparing and caring for the planted seeds, only to see each year's harvest strengthen the landowner's grip.

But something went wrong. Texas failed to live up to its promise. The spirituals sung in the Texas fields echoed those sung before the Civil War, with the promise of heavenly rewards to those denied opportunity on earth. The early vigorous hopes were slowly replaced by the same bleak outlook they had hoped to leave behind. Like those before them, their lives were filled with futility and despair.

Few sharecroppers found consolation in the grueling eighteen-hour days picking cotton, from hot, sticky July to dark, dreary December, when the ice-glazed cotton bolls literally stuck to blue frostbitten hands, as they tried to retrieve as many seeds as possible for the next season. More often than not, when the crops looked good and the plants were laden with huge white billowy puffs, cotton prices plunged. The big planters, whose crops glutted the market, could survive low prices; the poor could not. The Bradleys, in their frustration and despair, often longed for the security of their old plantation days. Though there had been no freedom, no chance ever to realize dreams and aspirations, at least they knew their families were fed.

In Calvert, as in other agrarian communities throughout Texas and the Southwest, it was only through long-term credit that families like the Bradleys managed to get through from one year to the next. Legal slavery had been replaced by economic servitude. Still, there were those who clung to the belief that the next year's crops would prove to be better. They preached and prayed for prosperity to bless all of God's children—all of those who had worked so hard and who had remained so patient, devoted, and faithful, year in and year out.

But patience seemed to fade with each passing harvest. Hope may have been a tonic to a weary spirit, but it didn't pay the bills, nor did it provide an answer for the ever-present question in the eyes of the children. Why did life have to be this way? Many came to realize that their vision of a bright future in farming was nothing more than an impossible dream.

As Lee Bradley reached maturity, there was little opportunity to do more than pursue the futile dream of sharecropping that his parents had known. He met and fell in love with a beautiful young woman from Beaumont, Texas, named Crenner Hawkins. The Hawkins family had been in Texas for some time, but their background of slavery and servitude was not greatly different from the Bradleys.

By the time Lee Bradley and Crenner Hawkins became husband and wife in Calvert, both had worked the cotton fields for many years. Neither had had a choice. There simply was no other work available for able-bodied people who had managed to acquire no more than a fifth-grade education. Their pockmarked hands, scarred by the stickers on the cotton bolls, and their left shoulders worn down by the weight of the cotton sacks were emblems of the futility of a sharecropper's life. But neither Cren-ner nor Lee would give up easily. Their determination was etched deep in the lines of their faces. They shared a belief that by working together they could build a future for their growing children.

Despite such optimism, Lee and Crenner saw their condition worsen each year. Bad weather and poor prices translated into deeper debts. Each fall after the crops were harvested, Lee dreaded the thought of another trip into town to see the cred-itors, of having to ask the storekeepers of Calvert for still another extension on paying his bills. At Christmastime, instead of going into town to buy clothes and toys for the kids or a new iron skillet for Crenner, Lee found himself each year begging for more time from the landlord.

The walk to town seemed longer during those trips in bleak December. There wasn't much to offer to those the family owed, so Lee was forced to borrow against next year's crops to pay off the previous year's lease. Anything left over was used to buy seed in the hope that next year's harvest would cover the debt, buy food, and pay the rent on their small log cabin. Though scarcely big enough for two to live in, the shack also sheltered the Bradley babies, five of whom were unable to survive infancy under such conditions.

The hardship affected every member of the family. The sur-viving children joined the parents in the fields to help as much as they could. At this time, there were only two—Lawrence Bradley, born in 1911, and Tom Bradley, born December 27, 1917.

In the years when cotton prices seemed promising and the outlook optimistic, the weather invariably failed. There would be drenching rains that went on for days, beating against the cabin's tin roof, each drop reminding Lee and Crenner of another day lost in getting the crop out. Other years no rain fell, and the leaves of the young cotton plants withered and died in the hot Texas sun.

Life in Calvert was full of hardships. Maybe God was trying to tell them something. Any way they added it up, it always came out the same—disaster, despair, and, for five babies, death. The only surviving female child, Willa Mae Bradley, was born in 1921.

The old shed where the family stored seed and supplies was more often than not virtually bare. Facing such obstacles year in and year out, Lee Bradley saw he was going nowhere. He concluded after yet another crop failure that he, like so many other sharecroppers of the period, had to face up to the situation. There was no future for him in Calvert—or, for that matter, in sharecropping.

He had to find a better way of life for his wife and three children. Maybe the city would provide the answers.

With the few belongings they had, the Bradleys packed up and moved to Dallas in 1921. There, Lee took on numerous odd jobs working as a cook, waiter, and handyman. He took any work that might help pay the bills for his growing family. Crenner found sporadic work as a maid. Yet she worried about being away from her children so much; she wanted to attend to the needs of her family. After two frustrating and difficult years, Lee and Crenner concluded that life in Dallas wasn't the solution. The opportunities were as bleak in their way as those in Calvert had been. Lee and Crenner now looked to the west to fulfill their hope of a better tomorrow.

The long cross-country journey was filled with all-too-vivid reminders of the segregated policies of the era. The Bradleys were forced to sleep in their old jalopy, as no boarding houses would allow blacks to stay overnight. Because of a similar "whites only" rule at coffee shops, Crenner went to grocery stores to buy ingredients for the bologna and mashed potato sandwiches she prepared each day to be eaten in the car. The Bradley children were becoming painfully aware of the stigma that dark skin carried throughout America.

In 1924, when Tom was six, the family arrived in the Arizona farming community of Somerton and moved in with relatives. There Crenner remained, enrolling the children in school, young Tom for the first time. Lee journeyed on to California, in search of a job in Los Angeles.

While in school in Somerton, Thomas developed an intense love of reading. There was no favorite topic. He simply devoured any text he could get his hands on. As Bradley tells it now, "While other students were out playing ball I would often slip into my seat during recess and read a book. Anything that gave me a new experience. *Moby Dick* was my favorite because [of] the adventure and determination in its pages." Bradley's life and that of his parents was full of both. And, as he remembers, he was taught from very early on that determination, channeled by a good education, was the route to a life that would offer more than the subsistence-level jobs his parents were forced to take. "Seeing me read all the time, my parents, especially my mother, nurtured this desire to work hard, to study hard."

But it wasn't just his parents urging him to a better life. Already, at six, he had had enough personal experience of the grueling, thankless work of a cotton picker to want something beyond that for himself. When he was too little to go to the fields, he had watched his mother and daddy, aunts, uncles, and cousins harvest cotton. He saw them bending over the long rows and stuffing the white cotton bolls into their torn bags. He remembered seeing the swelling fingers and sore hands, the bruises and cuts from the stickers on the bolls of cotton that would pierce the skin if you didn't pick it just right. When he was old enough, he joined the work force himself. One day, six-year-old Tom was in the field picking on a row, when one of his cousins quickly yanked his arm away from the next plant. A few feet ahead under the straggled branches of cotton lay a rattlesnake, coiled and ready to strike. His cousin killed the snake.

Already disinclined to a life in which each day's labor added up to twenty-five pounds of cotton picked and a few cents in wages, Bradley knew after the snake episode that he had to escape the meager confines of life in Somerton. He was glad when his mother took him and his brothers out west to join their father in 1924.

The period between 1920 and 1930 witnessed the greatest influx of blacks into Los Angeles. There were over fifteen thousand blacks out of over half a million population in Los Angeles (576,000) by 1920, representing a doubling of the black community in the previous decade. It would more than double again—to 35,000—by 1930. When Lee arrived in Los Angeles, he found the black population located primarily in Boyle Heights, the Ninth and Maple Street area, and in neighborhoods collectively known as the "East Side." Not too many years after that, Watts would become the nucleus for black immigration. According to noted historian Mary Jane Hewitt, the black concentration was so heavy in Watts that city officials moved quickly to annex the subdivision into Los Angeles. The reason? Fear that the community would "undoubtedly elect a black mayor."

The Bradleys' hope for a better life in Los Angeles would take a long time to be fulfilled. By the time Crenner Bradley and her children left Arizona for Los Angeles in the fall of 1924, Lee had been searching for employment for almost a year. During those months Lee, like so many others who had come to California, had looked in vain for a secure job.

Lee's pockets were near empty when Crenner and the children arrived in Los Angeles. The waves of immigrants had increased the keen competition for the few jobs that were available to the unskilled worker. To meet the immediate needs of his family, Lee was forced to be away for long periods of time, working as a porter on the Santa Fe Railroad and as a crew member on ocean liners that traveled up and down the coast. But his long absences did not diminish young Tom Bradley's feelings for his father: "He loved all of us kids and brought us treats whenever he was on leave from the boats he worked up and down the coast to Mexico and Washington. It was like our Christmas—we were always happy to see him come home."

Life continued to be a struggle for the Bradleys in Los Angeles. The family moved frequently, as many as four times in one year. In reflecting on this period, Tom Bradley comments, "Although I never asked why, I am sure some of the moves had to do with our not being able to pay the rent." Two more children were born to the family after their arrival in Los Angeles—Ellis, in 1929, who suffered from cerebral palsy, and Howard, in 1933.

In the attempt to meet the growing family's economic needs, Crenner Bradley worked as a maid, usually for a different family each day of the week. Leaving the house at daybreak, she returned after dark, compelled by circumstances to leave her children to fend for themselves. It may have been then that Tom first became aware of his ability to resolve conflicts. The mediation skills he used with his brothers and sisters would later distinguish his political career. With Crenner working most of the day and Lee away much of the time, the younger Bradleys had to learn to be on their own. Everyone had to contribute. Lawrence, Tom's older brother, dropped out of school and helped the family by working in the fields of the farms in Orange and San Bernardino counties. Although Tom was only the second oldest, it was he who took responsibility for running the house and making decisions. He seemed to take a special interest, and with Lee and her oldest away so much of the time, Crenner appreciated all the assistance she could get, especially in matters with money. Tom worked out how much they should spend on rent and food. He always tried to save some in the old jar—even a nickel or a dime—for a family rainy day. From a very early age he showed a dependability and maturity beyond his years, and Crenner came to rely on him more and more.

A serious child, he was more apt to spend his little free time reading than playing ball with his brother Howard and sister Willa Mae or with the other kids of the neighborhood. Crenner was pleased that it was Tom who took a special liking to Ellis, her third oldest boy, who had a noticeable handicap. There would be nobody picking on Ellis with Tom always at his side. Childhood friend Lowell Steward remembers that, if you picked on Ellis, it meant you would have to tangle with Tom. Sundays found Tom singing in the youth choir of the New Hope Baptist Church, which pleased his devout mother.

Absent from her family out of necessity, though thoroughly dedicated to their needs and wants, Crenner Bradley instilled in her children the importance of working hard and abiding by the Ten Commandments. She was proud of their hard-won independence, and even at the height of the Depression, she refused the relief money to which the family was more than entitled. She reasoned that there were poor people who couldn't work who really needed the money. After all, God had kept her healthy to provide for her children.

Tom Bradley still regards his mother as his major role model. "She made so many sacrifices to keep the family provided for," Bradley recalls. "She was not home except late at night when she would return from work every day, exhausted from cooking someone else's meals and washing clothes. But the first thing she would do was to fix a meal for us for the following day and ask about our school work." Tom's favorite food was his mother's sweet potato pie. However, he remembers, she had a "real artistry to take a cheap piece of meat and prepare it well—tongues, ham hocks, neck bones, beans. She made the most of what we had."

There was little time for the type of conversation and activities that characterize most middle-class families. The Bradleys were living in grinding poverty. But what they lacked in money, they made up in spiritual and moral riches, for Crenner was a living example of the Golden Rule.

One incident from his childhood is still fresh in Tom's mind. "Upon returning home from school one day, my friends told me about the storekeeper down the street who kept his candy out where it was easy to take. They had got plenty of it in the past." After surveying the situation, young Bradley capitulated to peer pressure and followed a friend into the store for some of the "free" candy. "But when I got home my mother asked me where I got the candy, and did I pay for it!" Bradley remembers the spanking he got and the terrible trip back to the store, where "I told the owner I had stolen the candy, paid him for it with money I had saved up from my paper route, and apologized."

Tom was a precociously responsible child, who from a very early age offered advice to his mother on many daily decisions. While all of her lot had been equally encouraged to make the most of school, Crenner noticed early that it was Tom who really wanted to be book wise. Far from regretting what many would regard as a lost childhood, Bradley says today that the deepest and fondest memories he has of his youth have to do with the relationship he enjoyed with his mother. She often read to Tom, Howard, Willa Mae, and Ellis particular passages from the Bible, and then expected each of her children to remember the verses. Usually Tom was the only one who could consistently recite the passage, and he came to know that the way to be sure he had done it correctly was to see the special smile she always had when she was pleased with her children. Tom would always remember that trait of hers. But even his mother's wisdom and goodness could not keep the evils of the world at bay.

One of Tom's earliest experiences of racial prejudice occurred shortly after the move to Los Angeles. Living in a mixed community with integrated schools in the West Temple area on the East Side, ten-year-old Tom enjoyed playing ball and studying at school with a new friend named Billy. But one day Billy didn't meet Tom to play kick the can. After school, the young Bradley asked his friend what was wrong. Embarrassed, Billy stared at the ground. He told Tom that his parents had warned him "not to play with any of the colored children on the block."

"I was shocked and didn't understand why our friendship had to end," Bradley recalls. Crenner had not discussed racial prejudice with him. When he returned home that evening, he asked his mother why people felt this way. She tried to comfort him, telling her son that some people didn't understand the Golden Rule. Although he and Billy continued to be friends, playing and studying where Billy's parents wouldn't see them, the recognition of prejudice helped shape Tom's character, impressing upon him at a very early age how damaging and painful racism can be to its victims.

But there were also positive experiences in those years. One of Tom's first teachers in Los Angeles, at the Rosemont Avenue Elementary School, he recalls, was "a loving, caring teacher, Mrs. Pearl Briley, who really took a liking to me. I think she noticed the potential and wanted to help shape it. She also helped out the family by bringing me clothing and shoes, because it was obvious that we were really poor." They were so poor, in fact, that Lowell Steward remembers that Tom wore overalls—which made the other kids call him "country boy"—and indeed sometimes did not have enough money for shoes.

Bradley credits Mrs. Briley with being one of the primary forces in his struggle for a good education. "She had such faith and was so supportive of me." Recalling the day when he was wrongfully accused of starting a fire in a vacant lot, he remembers that it was she who investigated the incident and cleared Bradley of wrongdoing. "It was very important to have that type of support during those early years," he now says.

If young Tom ever faltered in his commitment to school, Crenner Bradley was there to bolster him. One of her constant themes was how she and Lee had been confined to the most menial of jobs because of lack of opportunity to learn a trade or even to acquire a junior-high diploma, but that in Los Angeles in the 1930s, free education was available to all. She often reminded her brood of what it was like to pick cotton in the hot sun, telling them that education was their ticket out of the fields and to a better life. Tom, for whom she had the highest hopes, was urged to become a doctor.

To help provide outside income for the family, the two oldest Bradley children worked. With Lawrence in the fields, Tom obtained a paper route at the age of ten, earning $1.00 for every two hundred papers delivered in the downtown area. While other paper boys of the old *Los Angeles Record* were swiping pies from the local pie company and snagging free rides on the street-cars that then criss-crossed the downtown area, ten-year-old Tom followed a disciplined daily regimen. He would deliver his papers and then head directly home to study and complete the chores Crenner expected to be done when she returned at night.

On one of the rare occasions when he deviated from this daily pattern, Bradley recalls the price he paid. When he was about eleven, he and several of the other *Record* carriers decided to get back at an old man who had frequently threatened and screamed at the paperboys not to use the sidewalk in front of his house. The group approached the house and tossed some rocks onto the porch. The man appeared and chased the boys down the street.

Unfortunately for Tom, the man chose to follow him home, whereupon Crenner made Tom apologize. "And then when he left, I got the lecture of my life on respecting elders and the Golden Rule," Bradley remembers. Nor was there any arguing with Crenner, despite the way the old man had provoked the boys. "She had a way of just reaching down to your soul in the attempt to get her message across. Those lectures had a lasting effect and have remained a core part of my constitution ever since," Bradley adds. Still, young Tom did more than once make detours from the straight and narrow, and to this day he recalls with some pleasure his forays over the fence of a tamale and pickle factory near the family's home at 1369 Newton Street.

Tom attended Lafayette Junior High School where, like other members of the city's ethnic minorities, he was discouraged from entertaining lofty ambitions. "One of my most depressing memories," Bradley recalls, "is of the waste of talent that was a product of racial prejudice." Instead of pushing promising students to develop their potential, teachers and counselors urged Asians into stereotyped positions as gardeners and clerks, and "because there were no role models for people to emulate, blacks and Mexican-Americans were also channeled into the service professions." What it amounted to was a terrible waste of human resources. Here were talented people with no way out. Bradley states, "I often think back on all those gifted people with no outlet—so many ended up in jail or died of alcohol or drugs." But Tom himself was not discouraged. He never faltered in the self-confidence that Crenner had instilled in him, never doubted that persistence and a "can-do" attitude would pay off.

A favorite photo . . . running the quarter mile at UCLA, 1938. (Bradley Family Collection)

2

Tom's Key to Success—Education

*"Life is for dreaming dreams,
but few have the courage or will
to realize them."*

—Crenner Bradley

Even as a child, Tom Bradley seemed to attract people like a magnet, reaching beyond society's accepted boundaries. Perhaps part of his appeal had to do with his physical stature. Always taller and stronger than the other boys his age, he was constantly sought after by his peers. He had a natural aura of specialness, and his budding athletic abilities made him an immediate success on the playground, a force to be reckoned with. His early days playing football in the Central and the Slauson recreation centers began the discipline process that would later characterize his athletic and political careers.

His experience at those centers would be something he would always remember—a positive anchor in an environment of instability. "Perhaps it was these centers, whose role is so often overlooked as an important force in youngsters' lives," recalls Bradley, "where the program play-yard director influenced me to begin working toward all my goals in life."

The experience with the Central Recreation Center was "a critical turning point in my life!" remarks Bradley. It was at this center on 22nd and Central that Tom, with the help of an adept program director, began to tap into his athletic talents. "I realized early that this could be the only way I could hope to attend or even afford college. My only hope was an athletic scholarship."

Bradley began considering his educational future as early as the eighth grade. At the vocational counseling center at 14th and Hooper, where students received advice about what high-school courses to pursue, the 1930s attitude toward minority youngsters was evident. To Bradley, it was like hearing the same record over and over on the gramophone. He heard about the limited possibilities for minorities in modern society. He heard counselors tell even the most gifted students that there was little hope to break out of the menial job market. Bradley was told to give up his unrealistic plans for college, to take vocational training classes instead. But a determined Bradley resisted the call of "realism." As he reasoned, what was so unrealistic about believing in yourself? What was wrong with believing that the only real limits out there were those set by God?

This attitude baffled some of Tom's friends, and even his family. Lawrence admired Tom's spirit, but his years in the fields had somewhat dulled his own aspirations. Since he had little or no time for school, his aims were always toward jobs in manual labor. Howard wanted to believe that anyone could make it through effort and hard work, but he became more streetwise in his approach to life. However, Ellis—even with cerebral palsy— kept pushing on, perhaps in part to please Tom. Willa Mae was more like Tom—according to Crenner, they were "two peas in a pod"—and she was determined to have a career.

Yet, even many of Tom's physical education teachers expressed the same pessimistic outlook: "You are a good athlete," he was told, "but there is not enough opportunity out there for you to achieve success in sports. It won't be possible to get to college on a track scholarship." Each time the message seemed louder, but it was a message that didn't seem to sink in: ". . . my parents' faith in the importance of education was instilled in me so strongly that I constantly resisted that advice. My parents told me of the value of education. I believed them."

Despite all the time he put in helping his mother and working at odd jobs (once he and a friend grew okra and greens in a vacant lot to earn extra money) Bradley found time to continue his education on his own. Often, he would be allowed to borrow books from his mother's employers' libraries. There he read many of the classics, including *The Iliad,* much of Shakespeare,

Mark Twain, Zane Grey, anything he could find about the American West, and of course the Bible.

He read about the ancient Greek city-states, and was particularly interested in their Olympic Games, where even warring states put down their weapons in a spirit of competitive cooperation. He learned about the triumphs and tragedies of the European experience, of how Europe's peoples had endured the loss of homelands, the displacements of war. He was inspired by the Jews of biblical times, with their deep abiding faith under the cruelest of circumstances, and by the early Christians' persistence against the will of Rome. From his readings about the East, he grew to appreciate the discipline that had marked the Asian culture's ability to preserve tradition, warding off the onslaught of barbaric invasions. He was moved by the plight of both the American Indian and the coolie workers who had been imported from China to do the job of railway building, comparing it to the experience of his own family.

But it was the positive part of the American experience that most captured his imagination—stories of hopes and dreams, of a visionary people conquering a frontier because of the indomitability of faith, of the courage to take chances. Bradley identified with the American Dream, and from an early age saw a place for himself in it. Its lessons seemed familiar—they were the same ones his parents had drummed into him. But the frontiers to be conquered at this stage of the American saga were no longer physical. And the key to conquering them, just as his parents had said, was education.

One major concern Bradley had in preparing for high school was which school could provide him the most opportunities, which had the best facilities to further develop his academic, athletic, and personal attributes? And how could he get there? He set his mind to work. Bradley figured out a plan that allowed him to attend one of the city's best schools, Polytechnic High. The Bradley residence was then at 15th and Hooper in the Jefferson High School district, but Crenner worked for a family who lived only a few blocks from Polytechnic. Since Tom often helped with chores at the house and was well known to the family, they allowed him to list their address to school officials, enabling him to transfer out of his own district without a formal application. Tom had made an excellent choice. Poly was renowned academically and also had strong programs in football and track. According to Lowell Steward, who went on to Jefferson and later competed against Bradley in track and football, "there were only about one hundred blacks at Polytechnic at the time, and it was a much better school for those who wanted to get ahead. I tried to get in by using a different address. But they did not let me stay, because I was not a great athlete like Tom." Tom's experiences and success on the athletic field would later provide him with his ticket of admission to the best public university in the area—UCLA.

Attendance at Poly High in 1934 was a new and different experience for Tom, and not without its challenges. Bradley remembers that beneath his veneer of confidence, "I was a terrified youngster from the East Side of town the first day I walked into Poly." Soon he rallied, and his cooperative spirit helped him make new friendships. Tom found that the "acceptance accorded at Poly High helped life blossom, especially the help of the football and track coaches who paved my way to a scholarship at UCLA."

When he was just playing ball at the old White Sox Park, running track at Snyder's Playground, and scrimmaging at the YMCA, Tom had not only enjoyed sports, but recognized that they could buy him a future. Yet now that he had the opportunity to make the football and track team, he had to face the fact that he did not have the time required for practice. For years, he had delivered the *Record* each day. What he earned was not all that much, but it did represent his contribution to the family. It took everything that everybody could bring in just to pay the bills from one month to the next.

Tom mulled over his dilemma. And then, as he always did, he took the problem to his mother. Initially, she looked dubious. He thought for a moment that she did not approve of what he wanted to do. But that wasn't it at all. As Bradley remembers, "Her first question was 'what is football?'" Crenner had no idea what the sport was all about, what it could mean to his life. Her son explained it to her. "When I told her it could be the means of my getting into college, that was enough." Crenner immediately approved. The money from the paper route was secondary. Education was number-one.

Yet, never in all his years at Poly or UCLA did Crenner ever see her son in a single game or track meet. It was not that she wasn't proud of Tom's achievements. But she was always working, putting in the time needed to provide the money no longer coming from Tom's paper route. In fact, she took in extra ironing to make ends meet.

With his mother's blessing and support, Bradley now divided his time at school between mastering his academic subjects and capitalizing on his innate athletic talents. It all seemed worthwhile to Crenner, even the extra ironing, to be able to walk in the door and see her son laboring over his books instead of searching for another boll of cotton, as she and Lee had been forced to do at his age.

Tom became Polytechnic's new athletic sensation as he worked out daily on the track and football field. When others gave up in the hot Southern California sunshine, when they finally gave in to aching muscles, one figure remained, plodding on, knowing that every step he took brought him closer to his and his parents' dream of a college education.

In addition to his efforts on the playing field, Tom also tackled Polytechnic's racial barriers. As one of only 113 blacks and a smattering of Hispanics and Asians in a student population of 1,300, he faced a formidable challenge. Poly was going to provide him with the laboratory for his first experiments in politics. Here he would earn the respect and support of a heterogeneous constituency much like the one he would one day serve as the Mayor of Los Angeles. Displaying the approach for which he would later be known in his political career, Bradley quietly studied the new terrain, its dominant players and important groups.

One constraint was glaringly obvious, not only to Tom, but also to a significant number of students. As was the case in other schools at that time, blacks were forbidden to join or participate in the school clubs or organizations. As a result, many gifted students were frozen out of extracurricular activities. Bradley decided that the system would have to be changed, for his sake and for that of all those who suffered racial discrimination.

In his efforts to rectify the situation, Tom enjoyed the cooperation of a sympathetic science teacher, Mr. John York who helped develop a High Y organization for minority students. York's dedication to opportunity for minorities had a long-lasting impact on Polytechnic's new activist. Tom now recognized that there were those within the establishment who would take the extra step, who would help to widen the window of opportunity. "Mr. York never thought race or color were important factors in deciding who succeeded and who didn't," he recalls.

In retrospect, Bradley credits his experience at Polytechnic with providing him opportunities to prove himself as a mediator. Several times during his four years at Poly, there were disturbances that pitted whites against blacks, Hispanics, and Asians. Bradley's ability to analyze the situation, to empathize with the various points of view, and to facilitate communication among them was recognized by the school officials. Frequently he was called in to mediate, to ease the tensions between conflicting groups. He came to notice that people appreciated his low-key approach to resolution and leadership. Bradley was pleased and eager to continue developing this important skill.

The respect and recognition Bradley earned in incidents such as these, in his academic work, and on the playing field as Poly's most outstanding athlete, bolstered his confidence. They provided him with the credentials he needed to embark on his first political campaign for president of the Boys' League, during his junior year, a campaign which would be prophetic of his future contests, and would even at this early date show all the marks of a typical Bradley race. His success would depend upon his ability to create a heterogeneous constituency among the students at Polytechnic High.

His opponent, one of his football teammates, would, like most of Bradley's future political opponents, steer away from substantive issues. His theme would be "image" and appearance. There was no comparison of leadership abilities, as Bradley had hoped for. Instead, the message to the students of Polytechnic was that the winner would interact frequently with downtown businessmen, and that Poly deserved a president who would convey the right image. Young Bradley realized that the base appeal of the message was a subtle appeal to racism—a young black student simply wouldn't be capable of representing a school such as Polytechnic. After all, Tom Bradley didn't even have a proper dress suit.

Politically adroit even then, Bradley realized his vulnerability on the "proper attire" issue. As a matter of fact, there was only one suit in his entire family, and that belonged to his older brother. Bradley decided to try to meet the challenge the best way he could. He borrowed his brother's suit, which almost swallowed him, and remembers, "What I didn't have in suits, I tried to make up for in cleanliness." The first thing he did each day was to wash his shirt and take the suit pants down to be cleaned—a major expense given his finances, as well as a major inconvenience. He remembers that as being the real contest—running back and forth keeping his two shirts and two pair of pants always cleaned for the next day.

Identifying this episode as his "first exposure to negative campaign tactics," Bradley formulated a strategic response that was a blueprint of things to come. First he sought to take control of the campaign agenda, to redirect attention away from tangential issues and back to issues of substance. He outlined his vision for the student body at Polytechnic, a vision of fairness and equality for all students.

Bradley was an idealist, what he often terms an "eternal optimist," but he was also a realist. He knew the odds were heavily stacked against him. Yet he was determined that, when Poly students made their decision, they would know Tom Bradley's ideas. He had enough faith in the electorate to believe that, if they knew what he stood for, they would rise above their prejudices and deliver an honest vote on the issues. When they cast their ballots, they would base their decision on facts, not fears.

And he was right. On the evening of that first of many successful election days he would know in his political life, he announced to his mother that politics was rooted in his soul. They talked about what Tom's win could mean: In the immediate future, it would be yet another positive piece of data for admissions officers to consider on a college application that was growing more impressive each day.

Bradley's success in ending racial barriers at Polytechnic

went beyond election night. Throughout his four years of high school, he distinguished himself scholastically and athletically, becoming known as one of Poly's brightest and most active students. In his athletic career at Poly, Bradley set a new record for Los Angeles in the 440-yard-dash, and was named "All City" tackle in 1936. The following year he was "All City" and "All Southern California Track Champion" in the quarter-mile.

His old Lafayette Junior High pals, Paul Brown and Charles Scott, now found themselves going head-to-head against him on the varsity playing fields. As Brown remembers their battles on the football field, "When he'd get the ball, we'd go after him with a little extra punch." And high school chum Wilbur Harris, who would later work with him on the police force, remembers Bradley's "can-do" attitude on the track. "He and Wilbur Miller at Jefferson High had quite a rivalry in the 440-yard dash at the meets. Tom was determined that, if he put his mind to it, he could win those races." It was at such races that Tom would often see his father, who was by then separated from Crenner, living on Alvarado Street and taking odd jobs as a cook or carpenter.

It was a source of great pride to Lee that his and Crenner's own dreams might finally be realized by their children. But for him the economic strain had finally been too great. After years of struggling to support his family, he simply couldn't face not being able to provide for them. Hard as it is for those who haven't personally experienced such a defeat to understand, Lee did what so many other men in similar circumstances have done; he left his family. His attendance at Tom's sports events provided the two of them with a rare chance to see each other in a happy context.

Tom would often rush off after practice, without any explanation. Many of the athletes would go to the Elks matinee dance on Saturday evenings, or would take in a movie at the Lincoln, The Hub, or the Rosebud theaters. But, Tom seldom went along. He always said he had chores to do. Once when he ran into Bradley in a local grocery store, Harris found out why. It turned out that, in addition to studying, training, and keeping his mother's household running smoothly, Tom frequently helped older residents of the area with their shopping and errands. Bradley amazed everybody who knew him with his never-ending round of activities.

Even though Tom was successful on the playing field and in the classroom, one barrier still stood in his way at Poly. Honorary society recognition had been traditionally off limits to minorities. But during his senior year, when the Ephebian Honor Society named its new inductees, who had to be in the top ten percent of the class and to have a faculty recommendation, Bradley made the list. This was another first in the school's history. Tom's induction opened still more doors for minorities at Polytechnic. To the new Honor Society designate, it was the beginning of the end to racial discrimination at the school. After that, no one really dared to try to keep a student out because of color or creed.

Tom's high-school years were auspicious in yet another way. It was at this time that he came to know the one and only love of his life. Faithfully attending the New Hope Baptist Church since he was ten years old, Tom had long noticed the striking looks of the Church Superintendent's daughter, Ethel Arnold. Ethel had the most beautiful dark eyes and one of the most outgoing personalities he had ever known. There were times when he caught himself just gazing at her, songbook in hand—sometimes long after the rest of the congregation had closed their books for prayer. Young Tom was smitten.

The two became better acquainted at various church functions. Ethel gradually noticed that she was the object of Bradley's attention. Every time she read the minutes of the last meeting, she would glance up to find "those dark mysterious eyes of Tom Bradley on me." Personally, she was too busy for a serious relationship. And so was he. Theirs was a romance that would take time to blossom. At fifteen, Bradley had met the young woman he would ask to marry eight years later.

The second of seven children of a family of decorators, Ethel was born in Taylor, Texas, on February 9, 1919. Her family later migrated to Los Angeles, where her father gained a degree of financial security through his business. Ethel was described by her parents as "like a butterfly," because of her independent outlook on life and her determination to succeed and move beyond the traditional role models for women. Ethel had noticed Tom Bradley's stares at church, but even though she was stunningly beautiful, she had no interest in boys at the time. The spirited Ethel Arnold was concentrating on having a business career.

For the next few years, Tom and Ethel's mutual admiration and understanding grew. Both shared a strong sense of family and a deeply held religious outlook on what was right and wrong. Both were very ambitious, and they discussed their respective goals and aspirations at church dinners and afterward at the Arnold home. While eating homemade ice cream at church socials, Tom became more and more convinced that Ethel was the person he wanted to join him in realizing his hopes and dreams.

But in the early years of their acquaintance, it was the aspirations of the two that kept them from becoming too intense about each other. As a friend recalls, "they were just close friends. . . . Ethel was so busy with her activities in the neighborhood that neither she nor Tom were ready for any type of relationship beyond being good pals." Nonetheless, the common interests were established early, as were their mutual respect and admiration. Neighbors of the Arnolds frequently saw Tom, accompanied by his childhood friends Ernie Carr and Joe Campbell, sauntering up to Ethel's house. "Until they got their own girlfriends, the three of them were inseparable," remarked Ethel. "It was like being courted by the Three Musketeers."

Although Tom had long considered Ethel Arnold to be the most beautiful, special young woman he had ever met—energetic, full of life, and with high aspirations—it was not until June 1936, when he was eighteen years old, that Tom asked Ethel out on their first date. While many young women had expressed an obvious interest in Tom, his regimented schedule of school, sports, and work simply didn't leave time for much of a social life. His high goals and aspirations would require a most understanding and giving person. In Ethel he had met his match. Neither of them was interested in the standard high-school romance. Like Tom, Ethel simply didn't have the time for such narrow concerns. As she recalls, "I was so busy finishing high school and beginning college, taking care of the neighborhood, and getting ready with my own life that Tom's schedule was far from my own mind."

Ethel agreed to go out with Tom on their first date "only because he promised that I would get to see Jesse Owens run. So

I went to meet Tom at the Coliseum." But there was someone else on the track, Ethel remembers. "While I was waiting for Tom in the bleachers, looking for Jesse Owens, who did I also see running around the track, but the long legs of Tom Bradley!" The occasion was a dual meet of Ohio State and USC, and what Tom hadn't told Ethel was that interspersed throughout the college events were high-school championship races in which he too would be running.

Owens had been a great source of inspiration to Americans and to the free world when he embarrassed Adolf Hitler in the 1936 Olympics. Owens was the consummate role model for Tom Bradley. Tom admired him, and endeavored to acquire the same discipline on the track. Bradley also remembers the night he ran on the same track that his hero did, and credits his winning his race that evening (against Frank Jones, who would later set a world record in Junior College track) to Owens' presence. "That night Jesse Owens—my idol, a great inspiration to me—was also on the track, and I knew that this would help me run faster, which it did. I won that meet."

Before the meet, Tom had bet Ethel that, if he won the first race she saw him run, he would also win their first kiss. It was after that meet that Ethel told friends that Tom Bradley was hers.

As Tom turned his attention toward college, Ethel started up her own beauty shop in South-Central Los Angeles. She recalls that the shop enjoyed heavy business: "People would drive in from Pasadena and the Westside; it was always packed, and did we do hair!" Ethel opened up more salons throughout the city. The take-charge, independent style was a trait Bradley deeply admired in Ethel. She, too, was destined to move beyond traditional expectations. And they would transcend them together, in a mutually supportive relationship that would for each be their first and only love.

Bradley's performance on the playing field and in the classroom paid off. A former alumnus of Polytechnic, James LuValle, who was not only a star quarter-miler on UCLA's track team but was also Phi Beta Kappa, noticed the lanky, muscular star's quickness and talent at the city meets. After consulting with coaches Harry Trotter and Elvin "Ducky" Drake in Westwood,

*Then (1939) and Now (1985). UCLA Mile Relay team. From
left, Hal Sinclair, Tom Berkley, Carl McBain, Tom Bradley.*
(Courtesy of Carl McBain)

he talked with Bradley after school and gave him the good news—it was what he had worked for throughout his life. The University of California at Los Angeles wanted Tom to come to college on a full athletic scholarship. There was jubilation in the Bradley household. A dream had been realized. Tom would be running track and attending classes at UCLA.

Tom Bradley entered UCLA in 1937. A new educational environment once again broadened his horizons and introduced him to a new mentor. Just as Mr. York had inspired him in his early school days, Adeline Gunther, the head of a religious organization dedicated to promoting Christian values, would help shape Bradley's career during the early days in Westwood. He states: "She really served to rekindle all the ethical and motivational traits my mother had always taught me."

Tom was even more of an anomaly at the Westwood campus than he had been at Poly. Out of 7,000 students, there were only about a hundred blacks. But he adapted well. As he comments now, "The new setting was different, but it did not faze me." His first year he commuted to campus by bus each day, as no blacks lived on campus at that time. Despite the daily commute and the usual grueling Bradley schedule, the young freshman managed to form lasting friendships with fellow track team members. "I made many friends, some of whom I still have; we all loved the spirit of competition. In fact we still have reunions of just the track team in which we all compare our success now off the track."

Not only did Tom's physical separation from campus not impede his ability to make friends, it provided him with his first opportunity to respond creatively to the problems of mass transportation. During Tom's early college years, the Bradley family lived at 27th near Main Street, in the Watts area of Los Angeles, quite a distance from the crosstown Westwood campus. Working during summers and at odd jobs during the year finally enabled Tom to save enough money to buy his first automobile, a 1931 Model A Ford. "The car had a rumble seat, which made it large enough for five small people," Bradley recalled, "but I, more often than not, put six large people in. I suppose I had the first 'car pool' arrangement. We would all drive to UCLA, and each passenger would pay ten cents one way." Explaining the reciprocal benefits, Bradley explains, "As cheap as gas was, this charge was necessary for me to have a car. Still, it was a bargain to them and a great help to me." Crenner's son had the ability to put together a deal that would benefit all concerned parties.

He also continued to work as a photographer for comedian Jimmy Durante, a job he had obtained through Ethel's sister Maggie, who worked as Mrs. Durante's maid. During his high-school years, Tom had pursued an interest in photography and had shown considerable skill, fully qualifying him for the job. That had begun a long-lasting friendship between Tom and the Durante family.

Tom spent his college years in many of the same activities and involved in many of the same issues that would characterize his years in public service. He was active in the Bruin Club, made up of members of the Kappa Alpha Psi fraternity, and the Carver Club, named for the black spokesman who had done so much to promote equal opportunity. The Kappa membership was especially important, not only as a stage on which Tom could continue to practice his leadership skills, but also because it gave him the foundation for an important network that could later benefit his political career. College friend, Bill Elkins, remembers, "Tom ate, slept, and breathed Kappa." The black fraternity was an important nucleus for the small but growing number of black men on the Westwood campus. Kappa's motto— "Achievement"—served to further anchor Tom's deep-seated belief in one's ability to succeed against all odds.

At UCLA, most of the minority representation was composed of women. The simple facts of economics meant that most males during these Depression years were forced to find jobs immediately after high-school graduation. College was a luxury they could not afford. The school's strict academic standards also tended to exclude minorities from poor backgrounds. But once admitted, these students with the help of their families and friends worked very hard to stay there. Longtime friend and fellow classmate of Bradley's at UCLA, Jessie Mae Beavers recalls, "We were all part of a community effort where everyone just pitched in and did the work to help get us through. Sometimes there were two or three families living under one roof, but that was okay, because everybody did their part to help make it."

Bradley helped his family to make ends meet with a variety of odd jobs—stocking shelves, changing tires, shoveling scrap iron, working on construction sites.

The University of California at Los Angeles was more advanced in its integration policies than its crosstown rival at Exposition Park. There was no overt discrimination in any of its athletic practices. And academically, UCLA had boasted many fine black graduates like Ralph Bunche, who graduated in 1927 and went on to become the first black person to earn a Ph.D. degree in political science from Harvard in 1934. At the time of Bradley's attendance, UCLA had a solid and growing reputation for academic excellence. Tom, like many another ambitious minority student, was determined to make the most of the opportunities it offered.

But even the cooperative spirit at UCLA could not dispel the reality that segregation was still deeply imbedded within society. On a trip to Arizona, the entire Bruin team opted to ride in the cattle cars of the train because black team members were refused entry into the coach area. At Arizona, the teams stayed in private homes of the opposing team when black members of the UCLA squad were turned away at a hotel.

As committed as Tom was to a college education, by the time of his junior year he was becoming restless, eager to get on with what he perceived as the real business of living. Part of this had to do with his growing love for Ethel, who had begun to occupy more of the center of his life. He was thinking about getting married, starting a career, becoming involved in activities that could make a difference in the lives of other people. Although his mother still hoped he would become a doctor, he was leaning toward the teaching profession. Throughout his own life, teachers—first at home and then at school—had been sources of inspiration and guidance to him. To be able to do for others what his teachers had done for him, to make the difference for young students in search of their dreams—this was very attractive to him. By 1940, the teaching profession had begun to open up to minorities, and Tom liked the idea of being one of those who would push its doors wider still.

Of course, his time out of the classroom was methodically organized to maximize efficiency of track practice. Yet, although track was an individual sport, Tom would often spend extra time with his mile relay teammates, Carl McBain, Tom Berkley, and Hal Sinclair. Often the track meet would be decided by the mile relay, which was the final event. Tom accepted the pressure and made his best effort to show that he had, indeed, earned his scholarship.

But midway through his junior year, a move made almost on a whim changed the course of his life. Several of Bradley's friends had decided to take a city exam for entrance into the Police Academy. They joked that, if they got in, at least they would find themselves on the right side of the law. And if they scored sufficiently high, they could skip their last year of college and go directly into the Academy without degrees.

Without thinking much about it, Bradley accompanied them. Although he was aware that the Los Angeles Police Department was not known for its equal opportunity employment practices, he figured he had nothing to lose by taking the test, and perhaps he would learn something about what was required for police work. He took the exam, then finished out his junior year, and got started on his summer job. He didn't even tell his mother or Ethel that he had taken the test.

The summer of 1940 was unbearably hot. As Tom put in backbreaking hours shoveling scrap iron at the Hughes tire yard—his job on his time "off" from the forty-four hours a week he put in as a gardener, working beside teammate Carl McBain, at UCLA—he thought about Crenner and Lee at work in the cotton fields of Calvert, and not for the first time reflected on how fortunate he and his brothers and sisters were by comparison. Although he too had to put in grueling hours of hard labor, his work, because of his parents' sacrifices, had the potential to lead somewhere. Tom rededicated himself anew to realizing his goals for his parents as well as for himself—even as he remained undecided about what exactly those goals were.

3

The LAPD—A Commitment to Protect and Serve

"Law and order mean something deeper than the prevention of violence and the control of crime. They mean that every citizen in every neighborhood is safe and secure."

—Tom Bradley

A phone call during the summer of 1940 helped Tom Bradley make up his mind about his future. The voice on the other end of the line informed him that, out of the 5,000 taking the entrance examination for the Police Academy, he had placed near the top of the list. He could enter the Police Academy immediately without finishing college. Should he go? He considered what it would mean.

One advantage was that the Police Department would offer him the kind of stability his parents had never had. It paid good money, $170 per month, and provided a dependable retirement plan. But for a black man, long-term advancement and promotion would be tough, if not impossible. By this time, however, Tom was accustomed to facing and overcoming the obstacles that racism put in his path. He thought he could prevail, as he had done before.

His mother was surprisingly supportive of his decision to leave college. She had grown to trust his judgment.

The day he learned the good news—August 31, 1940—Tom

Ethel, an astute businesswoman, is a major factor in Tom's success. (Bradley Family Collection)

Graduation from the Police Academy was a success in itself. From left, Tom, Robert Greene, John Simmons, Perry Williams, 1941. (Bradley Family Collection)

stopped by to tell Ethel. It was just like Tom not to have even mentioned it to her. Now, with his 97 percent on the exam, he would be on the police force tomorrow. A visibly excited, but nervous, Bradley explained to Ethel that this was an important day—for both of them. Now that he had a secure job, he asked her to marry him. And she agreed.

It was official: Tom Bradley would be a cop.

A week later, with a secure, if not brilliant, future guaranteed, Tom took another significant step. He asked Ethel Arnold's father for his daughter's hand in marriage. Her family liked Tom. He talked more to them than to Ethel when he came over. But they still harbored some reservations about marriage. Ethel was, as her father said, the head of the pack of eight children, having graduated from Jefferson High School at the age of fifteen. After attending City College for two years, Ethel already owned and operated two beauty salons, one of them far away in Santa Barbara. Still, the Arnolds recognized that, once Ethel had her mind made up, no one could change it. Both parents agreed to Tom's request, and the wedding date was set for the following June.

The announcement of the wedding plans was big news in the *California Eagle,* a citywide newspaper serving the black community of Los Angeles. Tom didn't want to wait until June, however, and rushed the wedding, which was heavily attended by family and friends from the area, as well as by Kappa brothers from throughout the state. On May 4, 1941, Mr. and Mrs. Tom Bradley set up housekeeping on 57th Street in a small house in the Central area of Los Angeles, next door to Ethel's parents.

Tom's decision to join the police force when he did would have ramifications beyond the decision to marry. It would in all ways be a decision he would never regret. He says that he remembers only one bad day on the job—his first one, right after completing the Academy's courses. Bradley was relegated to directing traffic in downtown Los Angeles, a job that was boring to him. He felt he had not joined the police force to serve as a human "traffic light," but to protect and to serve the people.

For a black to make it through the Academy was a measure of success in itself. Of the seventy-two in Bradley's own class, only four were black. In his twenty years with the Los Angeles Police

Department, Bradley saw black representation on the force increase by only fifty-odd officers.

In recalling his early days on the force, Bradley points to several measures that were used to keep blacks out of the department. One of these was the physical examination. Upon completing the Academy and taking the physical examination, Bradley was informed by the departmental physician that he had a heart murmur, which would keep him from joining the force. It was news to Bradley, who insisted on a second opinion. Subsequently, the UCLA athlete was cleared for duty.

Another common roadblock for minority applicants was the oral examination, though it was no handicap for Bradley. He not only passed this test, but remembers candidly telling board members that he "intended to work hard to replace the negative view of the police department within the community, with a feeling of trust and respect." Even though everyone was aware of the public distrust of the department in many neighborhoods, it was not openly discussed within the LAPD, and especially not among the board. Such a straightforward statement from any police officer was rare; from a minority candidate it was a first.

The credibility of the LAPD had been seriously questioned during the administration of Police Chief James Davis, who resigned in 1938 as a result of scandals that engulfed the regime of his partner in corruption, Mayor Frank Shaw, who was also forced from office. Yet, the divisiveness that characterized relations between the community and the department was a product of far more than the Chief's personal indiscretions. It was rooted in his overall philosophy of law enforcement.

The Davis administration had established a "bum blockade" near California's desert borders to discourage indigents from entering the United States. As a result there was widespread abuse by police officers who beat up Mexican-Americans on the border as well as within the city. Davis had also organized a "Red Squad" to investigate "subversives" in the Los Angeles area. The Chief's obsession with the "Communist menace" and his racial prejudice were reflected in many of his programs and policies. He reported to the citizens of Los Angeles on what his undercover operations had "discovered." According to Davis, white Communist females were cohabitating with Negroes. Furthermore, he publicly predicted that Communists would overthrow the U.S. government in six years.

Despite Davis' severe shortcomings, the LAPD had become one of the first departments in the country to have black officers in uniform, though it remained profoundly racist in its policies, allowing black officers to work in only two areas, both of them in black communities. Bradley recalls, "The only other option was directing traffic downtown." Police patrols were also segregated, a policy damaging not only to the opportunities of minority cops but to the quality of service provided to the citizens of Los Angeles, and ultimately even to the safety of white police officers. If a white officer was sick, his partner was forced to patrol an area alone, even if a black officer was available to fill in. Black police officers were not allowed to patrol a white beat. Los Angeles' multi-ethnic, multi-racial, melting-pot population was not reflected in the make-up or philosophy of its Police Department.

The Los Angeles Police Department's history had by this time clearly established that regardless of talent or performance, the highest rank a black officer could ever hope for was sergeant. But Officer Tom Bradley viewed this for what it was—history. He had his own history—one of ceaselessly overcoming racial barriers in his rise to the top of whatever he undertook. He saw no reason to change. He had a positive attitude and an indomitable faith in his own merits. He remembers: "There was a lot of doubt expressed by the other minority cops; and for very good reason given the department's history. [But] I knew that when it came down to it, attitude was the most important asset we could have to break the back of racism in the department." This outlook would characterize his twenty-one years of work for the department—and his entire career, from the halls of Polytechnic to City Hall.

There was early evidence that Bradley's approach was working, whether because of remarkable luck, native ability, or a combination of the two. At that time the Department needed young blood to help with its juvenile delinquent program. After his first few days on the force directing traffic, Bradley, one of the youngest freshman officers of the Academy, was approached for an appointment to juvenile activities. His youth and his college background made Tom a natural choice for the job. Unexpectedly, he found himself with an ideal outlet for the talents he had intended to put to use in the teaching career he had been preparing for at UCLA. In charge of youths who had found themselves on the wrong side of the law, Bradley approached his new job as a teacher and a coach. Like his own mentors, he would strive to reach young people's minds.

Bradley began his career patrolling the Newton Street area, out of a station house across the street from where he had lived during part of his junior high school years. He was primarily responsible for cases involving the youth of the community, and he had a reputation as a tough but fair cop whom kids could relate to, an officer who favored dialogue over force.

His own background had given him insight into how family and environment could help or hinder the young as they grew into adulthood. Many of Bradley's own schoolmates had already lost the battle and become casualties of the slums. Here was a chance for him to steer the younger generation toward lives of promise and away from lives of crime. Here was a job that could utilize the sum of his past and present experience for the benefit of those he had long wanted to help. As Bradley himself says, looking back on his achievements, "I think my age and background really helped provide me with the needed insight to make a difference with these kids. . . . I often knew only too well the answers to some of the very questions I would be asking them."

Bradley felt strongly that all youngsters deserved a choice and a chance. He knew that many of them had assumed early in life that there was no other alternative to crime. He was determined to help stop the vicious cycles of poverty and deprivation. Something had to be done to change what was an all too predictable outcome.

Remembering what the athletic centers of his youth had meant to him, Bradley concluded that what was needed was an athletics program to channel the energy and talents of these troubled youths. Discipline, direction, and a sense of self-worth and satisfaction—traits desperately lacking in many of the young people he arrested—could be developed through sports. So the efforts of Citizen Bradley took up where those of Officer Bradley left off. Instead of enjoying his free time away from his job, Bradley devoted his off-duty hours to developing a sports program that could help make the difference for teens with a proclivity for trouble.

In organizing this citywide program, Bradley pieced together the type of public–private partnership that would later become a trademark of his leadership in government. Calling upon support from the local colleges and universities, he made football the major focus of the juvenile program, knowing that the schools would be interested in potential football stars. However, basketball, track, and baseball were also included throughout the year. "It really marked the first time that some of these kids were not in the ever-present company of drop-outs and more hardened criminal elements," Bradley remarked. "Having some of the college coaches and the stars involved—successful people whom these kids saw pictures of in the papers or heard about over the radio—really helped the kids to develop a 'can-do' attitude." The satisfaction and sense of worth that many of the youths began to develop in this program has continued up to the present. Today, Bradley frequently hears from many of those who began life anew as kids in the sports program.

Bradley's progress with the program did not go unnoticed. Charlotta Bass of *The California Eagle,* the oldest black newspaper on the West Coast, frequently commented on it and on Bradley's leadership. Tom Bradley was becoming well-known in his community as a symbol of hope and compassion. He and Bob Green, a partner on the force and a fellow Kappa, were increasingly active in community work. They became regular participants in Boys and Girls Days at the churches, at which a group of Kappas would provide the musical entertainment and Bradley would often speak.

When World War II broke out, Bradley made several attempts to enter the Air Force and the Coast Guard, but because policemen were at that time deemed more important to the national well-being than soldiers, he was turned down. Then Bradley received a letter informing him that he had been drafted into the

Army. It was the same week he learned that Ethel was pregnant with their first child. The prospect of fatherhood prompted him to reconsider his desire to enter the service.

At that time, Los Angeles was experiencing the infamous zoot suit riots. Merchants throughout the community were alarmed at the widespread violence and vandalism, and the police department's performance in quelling the disturbances seemed to aggravate the divisiveness within the city. Reportedly the police were attacking not only Mexican-Americans, whom they blamed for creating the disturbances, but also blacks. As had often been true in the past, a difference in color proved to be sufficient provocation to police action.

During this period of racial tensions and panic, the case of Officer Bradley came before the head of the Draft Board, a man who was a Watts real-estate broker and familiar with Bradley's work with juveniles in the area. Because of the situation in Los Angeles, as well as because of Bradley's prospective fatherhood, the Draft Board informed the young officer that he should continue with the police department and with his activities in the juvenile program. He was told to forget about the draft notice.

But tragedy was soon to strike the Bradley home. On May 4, 1942, their first wedding anniversary, Tom and Ethel's first child, Anita, died two hours after birth because of an underdeveloped heart. It was a loss that would take the couple many years to finally accept. Tom channeled much of his grief into his work with juveniles. Despite his own loss, he was more determined than ever to help save the lives of young people.

Given the gravity of the situation—the fact that many juveniles were becoming involved in the riots and gangs—Bradley's energies were greatly needed. Those familiar with the sports program testify that, while he often gave credit to others for its success, Bradley was the anchor, the mainstay, of the program during his five years working with it. As both coach and counselor, Bradley served as a role model to youth. They could readily see in Tom's life what a difference a positive attitude, dedicated effort, and a disciplined spirit could make.

Tom carried the spirit he professed on the playing field into all aspects of his life. In addition to reason and dialogue, Bradley remembers using his considerable athletic abilities to deal with troublemakers: "When you caught these kids doing something they shouldn't, they would immediately dart off and try to get away. Well, I guess my record in track paid off, because I would always catch them. They would be out of breath and just gaze up at me in disbelief. I guess after awhile I was known as a fast cop, because after a few incidents most did not try to escape."

His partner Wilbur Harris, who spent twenty-five years on the police force, describes Bradley as "very even-tempered." Harris recalls, "In all those years on the force, I can never remember Tom Bradley using his gun, he always preferred reason and dialogue over brute force. . . . But make no mistake about it, Tom Bradley was one hell of a tough cop."

While activities on the force were engaging him in more diverse types of responsibilities, Tom also saw his roles at home take on a new meaning. Two daughters were born to Tom and Ethel during this period. Lorraine was born on November 18, 1943, and Phyllis on June 16, 1945. Ethel would now be devoting full time to rearing two children, giving up her own career.

In 1946, after five years of noteworthy service in the Newton Street division, Bradley decided to try to join the handful of other minority officers who had made sergeant in the force. He succeeded in passing both an oral and a written examination. His selection served as further evidence that the system, even that of the LAPD, was capable of change. As he told his colleagues in the locker room, "Never give up, keep your thoughts and your mind always on the goal. Don't let them get you down to the level of dealing with what amounts to their attitude problem."

Bradley's promotion to sergeant should, of course, have been a routine promotion for such an extraordinarily capable officer in about three years. White policemen who had not even finished high school were promoted beyond sergeant to lieutenant and captain. But the fact remained that it was unusual in those years for a black man, no matter what his abilities, to make sergeant on the LAPD. There was no denying Bradley's outstanding qualities, however, even then. A 1952 review by his police captain reads, "I know no sergeant in the department who can excel Sgt. Bradley in the skill and personal qualifications necessary to make an ideal police sergeant."

After Bradley was promoted to sergeant he was assigned to

Outside their new home on 57th Street. (Bradley Family Collection)

Tom and Ethel's wedding in the home of Ethel's parents, May 4, 1941. (Bradley Family Collection)

Bradley's promotion to Lieutenant in 1958 evidenced a change in the LAPD's system. (Bradley Family Collection)

Tom, holding Phyllis, Ethel and Lorraine on a picnic outing, 1948. (Bradley Family Collection)

the Detective Division and moved to the Central Avenue community, which was widely known throughout the city as the heart of a bookmaking and gambling ring. Prostitutes operated freely in the area, servicing the bookmakers and their clients. Also a matter of public knowledge was the fact that several police officers were paid off regularly, in exchange for their pledge to look the other way at such activities. Bradley wanted to mop up the whole mess. Soon he was patrolling the old Florence and Lincoln Theater districts of Central Avenue, a welcome sight to neighborhood residents and workers.

He had long been familiar with the seedy nature of the Central Avenue area, having played ball as a youth at the Central Recreation Center and having worked with kids from that neighborhood when he was with the Juvenile Division at the Newton Street station. However, Bradley now needed to get to know the area very well and very fast in order to bust the gambling organization. He had to figure out how the operation worked and who its key players were.

One such incident involved a bookie operation working out of an apartment on Ninth Avenue. The apartment building was owned by Lowell Steward, Tom's old school chum, but he was unaware of his tenant's illegal activities. Steward recalls that Bradley threatened to break the door down if Mrs. Steward couldn't give him the key when he arrived for the arrest. Steward's wife called her husband at work, and he told her to provide Bradley with the key. Tom did the job, and he earned the reputation as the honest cop in the neighborhood.

Other cops on the beat gave Bradley tips, as did concerned citizens. Some of the very offenders he had helped to rehabilitate in the juvenile program also gave him information. Soon he and his partner knew enough to be able to carry out numerous successful raids. Ultimately they cracked the entire operation.

Bradley was earning a reputation as a cop who couldn't be bought.

Bradley's success in ridding Central Avenue of its bookmaking operation did not go unnoticed by the Police Chief. The sergeant received an appointment to the administrative vice unit in the Wilshire area. Here he worked directly with Chief William H. Parker, who had been appointed a year prior in 1950. The unit's responsibility was to ensure integrity within the department. Bradley and his colleagues would work to guarantee that divisional officers were not cooperating with criminal elements in the community. Sergeant Bradley wanted to broaden his horizons, to learn as much as he could not only about his profession, but also about the dynamics of Los Angeles.

Bradley's passion for detail became widely known. At departmental meetings, he provided expertise, instructing new officers on the intricacies of particular vice operations. His opinions were frequently requested in court. In circles outside the department and his own beat, Sergeant Tom Bradley was becoming ever more widely respected as a voice of reason, in a city where such a resource was in short supply. And he spoke widely, in a variety of settings, spreading his message of reason and tolerance.

Charles Lloyd, who would later be Tom's law partner, remembers how Bradley served as a role model for him. "I was majoring in police science at City College in 1953 and was overwhelmed by Sgt. Bradley's lecture." He explains, "Here was a black man giving a lecture to a classroom in which I was the only black, and he was so calm, charismatic and so bright. . . . Later when I followed his career it was obvious to me that he was the most qualified black officer on the force and one of the most outstanding of any color." Lloyd approached Bradley after the lecture, and began what would become a lifelong friendship.

It was also during these early years on the force that Bradley began to take an active interest in politics and in the Democratic Party. After working his beat and organizing the youth group's weekly agenda, he would rush home long enough to share a meal with Ethel, and then dash off to work as a volunteer for promising political candidates. His daughter Lorraine remembers, "After helping us with our homework and reading us a story, he and Momma would tuck us into bed about 8:00, and as far as we knew that was it. We never knew he then went out to the meetings or to classes."

Bradley's first political work was for Edmund G. "Pat" Brown's unsuccessful race for Attorney General in 1946. He then began working for a man who was destined to change history— Ed Roybal, who would be elected the first Hispanic member of the United States Congress from California in 1962. Beginning with Roybal's race for the City Council in 1949, Bradley was a Roybal supporter, in part because of the commitment the two men shared to the principle of minority judgeships. It was also through his Roybal campaign efforts that Bradley met a political volunteer who would be very important to him in his own political career—Maury Weiner.

In the following ten years, Bradley became involved in many community, state, and national causes, and was a member of 121 clubs and organizations in Los Angeles. A community leader described Bradley's role as being "not necessarily a focal leader, but rather a key player in numerous organizations. His mere presence induced the climate necessary to change."

One of the organizations that Sergeant Bradley became more active in was the California Democratic Council, dedicated to progressive programs within the party. Adlai Stevenson's bid for the Presidency in 1952 fueled the growth of local offshoots of the CDC, among them the Crenshaw Democratic Club. That club would, in turn, spin off two neighborhood groups in 1953, when its membership topped 600, at which time Bradley and Montana McNealy started the Leimert Park Democratic Club. Ruth Abraham, who would later play a decisive role in persuading Bradley to run for the Los Angeles City Council, vividly recalled his first visit to the Crenshaw Democratic Club, then the local chapter of the CDC. "I was President of the Crenshaw Democratic Club, and as we were discussing some issue I was a little scared when I looked up and saw this very large and impressive black policeman coming in the door in uniform." Bradley had to explain to an apprehensive group that he was in police uniform only because he hadn't had time to return home for a change of clothes after getting off work.

Abraham, an activist who had moved to California from New York and had quickly become part of the Los Angeles political network, was instantly impressed with Bradley. "It was his integrity and honesty, rare in politics, but obvious from the start in Tom Bradley." She and other Council members were pleased that he wanted to become more active in community politics.

Bradley became a regular member of the group. Abraham was impressed by his knowledge of the issues, his background, and his ability to work through the system for change. His involvement expanded to all areas of the CDC's activities—precinct walking on behalf of various political candidates, committee work, and recruitment. Not only did Bradley become active but he also urged his friends to become active. In 1961, when Bradley was President of the Leimert Park Community Democratic Club, his neighbor Leroy Berry also joined the organization. Berry remembers, "I eventually became President of the club, which was connected to the CDC, and it was all because of Tom's urging." Berry would later serve as a precinct captain in Tom Bradley's 1963 campaign for City Council.

In the effort to elect Eddie Atkinson as representative of the Tenth District in 1959, Bradley hit the streets to help. Atkinson was very popular within the district, but lacked the organization he needed to be successful. Nonetheless, the community attempted to raise money and help out in the effort to elect the first black representative to the Los Angeles City Council. But his campaign was badly hurt by an unfavorable story in the *Los Angeles Times* that mentioned his ownership of a tavern. Some saw it as character assassination. One person active in the Atkinson campaign points to the timing of the piece as typical of the strategies often employed against minority candidates: "It amounted to nothing short of a racial appeal that, as usual, came out about a week before the election to scare people in the majority regions from voting for a black."

But despite setbacks, the black community was becoming more politically aware and sophisticated. During the early 1950s, Bradley, along with Warren Hollier, Justice Vaino Spencer, Gilbert Lindsay, Jack Tenner, and Leo and Geri Branton formed the Democratic Minority Council, an organization that eventually grew to 600 people. The group's purpose was to mobilize support for a government truly representative of all the people. Dinners were held throughout the neighborhoods to help spread the word; church bazaars helped raise money. There was a new feeling of hope and excitement in the air as people began to see how activist politics could change their lives.

Given the mediation skills that Bradley often employed on the force and within the community to ease tensions, it was natural that he began to think about a legal career. He would be eligible for a pension after twenty years on the force—in 1961—and, with opportunities for advancement on the LAPD being so limited for a black man at the time, Bradley was eager to have other options. From 1952 to 1956 he attended law school at night at Loyola and Southwestern, so that when he retired from police work he would be able to shape the laws that he had once helped to enforce. He was interested in the law as a means of furthering Constitutional rights. A fellow classmate described Bradley, "He was so motivated, a real super achiever. He never once considered the handicap he might have because of his race. He seemed to be totally motivated to achievement, a true believer in the American Dream."

Bradley's steadfast determination and careful planning sometimes escaped even those closest to him. Recalling the day she learned that Tom had passed the bar exam, Ethel states, "I had no idea he had even taken the exam until I opened up a letter from Sacramento. When I read him the letter, it was the happiest I have ever seen him. He jumped so high he almost hit the ceiling."

His wife had witnessed how hard he had worked to pass the bar after working all day at the station. Bradley and David F. Cunningham had gotten a hotel room and spent the final few days there before the law exam, cramming in information. Ethel brought food and helped out, asking questions, doing whatever work had to be done. However, she had thought the exam was still to be sometime in the future. After hearing the good news, Ethel surprised Tom with one of the most memorable parties ever at the "Pacific Town," one of the nicest clubs in the area.

But even while putting in long days at work, attending law school, and continuing his involvement with his community, Bradley took time out for family. Wilbur Harris, who lived below Crenner Bradley's apartment, recalled, "Tom always came over two or three times a week and checked on his mother, and often helped pay the rent when she was getting too old to work." He didn't forget his love of football, either. He often took time out for family expeditions to the Bruins games. He and Ethel and their growing children would drive to Crenner's apartment near the Coliseum, park there, get her to cook one of her famous home-style meals of greens, chicken, and homemade pie, then go on to the game.

Tom also continued to care for other family members who experienced difficulty, including his younger brother Ellis who looked to Tom as not only his brother, but also the only father figure he had ever known.

Such activities were similar to those he had adopted during his early years, and it would take some time to move beyond the constraints of that period. Bradley recalls that having enough money for clothing and the essentials proved hard to become accustomed to after his childhood. "Every time I passed a store that sold socks, I'd go buy a pair." The result, as he recalls, was that "one day I noticed I had over 200 pairs."

4

Pushing at Racial Barriers

"Each time a man stands up for an ideal, or acts to improve the lot of others, or strikes out against injustice, he sends forth a tiny ripple of hope."

—Robert F. Kennedy

In their private as well as their public lives, Tom and Ethel Bradley were knocking on doors of segregation that continued to remain closed to thousands of citizens in Los Angeles. For years, they had put aside money from Tom's paycheck and from Ethel's beauty shop savings in the hope of buying their own house, a real home at least for their children, Phyllis and Lorraine.

They looked at a house in Leimert Park in the Baldwin Hills section of Los Angeles, and it suited their needs perfectly. The neighborhood was filled with small green and white frame houses on well-manicured lawns, along palm-lined streets. Home to many USC professors, it was a charming, well-kept, middle-class environment, perfect for family life. But there was a problem, and it was not the money. They had saved enough to buy the house on Welland Avenue. The problem was a more serious one. The people on the block did not want a black family in the neighborhood. At that time, there was a legal agreement, a restrictive covenant, that allowed owners to refuse to sell their property on the basis of race, class, religion, or ethnicity. The restrictive covenant and similar discriminative policies were common in the 1940s and 1950s, not only in Los Angeles, but throughout the country. Even to be able to look at the houses in the neighborhood, Bradley and Lowell Steward had to wear overalls and pretend to be workmen so as not to cause alarm among the residents.

At the same time that Tom Bradley was fighting the segregated policies of the Los Angeles Police Department, the struggle to outlaw such restrictive covenants was being waged in Los Angeles and throughout America. A Supreme Court decision in 1948 had ruled that racially restrictive covenants were unenforcable, and could not be used to exclude blacks from occupying property. But real-estate agents, local neighborhood associations, and zoning boards reacted to the ruling by formulating extra-legal procedures that would enable them to continue the bigoted practice. As late as 1953, restrictive covenants were utilized widely.

In 1964, the people of California voted by a two-thirds majority to pass Proposition 14, an initiative known as "The Fair Housing Act," which allowed a landlord with over four housing units to refuse to rent to anyone for any reason. Governor Edmund G. Brown, Sr., Tom Bradley, and others fought hard for its repeal. Eventually, in 1965, it would be declared unconstitutional, but even after the 1968 federal civil rights legislation that outlawed any racial discrimination in housing, many of America's neighborhoods continued to devise extra-legal plans to keep out minorities.

In 1950, when the Bradley family wanted to buy the house on Welland, the restrictive covenant was in operation. It threatened to cancel their plans for a new home. Ethel and the girls were extremely disappointed. The family talked about the problem. After listening to her father's explanation of segregated neighborhoods, five-year-old Phyllis told her dad that she didn't mind living in the neighborhood with people who weren't black. They all laughed at that, of course, while wishing life could be the way children see it.

As usual, Tom Bradley was determined to defeat the racial barriers standing in his way. He arranged for a white couple who were active in Democratic politics, Mr. and Mrs. John McTernan, to act as intermediaries in the transaction, following a procedure that was often necessary to enable minorities to buy houses in that era. Bradley recalls, "I realized that a black man's money wasn't good enough in those days."

During that period, lifelong Bradley supporter Jack Tenner worked as a lawyer to defeat restrictive covenants and other unfair measures, later serving as an attorney to Martin Luther King. He described how he and his wife often acted as "dummy buyers" for would-be homeowners: "During that time, we served as surrogates for a number of black lawyers, doctors, and judges, who wanted to buy particular houses, but could not, due to discriminatory practices." Tenner would look over the house, put down a deposit, start the escrow, and insure that the legal papers were in order. Then he would make a new deed and turn it over to the minority couple. "I remember one distressing situation where a black judge's wife wanted to see a house in Beverly Hills, and she had to pose as my wife's maid in order to see the house." As the only white lawyer in a black law firm, and as an attorney for the NAACP, Tenner occasionally turned down offers of money as high as $10,000—a lot in those days—from people eager to block these moves.

In 1950, when the Bradley family finally moved into their Leimert Park home, there were a number of ugly incidents. But Bradley instilled in his children the same indomitability that served him so well in all his battles. Daughter Lorraine, who was seven at the time, recounts one of these incidents. While walking home from school, she heard one of the boys across the street shout, "Nigger, get out of my neighborhood!" At first she ignored the remark; it wasn't the first time she had heard it. Then the boy approached her, and when he taunted her again, a fight broke out. She ran home with a bloody nose straight into her father's arms. "After I told him what happened, he sat me down, looked into my eyes, and said, 'Lorraine, you have two choices. One is to go out and continue to play, to make every effort to make this your home. The other is to stay here in the house all the time, afraid to ever leave, which in essence means that this hatred has beaten you.'" There was little choice to the Bradley's older daughter. Lorraine was outside within the hour.

Neighbor Leroy Berry, who moved into the area after Tom and Ethel did, used another tactic to help the Bradleys' daughter

Phyllis bridge the racial gap. "I remember teaching Phyllis football, and the three boys from the white family across the street joined in, and we had many good games of street football." Though that situation came to an end when the white family moved, the Bradley girls continued to make every effort to assimilate into the community. In fact, within a couple of months, Phyllis had not only made friends, but was a member of the neighborhood baseball team.

It was also a common sight to see Phyllis following closely behind her father as he mowed the Bradleys' lawn. Whether it was a Kappa barbecue or a scout meeting, activity was the norm at the Bradley home.

In 1955, Tom requested a transfer from vice to the Police Department's new community relations detail. Here he could mediate between a public that was still distrustful of its police and a police force that had made substantial progress since the corrupt Davis administration. This new unit was the nation's first police community relations program. With the approval of Chief Parker, Bradley became the entire city's community relations detail, though he would later be joined by Julio Gonzales. Bradley sought to further expand the unit's activities. He wanted to get the word out: the LAPD force was dedicated to its motto— "to protect and to serve." Facing problems of poor morale within the department and continuing communication failures between the department and the community, Police Chief Parker granted Bradley's request in hopes of bringing peace and harmony into a troubled situation.

In his new assignment, Bradley's broad experience in the city's various communities, along with the trust he had earned, helped to rally community support. Key groups and individuals began to join in the department's efforts to control crime. In order to encourage cooperation, not confrontation, between law enforcement and citizens' action groups, Bradley represented the Police Department in a variety of neighborhood organizations.

In the process of constructing this intricate network of neighborhood groups, Bradley forged alliances that would prove invaluable to him in the years to come.

Bradley's career with the LAPD exemplified the progress of

the Department's racial policies. In 1958, Sergeant Bradley became Lieutenant Bradley, a sign of promise to the few minority officers within the Department. Ethel Bradley vividly remembers that Chief Parker called the house with the news that Tom had made Lieutenant on a day when Tom was off fishing in Ensenada. Ethel hadn't known her husband had even tried for the promotion, and she decided to give him a surprise for a change, arranging for his new Lieutenant's uniform to be delivered to the house to be there when he returned home. She was delighted by the look on his face when he saw the uniform hanging in his closet. He was so excited he forgot to tell her about the fish he had left in the car. She discovered them the next morning.

Tom's new promotion was another step in the right direction by Parker, who had by this time been Police Chief for eight years. Before Parker, there had been numerous short-lived Police Chiefs since the scandal-ridden Davis administration had been driven from office.

Even though there was positive movement, the Department had a long way to go in ridding itself of discriminatory procedures. As Bradley describes it, the double standard was still deeply ingrained in the system. As a matter of common practice, minority officers were denied the promotional opportunities afforded to the rest of the department.

Because they knew that there was little likelihood of being treated fairly when it came to promotions, many of Bradley's minority colleagues lost their drive and their commitment to excellence. Again Bradley witnessed the waste of human talents and skills that discrimination can cause. But despite his anger and frustration, Bradley never lost his balance or his objectivity. Colleagues remember that, when someone at the station house tacked up a picture of Sammy Davis, Jr., and Swedish actress Mai Britt after their marriage, scrawling "nigger lover" across it, Bradley tried to dispel the tension. Although other officers vented their anger, people around Tom Bradley recall that his response was simply a shake of his head, even when he was the victim of racism. "He had a look somewhere between a smile and a grimace, but it was Tom's way of showing anger," said former colleague Wilbur Harris. "You never heard him say he was going to get even, he was always so noticeably calm and in control of the situation. That's what made him bigger than life to so many of us." It was as if Bradley realized that resentment or retribution delayed everyone from getting on with life. It was through moving forward that people could hope to overcome such obstacles.

Chief Parker was a disciplinarian whom Bradley grew to respect. As Police Chief, Parker had long outlasted the usual eighteen-month tenures of past chiefs. Bradley admired Parker's dedication to reestablishing the department's sense of dignity and his concern with guaranteeing the people of the city the protection they deserved. One particular trait Bradley valued was Parker's sense of fairness: "Up until Chief Parker, no one really knew if he would get a promotion or appointment, because the final decision was not based on the objective results of the examination. More often than not, people who had distinguished themselves on the examination would lose out to someone who happened to be a friend of the Chief." Parker changed that. If someone earned the promotion, he got it.

This was not to suggest that Parker's tenure marked a radical break with the segregated policies of the past. Parker was known to harbor hostile and stereotyped attitudes toward minorities. Often his behavior toward members of minority communities who blamed him for encouraging police abuse was arrogant. He had a tendency simply to shrug off public criticism. This got him into trouble with the community, a situation that Sam Yorty would exploit in his 1961 campaign against incumbent Mayor Norris Poulson, when he pledged to fire Parker if elected. This proved to be an empty campaign promise; Parker did not leave the LAPD until his retirement in 1965, at the age of sixty-three, after fifteen years of service.

By 1960, Bradley considered that his own stature within the department, combined with the changing political climate, might enable him to effect another major change in Police Department racial policies. This time his target was segregated radio cars.

The policy was costly, dangerous, and extremely inefficient. However, Bradley knew that many officers would resist changing it, and there was almost certain to be controversy. Nevertheless, he ordered that all the radio cars in his division in the Wilshire District were to be integrated. He asked Chief Parker to back him up and approve his new policy. To enforce the change, Bradley proposed that "If officers didn't go along with it, they would be out of a job, just like any other type of insubordination."

Parker refused to stand behind Bradley's orders. Without the Chief's approval, there was no threat of retaliation, so many officers called in sick, complaining loudly about Bradley's change. Throughout the LAPD, there were protests against the Wilshire division's integration plan. Those who favored the change were harassed and threatened. Without support from the top, the plan was doomed, at least temporarily. Bradley had realized that working through the system was the way to change the system. He had made the initial move, and was confident the segregated system was doomed; he felt that continuing to prod toward change would shorten the time until it was only a part of history.

His move did have a delayed impact. Within four years, Chief Parker announced that all squad cars would be integrated. When another round of protests ensued, Parker told renegades they could abide by it or turn in their badges. That was the end of segregated radio cars in the LAPD.

While working within the Police Department to open up opportunities to all officers, Bradley also assumed an increasingly activist role in community affairs. He joined with community leaders, many of whom he had met in the department's public relations work, to improve the quality of life and opportunity throughout the city. As Ed Roybal remembers, "Tom Bradley has always been a leader, not a black leader, just a natural leader of all the people." It was a characteristic more and more people were beginning to recognize. Fellow officers like Wilbur Harris also speculated that Bradley was coming to realize that there was no opportunity for a black captain—not even with his own distinguished record and education—in the LAPD. Bradley needed other opportunities.

It was shortly before he retired from the force in 1961 that Tom was approached with an unexpected request. Ruth Abraham, Warren Hollier, Rosalind Wyman, Cecil Morell, and Jack Tenner, all business and civic leaders in the black community, asked for the Lieutenant's help in an upcoming election. But this

time they wanted more from Bradley than just his usual commitment to put in long hours in behalf of a candidate.

The group told Bradley that they believed it was time for Los
Angeles to have its first black City Councilman. With the resignation of Tenth District Councilman Charles Navarro, who had
been elected City Controller, the community was in a unique
position to exert influence on the appointment to fill his unexpired term. There had been three other attempts to elect a black
councilman, including the effort in 1959 on behalf of Eddie
Atkinson, in which Bradley had been active. But this time, things
seemed different. Looking at the situation, they saw that Tom
Bradley was a successful policeman, a lawyer, and an activist
who knew the concerns and issues of the community. They
wanted him to seek the appointment. Lieutenant Bradley would
soon be retiring from police watch commander at the Miracle
Mile Wilshire station; as City Councilman he could continue to
serve his community, but in a different capacity.

The proposition that he try for the appointment came as a
surprise to Bradley. He recalls, "Running for office was not in my
mind, nor had it been in any of my long range plans." Long-time
friend Richard Boswell concurs, "I can tell you Tom was genuinely surprised at the idea to run for Council." Bradley adds,
"But after mulling over the possibilities, and the fact that it
would enable me to help out in a more active role in the community, would give me the credentials to propose policy changes
that were desperately needed, I decided to go for it." At this
time, as has generally been the case in his career, Bradley had
many people advising him, but as always it was he alone who
made the final decision—this time to forge ahead to a new stage
of his career in public service.

Bradley approached his decision at a time when the country
was beginning to wake up to new possibilities. Nationally, America was launching a space program, and John F. Kennedy (whom
Bradley had campaigned for in 1960) was launching what he
called the New Frontier. But the use of Kennedy's religion as a
campaign issue had been a sad reminder to Bradley that America
had a long way to go in living up to its ideals.

Bradley could sense that patience was running out among

some people. Blacks and other minorities, throughout the United States, had grown tired of waiting for equal opportunity. Even after the historic 1954 Brown Decision outlawing segregation in schools, there were still separate schools, north and south, east and west. People who had long been victims of discrimination were beginning to speak out. Minorities were calling for fair legislative district apportionment and demanding more representation. There was a need for new leadership in Los Angeles to help prod the system toward making changes. Tom Bradley was ready to put his legal training to work on issues of public policy.

The Tenth District was comprised of three distinct groups—whites, blacks, and Asians—with whites constituting an overwhelming majority. At that time, no district in Los Angeles had elected a black to the City Council. There had been pressure on the City Council from a number of organizations to appoint a black to serve out Councilman Navarro's unexpired term. Such a move would not only have been an acknowledgement of the growing political importance of minorities in the city, but would also have served as a visible indication that the City Council recognized the ten-year struggle for a black voice on the legislative body.

Certainly Lieutenant Bradley was an ideal candidate. One of the few minority lieutenants in the LAPD, and a long-time resident of the community, he had earned a reputation for being a pragmatic problem-solver, capable of dealing effectively with all elements of the neighborhood's diverse constituency. Bishop H. H. Brookins, then a young religious leader who had been recently appointed to one of the city's most prestigious black churches, identified these as the major reasons why Bradley was "the right person at the right time." Brookins concludes, "He was a moderate and forthright individual, a lawyer and competent about city government. He had strong support in the black community and credentials that brought him support from the white constituency as well."

Bradley also had a reputation for dealing constructively with the problems of troubled youth. In order to open up job opportunities for juveniles, he had laid the foundations for a partnership between government and business that was a model of how the public and private sectors could cooperate to their mutual benefit. In an era marked by conflict, Bradley had elected to work within the system, rather than advocate its destruction.

Bradley had long been active within the Democratic Party. Raye Cunningham, who served as a typist during his work in public relations at the Wilshire Station of the LAPD and who has been a member of his staff since 1963, remembers, "He used to go around as part of his job and acquaint himself with different organizations in the community to help in the police efforts, and that's one of the avenues that allowed him to know so many people and groups." Cunningham, like so many of Bradley's long-time friends and associates, also speaks of Bradley's inspirational qualities, recalling that it was he who got her to join the Democratic Club. "He was always trying to get new members to join. He has always been a real motivator."

Cunningham also recounts that it was Tom Bradley who urged her husband, a fellow police officer, to attend law school. "When Tom Bradley passed the bar the first time and my husband David didn't, Bradley continued to help him prepare for it a second time. . . . One day when we came home from the San Diego Zoo," Cunningham remembers, "all tuckered out after a long ride in a little old Volkswagen, with the kids and everyone mad, the phone was ringing. . . . It was Tom saying that David had passed the bar—it was great news, and especially then!"

Bradley's agreement to seek the Council appointment set off a flurry of activity. There were thirteen other candidates seeking the appointment, which meant that in order for a successful campaign to be waged, there first had to be a grassroots organizational effort.

Volunteers stalked the neighborhoods for the signatures needed to back a Bradley appointment. As Tom Bradley remembers it, "We went into the neighborhood and collected over seven thousand signatures, more than the number of votes required to actually win an election in the district." Rev. Brookins and others engaged the support of the churches on behalf of Bradley.

But the City Council chose to ignore Bradley's community support. As Montana McNealy remembers, "The community saw it as nothing short of a slap in the face, because even besides Tom, there were other aspiring blacks with considerable credentials, and none of them were selected either." Instead, the appointment went to Joe Hollingsworth, a wealthy Republican real-estate broker with no identity, visibility, or long-term interest in the heavily Democratic district.

Mayor Yorty's earlier public pledge to urge the appointment of a black to the Council had evaporated. When the appointment was being debated, the Mayor admitted he had no intention of getting involved. He told the press he would stay out of the deliberation. He had, as was his way of putting it, "gone fishing" instead of leaning on the Council to satisfy the needs and desires of the Tenth District.

The defeat of the people's choice for the appointment was met with widespread outrage. There was a campaign by district leaders H. H. Brookins, Warren Hollier, Ruth Abraham, Arnette Hartsfield, Jr., Opal Jones, Percia Hutcherson, Saul Reider, and Joe Wolf to recall the appointee. Though the candidate himself did not actively seek the recall, the effort lasted for six months, beginning in the late fall of 1961. Brookins remembers that the hard work resulted in over 13,000 signatures demanding Hollingsworth's ouster. Yet, through various questionable rulings by the City Clerk's office, including disqualification of specific wording, the petitions were ruled invalid and their thousands of signatures not legitimate, a charge that was vociferously protested in court.

In remembering the recall effort, Warren Hollier adds, "The City Clerk ruled that we used the wrong forms for the petitions, and the Superior Court held with the City Clerk's rulings." Yet the district's leaders' efforts did not stop. "We asked the Supreme Court to examine the matter, but it refused." Thus, despite the protests, Hollingsworth remained on the Council.

Bradley considers this to have been nothing short of a "conspiratorial effort" on the part of members of city government to discourage burgeoning political interest in the Baldwin Hills and Crenshaw areas. To all involved in the effort, Rev. Brookins' evaluation summed up the dominant feeling, "We are delayed, but not defeated."

The city's stonewalling served only to strengthen the resolve of Bradley and others to effect change on the Council. Bradley was determined that the election in 1963 would be one in which

the voters of the Tenth District—not the City Hall politicians—
would choose their own representative. He began preparing immediately for the election, intensifying his already heavy involvement in community organizations. In a period marked by divisive
rhetoric, Tom Bradley's low-key style became more widely
known and appreciated throughout the district. The objective
was not only to solidify support for his intended run for the
Council, but also to serve as a voice of reason in a period of fear
and uncertainity.

It was during this time that Bradley, who had worked with the
NAACP and the Urban League, attended an afternoon gathering
at the Beverly Hills home of film and television actor Anthony
Franciosa to help raise money for food and assistance for the
poor in the South. At the dinner was Anton Calleia, a reporter for
the *Los Angeles Times* who had been active in the civil rights
movement. During the course of the afternoon, as Calleia recounts, "Aaron Henry, a friend of mine from the NAACP in
Mississippi, introduced Tom Bradley." Calleia instantly felt that
what he was seeing in Bradley was a genuineness, a unique and
special force for good. "In such time of turmoil, a time to stand
up and be counted, Tom Bradley offered me an opportunity to do
something meaningful." It was the beginning of a relationship
that resulted in Anton Calleia's working as Press Secretary to
Bradley following his 1969 race for Mayor, and continuing as one
of Bradley's most trusted and valued aides.

After retiring from the police force in 1961, Bradley joined the
law practice of Charles Matthews, known as one of the brightest
attorneys in Los Angeles and the "Dean" of black lawyers because of his long practice for over three decades. Matthews had
known Bradley since his student days, had followed his career
closely, and—as a prosecutor for the District Attorney's office—
had had occasion to observe Bradley's frequent courtroom appearances as a witness for the LAPD. Upon hearing that Bradley
had decided to enter law, Matthews offered him an office at no
cost for a year. The two practiced out of an office on Crenshaw.

The community resentment over the Hollingsworth appointment continued to build. The community's commitment to re-
placing him was firm. Knowing how the large number of minority

candidates had divided the vote in past elections, local leaders, headed by Dr. Claude H. Hudson and Rev. H. H. Brookins, decided to hold a convention at the Alexandria Hotel to determine who would best serve the district, with the aim of uniting behind a single candidate.

There was considerable support for a Rev. Brookins candidacy, but the popular community leader felt that his responsibilities to his congregation would not allow him to devote enough time to the Council. The district needed someone who could devote his entire efforts for its constituents. At the convention, Brookins removed his name from consideration, and delivered what one supporter called the "most inspirational speech I have ever witnessed" in nominating Tom Bradley for the position. The convention ended with the entire black community in a rare display of unity.

The contest in 1963 would pit community choice Tom Bradley against political appointee Hollingsworth. The widespread disapproval of Hollingsworth—and of the 1962 power play that had put him in office—continued to fester. Nor was Hollingsworth's appointed deputy, Cage Johnson, any more popular than he was.

Maury Weiner was chosen to handle the precinct work for Bradley. Weiner was a canny political pro, who had earlier done the same job for Ed Roybal, a City Councilman from the Ninth District. Bradley had also been active in Roybal's campaigns for City Council and Lieutenant Governor, as he would be in Roybal's successful campaign for U.S. Congress in 1962.

The strengths and weaknesses of a Bradley candidacy were immediately apparent to Weiner: "Blackness in and of itself was considered radical." But Bradley's being a policeman balanced that. Furthermore, Weiner adds, "His not being publicly associated with any great controversial cause, although he was privately associated with many, was a plus, [because] the insiders knew of his conscientious efforts, but the general public did not. There was very little negative stuff they could throw at Tom Bradley."

Warren Hollier and Maury Weiner discovered, while organizing the precincts of the district, that the principal issue among the residents continued to be Hollingsworth's appointment to the Council in the face of a local mandate for Bradley. Also, Hollingsworth's record on the Council did nothing to endear him to his district. A glaring example was his outspoken opposition to a city ordinance for fair housing.

Rev. Brookins worked with Bradley on the writing and delivery of speeches. "He was a very shy individual and reluctant to push himself," Brookins remembers. "Because of my preaching background, I was able to be his lightning rod in helping him develop the skills to sell his leadership talents." Brookins' power in the community's churches also helped solidify support for a Bradley candidacy. He arranged for Tom to speak to church congregations and at church dinners and bazaars throughout the district.

The Bradley headquarters were located on Western Avenue. While Brookins and others provided strategy and advice, Ms. Teddy Muller was selected by Bradley to chair the 1963 contest, and recall veteran Frank Terry provided strategic input. To those who were familiar with politics, it seemed that in 1963 "we had the right stuff at the right time." There was a sense of imminent victory. Raye Cunningham collaborated with Madelle Watson from State Assemblyman Jess Unruh's 55th District office in the effort to get out the Tenth District vote. As Ruth Abraham remembers, when Unruh began sending some of his top lieutenants to help the Bradley campaign, "We began to feel real good because Jess Unruh was known for only backing winners." Also supporting the Bradley effort were Herschel and Pat Rosenthal, Norman and Dorothy Mattel, and Sheila Epstein, leaders in the district's Jewish community.

Bradley's campaign efforts went beyond the local grassroots organization. He was aided by supporters from the California Democratic Council. Another vital component of the Bradley effort was the support of his Kappa fraternity brothers from his days at UCLA. Ever since his student days, Bradley had been active in the organization. From 1964 to 1967, he held the office of Grand Polemarch of the fraternity, the first from the West Coast. He and Ethel were regulars in the weekly Kappa bridge games, and daughters Phyllis and Lorraine baby-sat for kids of fellow Kappas at the annual New Year's Eve party, as well as at other functions.

Respect for Bradley's character and convictions brought

many fellow athletes from UCLA days into the campaign. One was U.S. Congressman George Brown, who had been surprised to hear that the "ambitious cop" was pursuing a career in politics. They knocked on doors and distributed literature in the simple belief that, as Brown says, "Los Angeles needed more people like Tom Bradley."

One of Bradley's more dedicated supporters in 1963 was his first Field Deputy, Roland "Speedy" Curtis, who had been with him on the police force. Bradley describes Curtis as "my number-one advance man who could get any group of people's attention with just the right words." The duo of advance man and candidate worked well. Speedy worked the crowds "better than about anybody I have ever known," as Bradley recalls, then Tom would follow up with a pamphlet and a speech. Speedy also would be the official photographer for Tom during the ensuing years, attempting to fill the gap of the missing news reporter/photographer.

Bradley's support was like a patchwork quilt of groups from throughout Los Angeles. He received backing from numerous religious leaders, from influential businessmen, and from labor. Up to that time, no minority candidate had been endorsed by the city's largest newspaper, the *Los Angeles Times,* and Bradley was no exception. However, he did enjoy the support of the community paper, *The Sentinel.*

Bradley also received the unsolicited backing of a man he would later challenge for the leadership of City Hall, Mayor Sam Yorty. Mayor Sam's endorsement of Bradley stemmed more from the needs of his own political agenda—ridding the Council of those who openly opposed his policies—than any real agreement with the views that Tom espoused.

Bradley was, of course, extremely active in this campaign. "I remember running around giving out my literature and shaking hands from six in the morning until I almost dropped at night. . . . I think my rookie days on the force, directing traffic downtown on 3rd and Los Angeles helped out here. I would dart in and out of traffic, get on a bus and ride it for awhile, and make sure I shook everyone's hand and had given them a brochure."

The Bradley for Council effort also took advantage of another resource. Daughter Lorraine remembers that she and Phyllis had all their friends come over to the house on Welland: "We looked over particular neighborhoods on the map, and I told them where to put pamphlets on the doors." It turned out to be very hard work, but not unrewarded. As Lorraine tells it, "I remember opening the door, and seeing Daddy with a bag full of candy and a cake for all of us. It was like we had won the election right then. The next day we were all back at it, and after awhile we associated Speedy Curtis with hamburgers, because that's what we got after a hard day's work."

Bradley's grassroots style of campaigning included a tactic that had worked well for President John F. Kennedy during his successful run for Senate in Massachusetts:—community coffees, presided over by his wife. To the 25 to 100 wives who gathered at these functions, Ethel conveyed her husband's stand on the issues and interests of the Tenth District. She told those present how important it was for them to become active in the campaign—that, in the future, they could remind their children that they had been a part of electing Los Angeles' first black councilman, and that, because of their shared commitment and joint efforts, their children's future would hold more than just dreams.

Described by one of her closest friends as a "sharp, creative, charming person who has been a major factor and bedrock in Tom Bradley's success," Ethel Bradley was well-known and admired in the community. Her success as a businesswoman was second only to her devotion to her family and her husband. A former scout leader during her girls' younger years, an excellent cook and hostess, and a dedicated gardener, who even then was well known for her landscaping skills, Ethel had been campaigning for her husband in one way or another since his college days. She had been active in his successful rise to the top of the national organization of the Kappa fraternity. "Ethel would get up and give speeches like a pro, and used to get so mad when Tom didn't win, but, of course, that wasn't very often," a family friend remembers. The chemistry of the couple worked to their advantage. Tom's shyness had been offset on numerous occasions by Ethel's vivacity.

Now that her husband was attempting to become the first black ever to sit on the City Council, Ethel worked harder than ever to ensure his election. While some wives might have shrunk from a public life, Ethel Bradley did not. Jessie Mae Beavers describes her as "very happy and very supportive of Tom's decision to run for the Council . . . because, after all, this was a great step for a black man to be taking in those days." Despite her total commitment to Bradley's political career, Ethel's approach has at times been misinterpreted, but only by those who don't know her. As one close friend comments, "She sometimes sits back and watches, but she is very proud of everything he does, and I mean genuinely proud. Some people just might not realize that." The special bond between Tom and Ethel would be a source of strength for both in their journey from South Central Los Angeles to City Hall.

The Councilman candidate chose to run an issue-oriented campaign, thereby setting the tone for his campaigns in the future. He discussed subjects of immediate concern to all members of the community—not just Hollingsworth's failure to support the fair-housing ordinance, but nitty-gritty problems like the out-of-repair streetlights on Genessee Avenue, the lack of regular hours for street-sweeping, the need for playgrounds on La Brea Avenue.

There were signs that the campaign's message had struck a responsive chord. Ruth Abraham noticed, when she walked the Crenshaw area and one particular housing project, that people would not only accept the Bradley literature, but "pull me into the apartment and show me how to vote for Tom Bradley on the ballot." She remembers it being a wonderful experience, except for one problem. The interest in Bradley and the tendency for constituents to want to talk about him, delayed her in finishing the precinct walk on time. The result was that she could not keep to her schedule, which displeased the campaign staff. However, the important thing was that enthusiasm for the candidate was building. The grassroots effort was paying off. Abraham concludes, "I think the voters already knew that there was something inherently honest in Tom Bradley."

The Bradley effort was not without its setbacks. There were those who were still caught up in the politics of prejudice. Precinct walker and resident Leroy Berry remembers, "We would go to people's houses and they would open the small opening behind the door knock grate and see who it was, and then slam the door shut. They were really disturbed that blacks had moved into their neighborhood. A black person coming to the door and ringing the bell reminded them that blacks had invaded their community."

But Bradley forged ahead, campaigning on issues of substance, ignoring the politics of race, and pledging that he would "see to it that the Councilman of the Tenth District knows its problems, and represents the concerns of all of its people. . . . I live in this community. It is my home and yours. I've walked its streets as a cop, and practiced law on Crenshaw. I know what it means to have someone you can depend on. I think you know my record."

Bradley told the voters that he would be an active voice for the district: "We deserve a councilman who will always be available to hear your ideas, who will work together with you to open up opportunities for this district and this city, and to ensure these hopes are available to everyone."

5

Election to City Council

"The good of man must be the end of the science of politics."

—Aristotle

When the votes were tabulated in the April election, the cheers and laughter in the Bradley campaign headquarters told passers-by on Crenshaw Avenue that the 225,000 people of the Tenth District had spoken. To those who had appointed Hollingsworth the year before, the sound was deafening. Long-time supporter Arnette Hartsfield, Jr., remembers, "That night everyone in the election headquarters knew it was the beginning of something special."

Bradley's two-to-one margin represented a historical first in the City of Los Angeles. Although the appointment of Gilbert Lindsay to the Council just prior to the Tenth District race had cracked the color barrier (in a move by Mayor Yorty, which Maury Weiner speculates was designed to defuse the Bradley campaign), Bradley was the first black person elected to sit in the Council chambers at City Hall. He was soon to be joined by Billy Mills who was elected in May of 1963.

According to Maury Weiner, this marked the first time a black had been elected to office from a predominantly white constituency in any state west of the Mississippi.

The assessment offered by Sanford Sigoloff, Chief Executive Officer of the Wickes Corporation, seems an accurate description of the chemistry that had brought Tom Bradley to this point: "He's a guy who is the living image of what you can do if you really have the will to win, whether it's education or being a football star. He got an education and he got a law degree when you really had to be a hero of sorts in this country." The Tenth District's new Councilman was now on his way down a road that would find him, in Sigoloff's words, "running a small country— the City of Los Angeles."

At a time when many communities nationwide experienced race riots and the inner cities were blazing with fires of hatred, Los Angeles looked as if it might be able to weather the storm. The Los Angeles City Council now had three credible minority representatives from districts most susceptible to conflict. Yet beneath the veneer of progress was a profound resistance to real change, a racism that had gone underground but was still very much alive.

Bradley was determined to lead Los Angeles away from the confrontational tactics that characterized cities throughout the United States. To do so, he knew that he would have to be aware of the views of all the people and be prepared to utilize his skills at mediation. As Raye Cunningham put it, "from the very beginning, it was obvious that Tom Bradley's interests were those of everybody, not just blacks or any other constituency." The major emphasis in the process, according to Bradley, was compromise. "I'm not going to beat something to death that is not going to happen, and everyone has got to remember that I am Councilman of the entire district, not just one group of people." His insistence on finding what Cunningham calls "the common denominator, the currency on which to build trust and a consensus," has left Bradley open to the charge of being co-opted. Trying to represent all of the people all of the time often cost Bradley dearly, but it is one of the principles to which he has remained faithful.

While some have seen it as a weakness, Anton Calleia— speaking from over twenty-three years of experience with Tom Bradley—sees it as one of his great strengths: "As a realist and a very effective leader, Tom possesses the unique ability to create coalitions." Calleia adds, "Civil rights is really not a black issue any more than the holocaust is a Jewish issue. It's a human issue, and we are all part of it."

Bradley's ability to stay above the emotions of the political arena is a trait he has displayed on many occasions. It is, in fact, one of his most characteristic traits. Maury Weiner, who joined the Bradley staff in 1965 as a field deputy and who has been described by Bradley as a "strategic mastermind," recalls a vicious attack on Bradley by a fellow Council member during a session. Bradley did not respond to the harangue. When he returned to the office, Weiner asked him how he felt about the personal attack. Bradley's reply was "What personal attack? He had some people in the audience from his district and was attempting to make himself into a hero; don't pay any attention to that."

Many of his staff members, including field deputies Warren Hollier, Speedy Curtis, and Kitty Uyeshima, have been enraged by comments made about their boss, only to find Bradley unbothered by the attacks. Calleia remembers an incident that prompted him to rush into Bradley's office in a tirade about what some opponent had said: "Throughout the entire time I was there expressing my outrage, Bradley merely watched me." When Calleia finished and sat down, Bradley put his hand on Anton's shoulder and said, "When a man angers you, he conquers you."

The ability not to take attacks personally, to understand the diverse motivations operating in the political arena, and then simply go about his own business is one that both friends and opponents recognize as typical of Tom Bradley.

Bradley's view that each district influences the others, that the city is only the sum of its parts, became more widely accepted during his tenure on the Council. Some Councilmen continued to confine themselves solely to the needs of their own districts, but others, at least on some issues, opted for a more citywide approach. Bradley himself sees this as one of the major ways he came to be useful in "filling the void in mayoral leadership." On the national level, President Lyndon Baines Johnson selected Bradley as a member of the Peace Corps Advisory Board.

During Bradley's tenure, the Council established the Board of Grants Administration. Designed initially to meet the needs of poorer neighborhoods with federal dollars, the BGA later worked to obtain money from Washington for improvements throughout the city. "In order for the BGA to operate, each Councilman had to look at the benefits to the entire city and not just one area," Bradley explains. "The Mayor's office had been ineffective in cooperating with Washington, and getting the money we were eligible to obtain for such programs. We worked to turn it around."

By the summer of 1965, Bradley and other Councilmen were intensely aware of the frustration and despair growing each day in the South-Central Los Angeles neighborhood of Watts which was considerably south of Bradley's district, but very much a concern of his. The general opinion was that the city government was not doing enough to improve conditions. The facts supported his assessment. The Watts neighborhood of over 380,000 people was an area of chronic high unemployment, and it did not have a single employment agency. There were three separate bus lines that caused great confusion among the residents. The nearest hospital was two hours away by bus. While militant activists echoed H. Rap Brown's "Burn, Baby, Burn" proclamation, the Mayor's office seemed more apt to offer matches than increased opportunity to the depressed area. Los Angeles had been allotted a $2.7 million grant to the Youth Opportunity Board, but only $1 million had been dispersed by Yorty. Three thousand of sixteen thousand neighborhood youth corps jobs remained unfilled. Only 1,843 of the five thousand participants in the "Work Experience" program had been selected.

Councilman Bradley charged that City Hall was dragging its feet in allocating the federal funds. He joined with other Councilmen in calling for the immediate release of these funds. Bradley remembers, "One of the major reasons for the Watts disturbances was the lack of jobs and a widespread feeling of hopelessness and desolation. But it went farther than that, it was rooted in a lack of skills, the wasting of talent due to the absence of education."

Raye Cunningham, who at the time was office secretary for the Tenth District Councilman, describes the day Bradley went to Watts to witness the situation firsthand. Taking the bus to emphasize his identification with the people he was serving, he spent the day walking the streets and listening to members of the community. He visited schools and spoke to youngsters about their expectations of the future, talked to the indigent, and interviewed employers in the area about their job requirements. Prior to the trip, he had successfully persuaded several businesses to hire people from the Watts area, but now he realized that soliciting jobs was only one, and not the most crucial, answer to the problem. Training people to work in those jobs was another, and more basic, need.

Bradley was surprised at the lack of even the most elementary reading and writing skills, and he was moved by the depth of the hopelessness and the lack of self-esteem. He realized more powerfully than ever how much a job-training program was needed—this at a time when there were no funds for such purposes in Watts. Cunningham recalls Bradley returning to the office visibly shaken by the trip and more determined to develop a training program for the chronic unemployed. It was an idea that would not be fully realized until his own mayoral administration, when the city's efforts with the federal government's CETA program would meet with success.

At the time, Leon Washington, publisher of the black community paper, *The Sentinel,* advocated a black boycott: "Don't spend your money where you can't work." Thomas Griffith of the NAACP and leaders of the Urban League helped mobilize the community against the injustice of racism. One resident remembers, "There was also reaction against our efforts to improve the situation. Many crosses were burned on lawns in the 92nd Street area." Division was growing in the community. During a high-school football game between two schools—one predominantly white, the other black—a black student was burned in effigy at halftime. All the signs pointed toward a major confrontation.

During late July and early August of 1965, there were sporadic incidents of police abuse—both physical and verbal—in Watts. Police Department leadership failed to take the necessary actions to control the situation. There was no viable communication network with Watts' community leaders. Bradley knew firsthand that this was the critical time for the department to be working with community leaders in the attempt to defuse the explosive situation. But there was no leadership, no cooperation. Instead, the gap between the Police Department and the community widened.

The State Advisory Committee and the United States Civil

Rights Commission had earlier warned Mayor Yorty that mistrust of the police was a major problem in the Los Angeles ghetto. The Mayor's response reflected his inability to fully comprehend the issue; Yorty admonished that the Commission had been "raided by the Communist press."

To Bradley and others in regular contact with the community, the degree of mistrust and hostility in the Watts area served as signals of the danger ahead. Bradley sought to remedy the situation. He worked with other Council members to establish vitally important lines of communication. He introduced a motion within the Council, seconded by Billy Mills, to establish a Human Relations Board. But, as one member remembers, "The group of Valley Councilmen blocked its formation." As a former police officer, Bradley recognized the warning signs of impending violence all too well. He vividly described to his Council colleagues the deep-seated distrust of the Police Department by the black community. He and others proposed that the city should become involved in creating employment opportunities for the thousands without jobs.

Tom's political activism at this period was entirely motivated by his hope and belief that actions by the Council could forestall, or at least limit, the imminent racial explosion. Yet, as he and Councilmen Mills and Lindsay observed, the majority of the Council did not seem concerned. Why was the city establishment not taking the situation seriously? Why weren't measures taken to avert what seemed like inevitable confrontation?

Bradley argued that the creation of a Human Relations Board to mediate between the police and the community could dispel some of the mistrust in the black community. Bradley concurred that it could provide a continuing dialogue between the community and city government. But criticism from the Police Department for speaking out was the only response Bradley received. The Council voted the measure down, believing that the best way to handle the situation was to ignore it. The problem was surely not as bad as Councilman Bradley and his colleagues made it out to be.

This proved to be an extremely dangerous and misguided view. Tensions heightened, finally culminating in four days and nights of violence and bloodshed. A fifty-square-mile area of Watts became an urban nightmare. Police were unable to control the situation. The grim results of the riots left $40 million in property damage, thirty-five fatalities, and over one thousand wounded. So many businesses burned on 103rd Street that it became known as "Charcoal Alley." Over 1,800 people were jailed. Ten thousand National Guardsmen marched in a "state of insurrection." It was one of the most destructive uprisings in the nation's history. By comparison, the Detroit race riots of 1943 had resulted in thirty-five deaths and seven hundred injured. The deadliest such disturbance had occurred in 1919, a race riot in East St. Louis, Illinois, which claimed forty-seven lives.

City officials were quick to place the blame. Chief Parker stated that the riots started when "one person threw a rock, and then, 'like monkeys in a zoo,' others imitated the behavior." Mayor Yorty offered several explanations. First, he blamed the State Police for beginning the riot by making the first arrest, then the "Communists for agitating Negroes with propaganda over the past police brutality," and finally the bureaucratic bungling that had held up the city's federal anti-poverty dollars.

Nationally, President Lyndon Johnson remarked, "Rights will not be won through violence. . . . Equal rights carry equal responsibility." Martin Luther King and Senator Robert F. Kennedy looked toward the deeper meaning of the tragedy. King walked through the area and concluded, "There is a unanimous feeling that there has been police brutality." Kennedy told the press that too many blacks saw the present laws as the "enemy." Therefore, "obeying them simply did not make sense." National magazines such as *Time* pointed accusing fingers at Yorty's blatant disregard for the more than half a million blacks who made up fifteen percent of the city's population: "Like most of his predecessors, Yorty expresses paternalistic interest in the city's Negro population, but has made little effort to understand its problems or anticipate its difficulties."

The Watts riots were an extremely difficult time for Bradley. Throughout the days leading up to the disturbance, seeking as always to work within the system, he had suggested one measure after another to the Mayor's office, hoping to defuse the situation.

But Yorty did nothing. Even after the riots, the closest the Mayor got to the neighborhood was a bird's-eye view from the city helicopter he used frequently.

After the public hearings and interviews with hundreds of those involved, Councilman Bradley and others concurred with Martin Luther King, Jr. While they did not condone the acts of violence that had been committed by the residents of Watts, they charged that the Police Chief and the LAPD had erred seriously in their performance. Bradley was publicly critical of the well-documented police abuse that had occurred during the riot. He cited pages of credible evidence to back his assertions. But the Council chose to ignore the facts.

No one wanted to criticize the police. Therefore, facts, figures, and the eyewitness testimony of hundreds—the very requisites of the judicial process—were ignored. Having been a cop for twenty-one years, Bradley knew what constituted abuse and inappropriate conduct. In fact, it had been his job to investigate it at various stages of his police career. It was clear to him that, for the four turbulent days of the Watts riots, many officers had overreacted in the heat of the moment. Professionalism had broken down. Expansion of the department's community relations program was badly needed in this troubled area.

Bradley voiced his findings and was heavily criticized for them, but he stood firm, both in his refusal to excuse the crimes committed by the rioters, and in his overriding conviction that City Hall and the LAPD had badly overreacted.

Bradley and other Council members and civic leaders strongly argued that the Council's investigation of the Watts riots should focus on an examination of the causes and a discussion of steps that could be taken in the future to prevent a repetition of such a tragedy. They proposed that the Council assume a more constructive role by establishing an outreach network within the community and among the thousands left homeless by the destruction. They tried to use the riots as proof of the need for better education, transportation, and economic opportunities in the city's deprived areas.

Surprisingly, supportive of this view were the findings of the McCone Commission, appointed by Governor Pat Brown to look into the Watts situation. This commission was headed by John McCone, a conservative Republican; and, although it absolved the police of blame, it pointed to the need for resolving problems of health, jobs, and education in the area.

But the Mayor and most of the Council members were interested only in attributing blame, in naming individuals whom they could point to as having started the violence. Council speeches called for retribution, not understanding. But Bradley, Billy Mills and Gilbert Lindsay, among others, decided to make up for the Mayor's failure. They used the Grant Board Administration and other agencies to obtain funds from Washington, in order to rebuild the area. Their goal was to put hope and promise back into the lives of people left with nothing.

The issue of police brutality outraged Bradley. Throughout his days on the Council, he called for independent investigations into incidents where evidence suggested there had been use of excessive force by the police. Because of his background on the force, Bradley was able to offer specific recommendations for ways in which the Police Department could improve the quality of its service.

The overreaction by the police during the Watts incident was part of a nationwide epidemic of police brutality in response to inner-city rioting. Illinois Governor Otto Kerner, the Chairman of the President's Commission on Violence, would later create the term "police riot" to describe such actions.

Even with conclusive evidence of police abuse, the Council balked at issuing so much as a reprimand. To some councilmen, the police department was a sacred cow. In an era resounding with demands for "law and order from conservative members of the community," these representatives feared that they would be criticized, and they would have to face charges of being "anti-police" when they made their reelection bids.

In the wake of the death and destruction of the Watts riots of 1965, the Council did belatedly approve the Human Relations Board proposal. But, when Mayor Yorty announced that he alone would determine the Board's members, a good idea was transformed into just another ineffectual commission. Councilman Bradley reacted to this by fighting to withhold funds for the

Campaign Headquarters for Tenth District Council race in 1963: standing, Raye B. Cunningham, Abe Mandel, Robert Crane, Geri Smith, Warren Hollier, Richard Bruce; seated, Tom, Campaign Manager Teddy Muller, David R. Cunningham. (Courtesy of Richard Bruce)

Los Angeles City Council in 1965, standing from left, Billy Mills, Jim Potter, Ed Edelman, Tom Shepherd, Paul Lamport, John Ferraro, Marvin Braude, Tom Bradley, Ernani Bernardi, Louis Nowell. Seated, Bob Wilkinson, Gilbert Lindsay, L. E. Timberlake, John Gibson, Art Synder. (Courtesy of Los Angeles City Hall)

A good friend of Vice-President Hubert Humphrey, Tom campaigned for his election in 1968. (Courtesy of Los Angeles City Hall)

Councilman Tom and Ethel Bradley with Dr. Martin Luther King, Jr., Bishop H. H. Brookins at Southern Christian Leadership Conference, 1964. (Courtesy of Los Angeles City Hall)

Board's operation. "It turned out to be only another of the Mayor's public relations' toys, nothing like what was originally intended," Bradley explained.

Careful examination of Bradley's record on the City Council shows his involvement in a wide variety of issues that affected groups throughout the Los Angeles area. Certainly the Tenth District concerns that Bradley addressed most actively—Police Department and city government professionalism, fair housing, consumer protections, transportation, and equal opportunity—were of interest to all Los Angeles citizens.

But even on such issues as oil drilling in the Pacific Palisades, miles from his own district, Bradley was a leading voice. His intensive analysis of the proposal—and the questions that he raised about the terms of the permit that the City Council had granted to Occidental Petroleum—suggested that a serious reconsideration of the issue was in order. However, few people at City Hall were listening to Bradley or to the citizen action groups about the Occidental drilling permit. It was clear to Bradley that no one in the Mayor's office had given the matter serious thought. The drilling was to be done in an area susceptible to earthquakes; there were questions to be asked about the danger not only to the homes and businesses nearby, but also to California's state treasures—its beaches.

These concerns were debated heatedly by Bradley and other Council members. Much to Mayor Yorty's dismay, public opinion was also aired in these hearings. Yet neither the unanswered questions nor the speeches by homeowners prevented the ultimate approval of Occidental Petroleum's drilling proposal by the City Council.

But the controversy did not stop. Angry residents exercised their democratic rights, holding meetings with sympathetic councilmen and deciding to take the case to court. Eventually, the Council's decision was overturned.

The Occidental drilling issue continued to be disputed for years. In 1985, after Occidental finally changed its plans to take care of the objections of environmentalists, Bradley (as Mayor) finally approved a drilling permit. It was a move that his supporters cite as evidence of his flexibility, but some groups still oppose it and criticize Bradley for giving in.

Bradley's low-key approach to problem-solving was a direct contrast to the public performances of Yorty. "Mayor Sam," as he was called by his supporters, "Swingin' Sam" by his adversaries, tended to favor the thrill of the flashy fight (and the media attention it generated) rather than a behind-the-scenes leadership role of mediation and reconciliation. In his 1961 campaign for Mayor, Yorty had earned the nickname of "Trash Barrel Sam" by focusing almost exclusively on consolidation of garbage collection as his major campaign issue. The candidate called upon all citizenns to break up the "tin-can monopolies" of the day, and on that basis was elected Mayor.

As quiet as Tom seemed, he was not about to be thwarted by the "maverick" Yorty. When the Mayor rejected as too expensive the Council's calls for programs to put people to work and improve the quality of life in the city's neighborhoods, Councilman Bradley, who had become known as a fiscal conservative, was prepared to show that the problem was not so much in the size of the budget, but in its management. He had become more and more convinced from the twelve-hour days he put in on the Council that an adept administrator could shave millions of dollars of bureaucratic waste and duplication from the city's budget.

For example, Bradley had carefully analyzed the bureaucratic overlap of city and county programs during his early days on the Council. Councilman Ernani Bernardi's cogent analysis of how the city and county were both involved in the same areas of health care had impressed him. Bernardi gave detailed examples to his colleagues of services rendered by both sets of government agencies. Bradley joined Bernardi in calling for a merger of the overlapping agencies, arguing that millions of dollars could be saved each year.

Bradley pored over the bureaucratic structure of the city and county. As a member of the Southern California Association of Governments, Bradley was aware of the pitfalls of such overlap. He reviewed the functions of each arm of government, and was struck by the duplication of tasks and services. Health care, the issue addressed by Councilman Bernardi, represented only the tip of the iceberg. The same type of overlap existed in numerous other areas. The result was needless spending of scarce funds that could be put to far more efficient use in programs that had been previously neglected.

Why had nothing been done to begin the long overdue merger of the county and city? Bradley and his staff investigated. The answer was that government was bogged down by the reluctance of either the city or the county to initiate action that would mean cutting jobs, money, or power. Neither the Council nor the County Board of Supervisors were anxious to meddle in questions of jurisdiction, because of the political controversy that would inevitably result. Nor was the Mayor's office willing to offer any initiative.

But Bradley's standards of performance were different. Even in a situation where his personal interests were most directly at stake, such as the Council's vote on a police pension plan that would fluctuate with the rate of inflation (and other variables) Bradley voted from his principles, not his pocketbook. Although, as a retiree from the Police Department, he would have personally benefitted from the change, Bradley attacked the measure as too costly to the city's taxpayers.

However the temper of the times dictated that virtually any request made by the police would win uncritical approval. The pension measure passed the Council, and was then approved by voters at the polls. As Bradley points out, "the public later paid for this mistake with higher taxes."

The shortsightedness and the lack of vision by the Yorty administration was evident to Councilman Bradley on numerous other issues. As an example, Bradley recalls the construction of the $20 million Convention Center in 1966. While the majority of the Council favored construction of the facility as a means of attracting business to Los Angeles, the debate centered on its location. "The Mayor and his supporters first wanted to build it on a park site already owned by the city," Bradley explains, "which was near the Elysian Park area, and I along with several others voiced a strong protest. We thought that we needed to leave the park for the people." The Council was pressed to look for another location, and Bradley suggested that the Center be constructed in the USC area, adjacent to the Memorial Coliseum and Sports Arena complex, because that location could easily offer the necessary parking, as well as proximity to related restaurants and the freeway system.

Furthermore, there would be reciprocal advantages. The Center's construction at the site could have been an enormous economic boon to an area that was very depressed at that time. Bradley presented these and other arguments in Council and received some support from his colleagues. But, when the final decision was made, Bradley's arguments did not garner the support needed for adoption. The final site selected was not Exposition Park. Instead, the impressive 200,000-square-foot Civic Center project, covering thirty-one acres, was constructed in the central city downtown area on the Pico–Figueroa site, because of the accessibility to residential areas and to the Santa Monica and Harbor freeways.

Waging the battle, fervently debating the issues only to fall short when the final votes were tabulated, seemed to be, at times, an all too predictable pattern for Councilman Bradley. Yet fellow workers and friends testify that setbacks tended to spur him on rather than to frustrate him. His experience in trying for a Council seat was typical. Defeated in his first bid for it, he went after it with even greater resolve the second time around and won. Failure seemed only to strengthen him, never to embitter him.

Many of the proposals Bradley sponsored or supported in Council—the Human Relations Commission, the Consumer Affairs Bureau, specific mergers in county and city government, and others—were initially rejected, but later—after Bradley reintroduced them and made effective arguments on their merits— were eventually accepted. Sometimes his fellow councilmen changed their minds only after dire events proved their value, such as the destruction and deaths experienced in Watts. Other times, an idea that seemed radical at first (like integrated radio cars, to harken back to Bradley's days on the police force) went through an incubation period before it was seen as the sensible course of action.

After many such struggles, Bradley came to have a keen appreciation of the importance of timing in public policy. There were times when his constituency or the Council were not yet ready to face up to an issue. The political facts of a given period might clearly indicate that the possibility was remote for passing and implementing a measure Bradley considered crucial. In these cases, Bradley knew that he needed patience, but he would put the deliberative process into motion, inviting discussion on the issue, knowing that eventually it would prevail.

However, there were other times when Bradley felt that waiting for the right moment was simply not possible. When he tried unsuccessfully to argue for the right of anti-Vietnam protestors to address the Council after a large demonstration in Century City, Bradley's convictions about what was right overrode considerations of what was politically timely or expedient. He firmly believed in the right of people to present their opinions. Freedom of speech is one of the chief guarantees of this country and its Constitution, and Bradley was more concerned about honoring that promise than about whether it would be a popular move. Unfortunately, the majority of the Council and Mayor Yorty disagreed with him. Yorty's contempt for dissenting opinion on the Vietnam War was widely known. He had been so vocal and adamant in his support of America's role in Southeast Asia, that he had acquired another nickname for his long list—"Saigon Sam."

Neither the Council nor City Hall cared to hear the voices of the protestors. The predominant view was that America had a mission to rid the world of Communism, and Vietnam was our Alamo. We had to make a stand. In this, they merely echoed the President of the United States in his narrow view of foreign affairs. The democratic process was thereby severely handicapped, the result being the loss of an entire generation's faith and respect. Bradley sought to join Eugene McCarthy, Robert Kennedy, and Martin Luther King, Jr., in restoring hope to a land badly in need of moral leadership, on matters of both domestic and foreign policy.

The Tenth District's satisfaction with Bradley as their Councilman was evident. In 1967, he ran unopposed for another term and received a strong mandate from voters on election day.

6

Running for Mayor

"Tom Bradley has plans for a greater Los Angeles. He can give people everywhere hope for the future of our city."

—Adlai Stevenson

The year 1968 was one of turmoil in America. Two leaders who inspired hope in millions of Americans were gunned down within weeks of each other in senseless acts of violence. One man, Martin Luther King, had believed and demonstrated throughout his life that social progress was possible through peaceful protest, and that the confrontational tactics and acts of violence advocated by militants would only aggravate the growing gap between people. But King's dreams for America received a great blow with his murder at a Memphis motel.

The other man had also been deeply concerned about this country's movement toward what Governor Otto Kerner, in the report of the President's Commission on Violence, had described as "Two societies—one black and one white." But Robert Kennedy's hopes and aspirations for a united and just society also ended in an explosion of gunfire, this one in Los Angeles at the Ambassador Hotel.

Tom Bradley had learned of the shooting after having deciding to pass up the election night festivities at the hotel in order to accompany his wife Ethel to a Los Angeles Dodgers game. He spent the entire night sleepless with despair over the violence that was convulsing his country. In the wake of the assassinations, cities all across the nation were burning.

The war was dragging on in Southest Asia. Each day, Bradley read the morning news, staring at the grim body count of the young Americans killed. He had backed the candidacy of Senator Kennedy and campaigned actively in his behalf in the California presidential primary, believing that Bobby would end the war and could offer hope and inspiration to a troubled land.

Bradley was a delegate to the 1968 Chicago Democratic Convention, where amidst the barbed wire and barricades, Hubert Humphrey was chosen to run for President against Richard Nixon. As a good Democrat and a good friend of Humphrey's, Bradley campaigned hard in the doomed 1968 electoral effort.

For Bradley, one good thing did come out of the 1968 convention—his meeting Stephen Reinhardt, an articulate political strategist from California and of the National Democratic Committee. Soon Reinhardt would begin advising Bradley on political decisions. His political prowess within California later proved to be an advantage in Bradley's quest to oust Sam Yorty from City Hall. To Reinhardt, Bradley's unique ability to unite people was apparent from their first meeting.

Reinhardt spoke on behalf of all the officers of the Democratic State Central Committee, the Democratic County Committee, and the Democratic clubs in Southern California, endorsing Democrat Bradley instead of Democrat Yorty. He stated: "We do so with enthusiasm, with pride, and with increased determination to help insure his victory May 27. It is pathetic that Sam Yorty cannot, or will not, face up to the fact that Democrats and Republicans alike are supporting Tom Bradley—not for ulterior motives [of attracting black voters], nor as part of a sinister conspiracy—but simply because they believe Tom Bradley is by far the best choice for Mayor."

Tom Bradley was growing increasingly concerned about the lack of direction and vision from Mayor Yorty's office. Los Angeles was floundering, failing to capitalize on its potential as the nation's gateway to the Pacific. Rather than taking advantage of federal programs, Los Angeles, under the Yorty administration, seemed to be content to languish in the warm western sun. Yorty didn't act, he reacted, thus losing what Bradley saw as the opportunity to actively shape policy and control events. The apathy and inertia were compounded by Yorty's work habits. In Bradley's words, "He was no more than a part-time Mayor. Most of the time Yorty wouldn't arrive until mid-morning, and then he was gone by mid-afternoon."

Yorty reveled in the perquisites of office—helicopter rides to and from work, and his frequent trips to Europe, the Middle East, the Far East, and Mexico, which had earned him yet another nickname, "Travelin' Sam." Many people were concerned that Los Angeles should have more than an absentee chief executive. The fastest growing city on the West Coast needed a mayor who matched its vigor. In 1967, Bradley tried to tackle the problem by proposing a Council resolution that would limit the Mayor's tenure to only two terms, but the resolution failed. The evidence suggested that the reason was more out of a personal concern of the Council members that their own jobs might become jeopardized by similar legislation limiting tenure on the Council. Since it was clear that Yorty was gearing up for a reelection bid, Bradley contemplated the possible alternatives to a Yorty candidacy. But who could oppose Yorty, to bring dynamic new leadership to City Hall in 1969?

At a meeting with his key advisors, after his reelection to the Council in 1967, Bradley had mentioned the possibility of his running for Mayor. He recalls the group's reaction to his suggestion: "Well, at first they thought I was joking." Warren Hollier reminded his friend and Councilman of the political reality of Los Angeles—blacks had been on the Council only for five years. It would be impossible to elect a black as Mayor of Los Angeles. At a time when television screens were filled with news stories on black militants threatening to burn down the country, even the most ardent Bradley supporters were dubious about his chances for becoming Mayor of the third largest city in the United States.

But lifelong supporters such as Lonnie Wilson urged him to make the race: "It was like part of the natural progression, and I always though it it was a good idea for him to run. To dive in and take a chance. . . . That's my nature, and I think it is the very same with Tom Bradley—a willingness to take the chance to be a force of good in such a troubled time. Nothing but determination beats a child of failure except that you just have to get out there and try."

To Tom Bradley, tackling impossible odds was a familiar scenario. He had been doing it all his life. He wasn't willing to take "no" for an answer. Though he was realistic enough to know the odds against him in a mayoral race, something within him wanted to take the chance, to make the try. He had faith in himself and in the ability of the Los Angeles voters to judge the candidates on their records rather than on race.

Except for his own deep-seated hunch that he should run, however, there were few other encouraging signs for a Bradley for Mayor campaign. Private polls in early 1969 revealed that, despite his involvement in issues outside the Tenth District, Bradley was virtually unknown citywide. Also, there were thirteen other candidates in the April 1969 primary, including Republican Congressman Alphonzo Bell, popular television commentator Baxter Ward, and liberal Democratic Congressman Tom Rees.

A definite handicap was that all of those vying for Yorty's job were also vying for the same sources of financial support. Many prominent contributors who praised Bradley's record were dubious about his chances of a mayoral candidacy in a city where only seventeen percent of the population was black. At all levels, serious doubts were expressed about Bradley's prospects. Hale Champion, a cabinet member in Governor Edmund "Pat" Brown's administration, remembers: "Anybody who seriously thought that a black candidate had *any* chance for winning any office in 1969 was looked upon as *crazy*." Charlotte Asberry, who worked in Mayor Yorty's office at the time, recalls, "In the primary, the major figures in the office didn't seem too concerned, especially about Bradley." A Bradley fan, Asberry remembers "wanting him to win, but wondering in the back of my mind if he had any chance of being successful. . . . I personally did not think he was going to win because of his race." Stafford Grady, head of the State Insurance Commission in the 1960s recalls, "Having heard Bradley adeptly argue cases before the commission representing his clients, I knew that on merit he certainly would be an outstanding candidate for all of Los Angeles."

But what Bradley initially lacked in funds and in credibility as a citywide figure he made up for in friends—especially those willing to provide the campaign with personal loans and with the hard work that a good old-fashioned grassroots campaign needs. Over five thousand volunteers went door to door, spreading the message about Tom Bradley throughout each and every neighborhood of Los Angeles.

His old supporter Rev. H. H. Brookins rallied the forces of the black community on behalf of a Bradley candidacy. Repaying his old friend's favor, Representative Ed Roybal praised Bradley and personally campaigned in his behalf, citing the candidate's "thorough knowledge of city government." Gerald Hill announced that the ten-thousand-member California Democratic Council, of which he was president, was "going all out for Bradley." And in the primary, the AFL–CIO, the Teamsters, and the Building Trades Union endorsed him.

Expanding his geographic range, Bradley acquired supporters from the San Fernando Valley. Dodo Meyer, an activist and founder of the "Women FOR," had worked with Bradley on the Bobby Kennedy campaign in 1968, when she "began to think about the promise of Tom Bradley, of how this city could grow under his leadership." She became an early supporter of a Bradley bid for City Hall and headed the Women's Committee for Bradley for Mayor. Her good friend Bee Canterbury Lavery also supported Bradley because of his leadership in South-Central Los Angeles and his concern for issues throughout the city. Lavery recalls, "This man was helping to resolve the Van Nuys Airport controversy even though it was clear across town and out of his district; he seemed to really care, which is a unique trait for politicians, especially in those days and with the Yorty administration."

Along with Fran Savitch, who had been Campaign Manager in Yvonne Brathwaite Burke's campaign for U.S. Congress and who had known Bradley since their membership in the Leimert Park Democratic Club, Meyer and Lavery got behind the Bradley effort, helping to increase his visibility citywide. They saw to it that Bradley was featured at group meetings in the Valley and in other areas outside his district.

At a dinner at Dodo and Stanley Meyer's house late in 1968,

with Congressman James Corman and Senator Alan Cranston present, Councilman Thomas Bradley made it official. He was a candidate for Mayor of Los Angeles.

Even though the campaign for Mayor was on a much bigger scale than any campaign he had previously been part of, Bradley maintained a constant awareness of the contributions made and the problems encountered on his behalf by his many supporters.

Valerie Fields agreed to help cut costs of the campaign by personally planning a major fundraising dinner at the Hilton to be chaired by Gregory Peck. She remembers that she "and about ten other women were meeting every evening to work on the seating and menu." This went on for about six days. "After awhile it took its toll on my husband, an attorney who expects to come home every day to the comforts of home and family." Finally there came a night when attorney Jerry Fields looked into their kitchen, where his wife was working with the others on choices for the main course, and asked to speak with her alone. When she went to greet him in the adjoining dining room, she found a livid husband who said, "Valerie, I want these damn women out of this house *now!*"

The next morning she received a call: "Hello Valerie, this is Tom Bradley. I just wanted to know if those damn women are out of your house?" To this day she doesn't know how Bradley found out about the scene with her husband. But she calls this vintage Tom Bradley, both for his uncanny ability to be aware of everything going on and for the tact and consideration he always shows. He went on to apologize for the strain his campaign had put on her family life, and to thank her for all her work.

As the primary contest got under way late in 1968, Bradley was approached by party officials including key Democratic fundraiser Mark Boyer, who were concerned with mounting the strongest possible challenge to Yorty. They wanted Bradley to withdraw from the primary. Of the thirteen candidates, they explained, only Tom Rees would have a realistic chance of beating Yorty. But Bradley refused, and his key advisors stood by his decision. He would neither disappoint his followers nor betray the faith he had in himself. Eventually Rees was the one to drop out of the primary, with most of his support, including Boyer's, going to Bradley.

Voters learned more about Bradley's record as a Councilman and heard the specifics of his plans to be a full-time working Mayor. Polls in February of 1969 showed that the campaign was taking hold—there was a dramatic increase in his support.

He needed to achieve a coalition of groups, and that seemed to be within his grasp. Liberal Jewish voters were impressed by his stands on equal opportunity and heard Gene and Rosalind Wyman, among others, speak on his opposition to acts of anti-Semitism while on the Council. Those who attended the coffee-klatches organized by Pat Rosenthal, Aileen Woodson, and Lucille Boswell were also reassured by what they heard about his many years of work on the police force. *The Heritage Southwest Jewish Press,* Los Angeles' Jewish voice since 1914, printed a special supplement weeks before the election entitled "L.A. Jewry All-Out For Bradley." Mexican-Americans heard Ed Roybal and other leaders in their communities exclaim, "Viva Bradley!" His longtime support for Chicano representation on the City Council was in part responsible for the warmth of his reception among them. And Rev. Brookins enjoyed considerable success in his organizing and mobilization of the black community. Blacks viewed Bradley's candidacy as not only an improvement in leadership at City Hall, but also as an important symbol for their children of what was possible if one worked hard within the system.

But there was criticism too, including some from members of the black community who thought that Bradley should concern himself exclusively with black issues. But Bradley had never restricted himself to black priorities. Even in the Council, he had been a voice for his entire district and for the city as a whole.

Despite criticism and skepticism, Bradley was tireless in pursuit of his goal: "It was an incredible experience, an overwhelming campaign," remarks Phil Depoian who served as the Councilman's driver in the 1969 campaign. Depoian, a young, idealistic college student at the time, had worked in Senator Kennedy's campaign and then joined the Bradley campaign, beginning an association that would shape his career and his life from that point on. "I'd pick him up at six in the morning and drop him off at his house at ten or eleven that night. It was the same schedule, *seven* days a week, for months on end. I've never seen another campaign like that one in my seventeen years of campaigns, and never will again."

Unlike Bradley, Mayor Yorty was not running hard. His billboards proclaimed him as "America's Greatest Mayor." Although confronted with a campaign that was clearly taking off, he remained unconcerned. "I didn't spend hardly anything in the primary, because I knew that people knew me and my record," explains Yorty. Even Bradley's most fervent supporters knew how long the odds were against a black candidate. As Depoian says, "I thought it would be astounding if a black was just able to break out of the pack and win the primary."

Confounding all conventional expectations, the primary election on April 2, 1969, witnessed a stunning victory for Bradley, who led the field of candidates with 42 percent of the vote. Yorty was a distant second with 26 percent. Baxter Ward received 17 percent and Congressman Alphonzo Bell, who had out-spent all his rivals, polled 14 percent. What once seemed like the impossible dream now looked more and more like tomorrow's reality.

Yet, while many were jubilant about Bradley's stunning success, his campaign manager was not. The Bradley organization had been superb, but it had failed to deliver the outright majority that would have knocked Yorty out of the race. That made Bradley vulnerable to a Yorty comeback. And Weiner was expecting a no-holds-barred campaign from Swinging Sam for the runoff. "I knew, as did Bradley and the staff, of Yorty's history of negative campaigning and ruthless smearing of any opponent," recalled Weiner. "I was less optimistic for the runoff because I knew that he would run a racist campaign. Everything about Sam Yorty suggested to me that he would not care if another uprising or riot occurred as a result of his harangues. . . . Yorty is totally without scruples, and he would do *anything* he had to do to get elected."

Yorty denies this. "I never did anything racist in my life; it was the papers that portrayed me as racist," he insists. But as early as primary victory night, material was being gathered for a campaign with distinct racist overtones.

On that night, Democrats, Republicans, whites, blacks, Jews, Hispanics, Asians, and American Indians gathered at Bradley headquarters to celebrate. Staffers hoped that media accounts of the crowd would put to rest any lingering notions that Bradley was a candidate supported only by blacks. Key advisor Stephen Reinhardt clearly understood how important it would be to the future of Bradley's candidacy that the heterogeneous nature of the crowd be accurately conveyed in the press.

However, as he recalls, "For some reason when Bradley began his speech and the cameras started flashing, there were only blacks on the platform." The Democratic advisor instantly knew the image would mean trouble. And the next day, when Reinhardt checked the papers, there it was—a picture of Bradley surrounded by faces that were all, with the exception of Reinhardt's own, black. "But although I thought it was the last time I would see that picture, I was wrong. Miraculously, the picture appeared on a Yorty mailer the weekend before the general election—but there was one difference, my face was colored in black, and the message underneath read, '*We* need a mayor for *our* city!' "

One of the first efforts of the Bradley team was to mount a conscious effort among the losing candidates to persuade them to endorse Bradley in the runoff. At 4:00 A.M. of victory night, Reinhardt was on the phone with his good friend Congressman Jim Corman, asking him if he would talk to his fellow Congressman Alphonzo Bell, who had come in a distant third in the primary, about endorsing Bradley. Reinhardt told Corman that, in defeat, Yorty had "already gone on a racist tirade," and suggested that "Al Bell would be the best person to counter that type of smear." Corman reminded Reinhardt that Bell "had just lost an election," but said he would speak to him.

Within hours, Bell called Reinhardt to schedule a press conference for that morning, at which Bell blasted Yorty's "appeals to fear and hate." Congressman Bell, according to Reinhardt, "knocked himself out for Bradley over the next few months, because he believed Yorty was a racist." One result of Bell's enthusiastic support of Bradley was that many of his staff joined Bradley's campaign effort. Speaking of the differences in organization and style between the two groups, one campaigner recalls "It was sort of like Brooks Brothers meets Levi Strauss." The Bell staff were astounded both by the numbers of volunteers ready to work for Tom Bradley and by the disorganized nature of the runoff effort, which was in need of immediate attention.

Bradley moved quickly. Key changes were made in structure and personnel. Lu Haas, known for his successful work with Senator Alan Cranston, was brought on board as press director. William King, a former Republican strategist who had aided Alphonzo Bell's campaign, joined the Bradley campaign in the effort to attract GOP voters who, according to polls at the time, favored Yorty over Bradley.

The runoff campaign now seemed well-launched. Bradley was getting more national media attention. Testifying in Washington in May before a House subcommittee he was praised by the bipartisan members "for [the] thoughtful and imaginative character of [his] testimony." Locally, the *Los Angeles Times,* which had been favorable toward both Bradley and Bell in the primary, now endorsed Bradley for the first time in his political career. The city's most respected newspaper singled out Bradley as "a man of integrity, of principle, of the sort of vision that is so badly needed by Los Angeles." By contrast, the paper mentioned the Yorty administration's "cavalier attitudes of . . . planless drift, record absenteeism, angry discord, and outright corruption. . . ."

To Yorty, this didn't mean "that the *Times* liked Tom Bradley—they just hated me and always had hated me. They would do anything they could against Sam Yorty and everything possible to get me out of City Hall. They tell Tom Bradley what to do." In 1969, after losing the primary, Yorty offered the following assessment of the *Times'* endorsements: "(The *Times*) would endorse a mad dog against Yorty. . . . They have no principles and no ethics. . . . anyone to beat Yorty."

With the primary's success came an increase in interest in Tom Bradley. Fundraising was no longer as difficult. There were even offers of personal financial help for the candidate and his family, but Bradley refused all money except that intended for the campaign.

Beneath his veneer of confidence, Yorty had been shocked by the primary results. Those who knew the "Maverick Mayor" (as Yorty liked being called) now waited for him to come out swinging.

One of the incumbent's strongest political assets was his keen sense of gauging public opinion, his ability to be a quick change artist, saying whatever he thought the voters wanted to hear. In his climb to the top of city government in Los Angeles, he had begun as a liberal, and by 1969, had become a staunch conservative. His political odyssey had taken him along a road that included bids for state and national as well as local office. As a young lively liberal in 1934, Yorty had been elected at the age of twenty-seven to the State Assembly. Then there were unsuccessful bids as a perennial candidate for numerous offices—including Los Angeles City Council in 1939, U.S. Senate in 1940, and Mayor of Los Angeles in 1945. He eventually was reelected to the State Assembly in 1949 and to the U.S. Congress in 1950. Yorty again lost races for U.S. Senate in 1954 and 1956. In 1960, he defected from the Democratic Party to support Nixon. His theme, "I Can Not Take Kennedy," was seen by many as an unscrupulous attack on John Kennedy's Catholicism. In a scathing twenty-seven-page campaign pamphlet, he accused Kennedy of taking "undue advantage of his religious affiliation." He finally won election to Mayor of Los Angeles in 1961, and reelection in 1965. In 1966, he challenged Governor Pat Brown for the Democratic nomination for Governor. In 1970, he again tried unsuccessfully for the Democratic nomination against Assembly Speaker Jess Unruh. He would even run for president in 1972.

Facing an uphill struggle in the runoff, Yorty now unleashed the kind of campaign for which he was well known. He had a long history of using smear techniques. On the night of the primary, Yorty hinted at the campaign approach he would adopt for the runoff: "I have not let loose on him yet. . . . We need to let the people of Los Angeles know who Tom Bradley really *is*."

Yorty proclaimed on primary election night that Bradley's campaign was backed by "black militants" bent on "taking over City Hall." Furthermore, the Bradley camp was riddled with "Communists," a favorite term used frequently by Mayor Sam. In a practice reminiscent of his past campaign tactics and those of the McCarthy era, the incumbent Mayor offered the voters proof of his claim that there were "Communists" at high levels of the Bradley campaign. Yorty claimed that Bradley's campaign Field Organizer Dan Rothenberg had once been a member of the Communist Party. There it was, according to Mayor Sam, the "smoking gun." Now the voters would know who really was behind the Bradley for Mayor organization—the very people responsible for SDS and other radical revolutionary groups.

The charge against Rothenberg did indeed prove to be correct. Unknown to Bradley or anyone else on the campaign staff, Rothenberg had been affiliated with the Communist Party in his youth. But now his political past was headline news, at a time when much of America blamed the Communists for the political unrest convulsing the country. Yorty's political antennae were, as usual, in good working order.

As the press repeated the charge in its daily headlines, many of Bradley's campaign strategists urged him to fire Rothenberg. They argued that Rothenberg would seriously jeopardize the efforts to bring Republicans over to Bradley's campaign.

Bradley stood firm. From conversations he had with his field organizer, it was clear to Bradley that Rothenberg no longer subscribed to the Communist perspective. "It would have been politically expedient to have gone along with those who wanted his resignation, but I just couldn't," Bradley said, explaining his feelings about the episode. "His past actions had nothing to do with the campaign and did not reflect his current philosophy." Bradley saw the incident as another gutter-level tactic by Yorty, designed to keep the focus off his own record as an absentee Mayor, and he was determined not to lower himself to Yorty's level. Paradoxically, he was encouraged by the very shrillness of Yorty's rhetoric, since it showed that the Mayor was running scared.

During the runoff, Mayor Sam courted racist as well as anti-Communist feelings by charging that Bradley had waged a "racist" campaign in the primary, appealing "for a bloc of Negro votes." In a strategy that would be used by Bradley's opponents throughout his political career, Yorty simultaneously deplored and exploited race as a campaign issue: "I am not going to make racism an issue, but I do state as a fact that Bradley ran a racist campaign among Negro voters and it was effective."

Yorty even attempted to portray Bradley as a black militant. He appeared on television saying, "This extremist group put up a black man for the purpose of polarizing the community." In response to questions on the identity of "this group," Yorty's answer was, "This whole bunch—the SDS, the black militants, the gang behind Bradley."

During the primary, Yorty's billboards had proclaimed him "America's Greatest Mayor." But in line with the changing tone of his rhetoric, during the runoff election they said "We need Yorty now—more than ever." Advertisements asked voters, "Will Your Family Be Safe?" Charlotte Asberry remembers one ad during the last week of the campaign in the *Times'* magazine as typifying Yorty's appeal. Beneath a big picture of Tom Bradley, the message read, "Will your city be safe with this man?" Speaking of herself and of many others in Yorty's office at the time, Asberry recalls, "While most of us did not subscribe to the tactics being used against Bradley, we were not a part of the political organization."

Commenting on these tactics today, Sam Yorty denies personal responsibility: "I had very little to do with the campaign itself." The Mayor points out that "my deputy mayors, Joe Quinn and Eleanor Chambers, were in control. I merely went around and spoke at the engagements I was scheduled for. . . . I certainly don't remember personally using any racist tactics. In fact, I simply do not believe the *Times* and my critics who claim that I did."

Whoever orchestrated the Yorty campaigns—and no one from Yorty on down is willing to take responsibility for it in retrospect—it was a divisive campaign that heated up a potentially explosive situation. Bradley Press Secretary Bob Kholos, remembers that Bradley staff meetings at his campaign headquarters were held downstairs, and the windows upstairs were always locked. When asked why the group did not meet upstairs in the larger room, Bradley's campaign manager replied, "because we'll be able to hear if someone throws a bomb or Molotov cocktail through the window, and have enough time to clear everyone out."

Another Yorty tactic was to portray Bradley as "anti-police." The Councilman's criticism of well-documented examples of police abuse and his opposition to the police pension fund proposal were examples of how Bradley was "no friend of the keepers of the peace," according to Yorty. It stood to reason, according to Yorty, that if Bradley were elected Mayor he and his "extremist-militant" backers would destroy the department. Despite his twenty-one years as a cop, Bradley, according to Yorty, "always has been a bad cop and anti-police and always will be."

Taking his cues from Richard Nixon's 1968 "law and order" campaign, Yorty exacerbated the already serious racial tensions in Los Angeles, warning that a Bradley win would leave the city defenseless against crime. The city would be safe for no one. Hoodlums and black militants would reign in a system of anarchy. Given what Yorty described as Bradley's "lack of support of the Police Department" in the past, the Councilman's election would mean that "hundreds of police officers would simply quit." At a time when revolution was in the air, Los Angeles would be the only major city in the country without adequate police protection.

The typical Yorty harangue concluded with a plea that echoed his advertising slogan—"A Mayor for *all* the citizens of Los Angeles." Yorty told white audiences, "So I hope that our people will wake up. I'm doing my best to tell them, and I need your help in doing it, because it's not just my city, it's our city, and I think we want to keep on governing our city." This message came complete with "evidence" of how Los Angeles under Yorty differed from cities with black mayors. In Cleveland, Ohio, for example, the Mayor was fighting with the Police Department; in Gary, Indiana, part of the city was trying to secede. Through fear, hate, innuendo and prejudice, Yorty hoped to convince the citizens that a Bradley victory would reap disaster for Los Angeles.

Voices within the Bradley campaign urged their candidate to strike back. One obvious way of undermining Yorty's "law and order" campaign would have been to run their own, emphasizing

Bradley's twenty-one years on the police force. As Stephen Reinhardt recalls, "Weiner and I wanted to run an ad in all the major
newspapers featuring a very official police photo of Bradley in
his uniform." But the ad never ran because there was no consensus on this tactic within the inner circle of advisors.

Another tactic of the Yorty campaign was to try to weaken
the broad-based coalition that Bradley had put together for the
primary. There was little likelihood that any effort would draw
away support from the black community. But the Mayor did make
a concerted effort to draw away Bradley's support within the
Jewish community by distributing pamphlets decrying anti-
Semitic statements made by prominent black officials in the
East.

The Mayor proudly displayed an endorsement from a small
group of conservative Rabbis to show that he, too, was popular
within the community. And he pointed out that it was under his
administration that the Israeli city of Eilat had been added to Los
Angeles' Sister City program.

Maury Weiner concurred with Bradley on the need to give a
strong speech condemning anti-Semitism, and outlining the can-
didate's long history of working against it as part of his campaign
for civil rights for all citizens, regardless of race, color, or creed.
The April 28 speech was on target. Weiner remembers that "the
Jewish community responded with the greatest understanding of
Tom's plight. They just felt an instant camaraderie with him."
The impact of this relationship would be long-term. Weiner adds,
"From that day forth, Tom Bradley realized that this bond would
be special. He has always received the utmost respect and sup-
port from the Jewish community which formed an important
cornerstone of his political base."

Immediately, a large number of moderate and liberal Rabbis
publicly endorsed Tom Bradley in a special election issue of a
paper disseminated throughout the community. Furthermore, in
late April, Max Mont, one of Yorty's Jewish appointees, resigned
his city position in protest of "the false charges of anti-Semitism
emanating from the Yorty campaign." Ever since the 1969 campaign, Bradley has enjoyed unusually close ties to the Jewish
community of Los Angeles, which at that time comprised ten
percent of the registered voters.

The Asian community leaders who supported Bradley became concerned about Yorty making inroads among their constituency. George Takei states, "We felt that in the Japanese-American community there was an undercurrent of racism prevalent, and we felt the best way to combat it was with Tom Bradley himself." Takei and others organized appearances for the candidate in the Little Tokyo community. The response was very favorable, as Takei recalls: "We were able to get one of the Republican property holders to donate space for a 'Tom Bradley for Mayor' sign, ideally located on the wall clearly visible to all traffic in the Civic Center area"—a first in Little Tokyo, according to Takei.

Although many Bradley supporters were concerned about the effect of the Yorty campaign, the polls were encouraging. According to them, Bradley was increasing his lead over the incumbent Mayor. Perhaps the politics of racism and fear would fail after all. Bradley himself continued to think so, and insisted on continuing with a very positive, issue-oriented campaign, instead of dignifying his opponent's slurs with a response.

7

The 1969 Mayoral Campaign

"This is an outrage!"

—Ethel Bradley

The mayoral hopeful outlined programs that he intended to develop at City Hall, pledging to improve the educational and economic opportunities for all of Los Angeles' citizens and to begin to develop plans for a mass-transit system. He promised to be a full-time Mayor and to offer a vision of a city in which people could work together rather than against each other, as had been the case during the Yorty years. In public appearances, Bradley highlighted specific examples of the ineffective leadership and the widespread corruption of the Yorty administration.

He stated, "Do we really need to spend $105,000 on Mayor Yorty's Los Angeles to Paris Exposition? Are his Los Angeles in German Folk Fest and his Japan Exposition really worth $455,000? Can we not forego his $2.5 million ornamental bridge from City Hall to County Mall? In Los Angeles today, 'commissioner' has too often meant corruption. Briefings on zoning or harbors have too often meant bribery. And Civil Servant has come to mean conflict of interest."

He told the voters about the federal funds targeted for other major cities, asking where Los Angeles was on this important list. It was, he pointed out, near the bottom. When the "model cities" program was first initiated in 1967, he announced, Los Angeles was the only major city whose application had been rejected by HUD officials, and the city had still failed to receive its rightful share of such funds in 1969. The city's share was short by almost $600,000, due to failure of the Yorty administration to comply with the application process. If incompetence was not enough, there were numerous scandals involving graft and corruption of Yorty's appointed commissioners.

Yorty attempted to refute the Bradley charges with humor: "Of course I can't guarantee the absolute integrity of 40,000 people who work in city government. As Mayor Joseph Alioto says in San Francisco, even Jesus in picking the apostles got one that turned out bad. So you're going to have that once in a while. But it's very minimum."

Bradley sought to compare the candidates' two styles of leadership. Yes, Bradley would travel, but the focus of his trips to Sacramento and Washington would be on finding solutions and funding for particular projects. In contrast, the city's travel records revealed that Yorty's frequent trips had primarily been to cities abroad that the Mayor had designated as "Sister Cities," trips that even his staff admitted were primarily for pleasure.

By contrast, in early May, three weeks before the election, Bradley made a working trip to Washington where he met with George Romney, Secretary of Housing and Urban Development, to try to arrange for federal dollars to be earmarked for Los Angeles.

Public recognition and approval of Bradley was broad-based. The majority of those City Councilmen who revealed their personal choice announced their support for him. Both of California's U.S. Senators—Alan Cranston and George Murphy—endorsed Bradley, as did Assembly Speaker Jess Unruh who was well-known for successful coalition politics and who had been a Yorty supporter in 1965.

Support came from many national leaders as well. Some had pledged their support during the primary, but even more jumped aboard the bandwagon for the runoff election. Bradley was preferred by prominent leaders of both parties, including former Vice President Hubert Humphrey, Senators Eugene McCarthy, Jacob Javits, Edward Brooke, George McGovern, Charles Goodell, Fred Harris, Charles Percy, and Edmund Muskie. Republican Senator Javits identified Bradley as a "remarkable American" in the "struggle against poverty, blight, bigotry, and hunger in our nation's cities." Senator Edward Kennedy of Massachusetts was prominently featured in campaign literature: in a television endorsement he compared Tom Bradley with his late brothers: "He shares a common ideal with them about the kind of city he wants Los Angeles to be, the kind of state he wants California to be. . . . I think Tom Bradley can bring dignity to the office of the Mayor of Los Angeles. I think he can bring reconciliation to the people in Los Angeles. I think he has the character, the motivation, and the integrity to be one of the great mayors of a great city."

Former presidential candidate Adlai Stevenson told residents in a radio spot: "I'd like to add my personal support to the many hundreds and thousands of citizens who are working for the election of Councilman Tom Bradley as Mayor of Los Angeles. . . . In Tom Bradley you have a man of real integrity. He has plans for a greater Los Angeles. He can give people everywhere more hope for the future of our city. Your vote is important on May 27th. I hope you'll elect Tom Bradley Mayor of Los Angeles."

Former Republican Senator Tom Kuchel of the Golden State added his support: "The people demand clean, strong, and honest American government, with equal justice and equal opportunity for every citizen. . . . Tom Bradley has high credentials for leadership. He has courage, wisdom, and humility."

The Hollywood Committee to Elect Tom Bradley boasted some of the top entertainers in the land. The list included Steve Allen, Burt Bacharach, Barbara Bain, Gene Barry, Milton Berle, Sid Caesar, Jack Cassidy, Jackie Cooper, Bill Cosby, Tony Curtis, Sammy Davis, Jr., Angie Dickinson, Tony Franciosa, Samuel Goldwyn, Florence Henderson, Quincy Jones, Shirley Jones, Jack Klugman, Burt Lancaster, Martin Landau, Norman Lear, Jack Lemmon, Henry Mancini, Jayne Meadows, Leonard Nimoy, Gregory Peck, Brock Peters, Sidney Poitier, Carl Reiner, Debbie Reynolds, Gene Roddenberry, William Shatner, Martin Sheen, Dinah Shore, Frank Sinatra, Robert Stack, Barbra Streisand, Elizabeth Taylor, Dick Van Dyke, and James Whitmore, among the over one hundred stars backing the Councilman.

Endorsements also came from prominent diplomats. United Nations Deputy Undersecretary Ralph Bunche, who claimed Los Angeles as his hometown, told the press, "I am appalled by what I have seen of Mayor Yorty's campaign." The former Nobel Peace Prize Winner lambasted Yorty's "demagogic appeal to base emotions and crude attempts to instill fear [as] sickening and utterly irresponsible."

But the support of such diverse groups throughout the nation did nothing to blunt the attacks waged by Yorty. The feisty incumbent offered this interpretation of the motives that had lead so many leaders to endorse Bradley: "[They are] opportunistic politicians who are trying to appeal to the Negro vote in their own areas by endorsing a Negro here—because they don't have to come and live under Mr. Bradley."

In an effort to mute the force of Yorty's attacks and appeals to racism, civic groups and police officers praised Bradley's record. But the Mayor smelled success with his strategy, and he charged that, in other cities with black mayors, chaos paralyzed city government.

There were even blackmail threats aimed at the Bradley organization. Raye Cunningham remembers that, as she was working at the headquarters one day, "A group came in to see me with a picture of a black fist and the words 'Black Power' scribbled below." The individuals told Cunningham that they knew the source of the printing and could stop it if the price was right. The longtime Bradley supporter recalls, "I took it over to Tom Bradley, who was at the headquarters and explained to him what the group had said." Bradley's only response was that he was "not about to be blackmailed." The group left, and the posters appeared throughout the city during the last weeks of the campaign.

Irene Winston, a Woodland Hills resident, recalls that, during the last two weeks of the campaign, people began to take notice of the Yorty fear tactics: " 'Liberal Democrats' in my home neighborhood started saying they couldn't vote for a black because the neighborhood would no longer be safe."

Bumper stickers proclaiming "Bradley Power" above a clenched black fist were prominently displayed on cars driven by blacks cruising through mainly white districts of the San Fernando Valley and were posted on street-signs and buildings. The words were an echo of Stokely Carmichael's controversial book, and the image also recalled the two black athletes who had used it in the 1968 Mexico City Olympics. Natalie Friedman, a Bradley supporter who lives in a white neighborhood in the San Fernando Valley, recalls finding what looked like a Bradley campaign brochure with the headline "Make Los Angeles A Black City" on her doorstep.

As election day approached, there were slight alterations in the message. The clenched black fist was accompanied with a "Bradley for Mayor" slogan. Many such bumper stickers were affixed to cars in parking lots without permission from their owners. It would be hours or even days before the owners noticed. When they did, they made calls to Bradley headquarters, complaining of the incident. After being told that this was not a Bradley campaign product, several callers hung up, worried about what it meant. It was best summed up by Bradley's Press Secretary, Bob Kholos: "We knew. . . . We knew who was responsible. We *all* smelled a rat."

Other last-minute "hit-piece" mailers displayed pictures of black militant leaders and of looters in burned-out urban areas. Los Angeles newspapers carried stories the week before the election of "black militants disrupting church services and other meetings throughout the city." Suspicious advertisements, unknown to the Bradley campaign, appeared in papers on the predominantly white Westside, listing Black Muslims and some Black Panthers as key Bradley supporters. According to Weiner, "There was no doubt, all stops were being pulled by the Yorty gang."

Accusations flew on television and radio, and in print, coming from second- and third-hand sources. Some were too ludicrous to answer. Most, in retrospect, were too ludicrous to believe. But, the anti-police charge continued. When the press asked for evidence to support his assertions, the Mayor responded, "I believe it. And so does Police Chief Parker." That was the extent of the evidence Yorty offered, though he went further, charging that the real story was to be found in Lieutenant Bradley's police file, implying that there was something sinister in that record. Since police rules forbade the disclosure of personnel files, even if the officer in question approved, Yorty was able to raise suspicions about his opponent that Bradley couldn't counter, even though he denied that there was anything amiss in his file.

At times, action and reaction seemed better choreographed than most stage shows. For example, after church services were disrupted downtown by black militants, Yorty proclaimed: "We will take every action we can to protect the churches and synagogues from similar efforts to disrupt the services and make unreasonable demands from the worshippers." He then directed the Police Chief to conduct closer surveillance on places of worship. The suggestion was that, with Bradley as Mayor, churches and synagogues might require the presence of police officers, which in turn would mean fewer police on the streets. Many of these activities were later linked "directly to Mayor Yorty's campaign." The result for the campaign was a heightening of the race issue and the spreading of paranoia and fear.

Like Natalie Friedman, Bee Canterbury Lavery found a brochure on her doorstep in the Valley. This one arrived on election day and it depicted Bradley with his arm around Eldridge Cleaver. Lavery recalls, "Well, Tom Bradley had never met Eldridge Cleaver, and I got on the phone and inquired about the smear piece." It turned out to be a doctored photograph, its intended message only too clear—Bradley was a good friend of black militant Eldridge Cleaver, a man who was frightening to many Americans.

Despite the attacks by Yorty, the polls continued to show Bradley ahead, and this had a negative effect. In the words of Stephen Reinhardt, many members of Bradley's staff "thought we had it won," prompting them to dissipate their energies in arguments about whether Mayor-elect Bradley should make his first post-election appearance on *Face the Nation* or *Meet the Press*. Reinhardt, Brookins, and others were dismayed by the distraction. They knew that valuable time and energy were being lost.

The candidate himself was responsible for one of the other handicaps of the campaign. Dodo Meyer explains: "The big problem then and now is persuading Tom Bradley to allow us to get the message out about his record. . . . His whole style is to do things in the background; he is a conciliatory man. He doesn't like confrontation, is a master of negotiation and compromise— and that's just the Bradley approach. . . ." Some consider this to be Tom Bradley's greatest weakness as a campaigner, but it is a characteristic that is deeply rooted in his personality, and he cannot—or will not—change it.

Regardless of whether this route was the politically effective one, it was the one Bradley had chosen. And now the campaign was coming to an end. The voters would speak in the voting booths, and Bradley had confidence that they would say "no" to what he called "the dirtiest campaign in the city's history," and would turn out of office "those who seek to divide us . . . , those who set race against race . . . , religion against religion, [and] sow the seeds of lawlessness." He firmly believed they would endorse his goal, which was "to make this city a city of peace, free from violence and hate."

At Bradley headquarters, optimism remained strong. The day before the May 27 runoff, the final poll of the *Los Angeles Times* reported Bradley with a comfortable fifteen-point advantage.

Election Day arrived. It would be a very long day, a day of anticipation, of terrible ups and downs. Stephen Reinhardt remembers something that happened just a few hours prior to the closing of the polls, as he traveled with Bradley and a *Times* reporter: "When we stopped by Bradley's house for a couple of minutes, the reporter from the *Times* asked, 'How do you spell your name?'" He answered the question, and asked why. The reported looked at Reinhardt and said, "I just wanted to get it right in case anything happens tonight and Bradley gets shot, I'd like to have your name right."

Reinhardt had been at the Ambassador Hotel when Bobby Kennedy was killed, so assassination was not an abstraction to him. Still, he was stunned to hear reporters exploring this possibility on such a night. The candidate himself seemed perfectly calm as the three passed by the Palladium, the headquarters for the Bradley campaign celebration, and entered the nearby Columbia Pictures building, to await the results in Mike Frankovich's office.

Anticipating the victory predicted by the pollsters, over five thousand supporters had gathered to hail Bradley's arrival at the Hollywood Palladium. The crowd, an accurate reflection of Bradley's constituency, was a mixture of whites, blacks, Hispanics, Asians—young and old, Republicans and Democrats. All had come together to witness history in the making—Los Angeles' selection of a new voice and a new direction.

Looking out over the crowd, Neil Barry noticed home-made signs saying "We did it, Mayor Tom!" and "The Dream Never Dies, Tonight it Lives!" A group of children were already dancing and singing in celebration of the expected victory, as was a man who had to be at least eighty years old who was doing "the Bradley." Some people wore badges that presaged what many were already discussing—even bigger things for Tom Bradley. Willis Edwards, a precinct walker, saw one button that combined two great hopes, white and black—"Teddy and Tom in '72!"

As Bradley sat in Mike Frankovich's fifth-floor office at Columbia Pictures, some five blocks from the Hollywood Palladium crowd, surrounded by friends and family, he watched the early inconclusive returns, contemplating the significance of this night. Ethel was at the Palladium, along with his mother and his daughters. He thought once more about the speech he would soon be delivering. Without confiding in his aides, he had written his victory speech, practiced it, and carried it with him throughout the day, since 8:00 A.M., when he and Ethel had voted. Its message was not just about his own journey, but about the spirit that characterized his campaign, the "can-do" attitude that had given him strength when he wanted to quit. This was something he wanted to share with everybody tonight, because it described not only his own goals and hopes, but the American Dream itself. He planned to say, "The election was a victory—not of a man, but of an idea, an attitude—proof that our democratic system is capable of peaceful change, a testimony that people should not live by fear but by hope, not by hate but by love. . . ."

Suddenly, his thoughts were interrupted by someone nudging him. It was Maury Weiner, who was upset about something. It was about 11:00 P.M. The news was in, and it was very hard to take. Something wasn't right. Reinhardt told Bradley that "from the reports, the trend wasn't going to change." Furthermore, the Fire Marshall had informed Sam Williams that the crowd at the Palladium was becoming unruly, waiting to hear from Bradley. Depoian remembers: "People were crying, others were angry." The eighty-year-old man, who had entertained the crowd for hours, sat on a stool shaking his head. To Reinhardt and Weiner, the five-block drive to the Palladium was one of the longest journeys either had ever made. Bradley looked calm. Anton Calleia noted, "He was totally collected, and didn't show any emotion, even when those around him were drained by the moment."

"The scene at the Palladium was incredible," remembers Bob Kholos. "Here was a place where they filmed *The Lawrence Welk Show,* but this time it was filled with hundreds of young idealistic people, black and white, proclaiming the history of the moment." George Takei, leader of the Japanese-Americans for Bradley, remembers that even though the reports had been bad, the crowd was still "positive, so optimistic, and still somewhat confident. They wanted to hear Tom Bradley speak."

At the same time, the Hell's Angels motorcycle gang was outside, circling the arena, threatening to break up the Palladium crowd and "cause hell if the black man won." Also present outside were the Street Racers, a neighborhood gang, who had come to protect Bradley supporters after hearing of the Hell's Angels' plans. According to one policeman present, "it looked like the makings of a very bad scene."

Supporter and long-time friend Sam Williams recognized the need to control the crowd, whose passions were increasing and frustration and anger mounting with further news of Yorty's victory. Williams urged the Councilman to address the crowd to help defuse the explosive situation.

Bradley knew he had to make some statement. He decided that disappointment should not lead to violence. That he should explain that there would be no celebration that night—that they should remember what they had worked for and look toward the future.

How had it happened? Among the Councilman's advisors and family, there was dismay and disgust. Ethel Bradley could not believe what was happening. "This is an outrage! They've stolen the election from us," she insisted. Dodo Meyer remembers that there was some evidence to support Mrs. Bradley's claim. "Some of our staff heard reports all that evening of irregularities." The computerized machines broke down, and the Police Department was responsible for transporting the ballots into the City Clerk's office. Meyer adds, "We could not trust the police because the Chief at that time unequivocally supported Yorty."

Reports were phoned in about ballot boxes that hadn't been properly delivered to City Hall. Meyer remembers one distraught supporter reporting that "they had seen police helicopters dumping ballots into the Los Angeles River." While there was corroboration of some strange happenings on election night and of ballots being incorrectly counted, Meyer adds, "we just did not think that we had the opportunity to investigate, because the city election officer's deck was just downright stacked against us."

"I'll never know what actually happened," she continues. "But it certainly did not faze Tom Bradley." He listened to the reports and offered his consolation to those who grew disappointed and upset as the evening progressed. But to those who knew him, there was no doubt that Bradley was looking at what happened so that he could learn from it.

When the final votes were counted, the dream had faded away. Tom Bradley lost by about 55,000 votes out of close to 850,000 cast, a turnout of over 75 percent of the registered voters of Los Angeles. Yorty commanded 53.3 percent of the vote, with about 449,500 total. Bradley garnered 46.7 percent, with about 394,000. History, indeed, had been made, but not as the press and Bradley's supporters had expected. Mayor Sam Yorty was now in the history books as the city's second Mayor to win three straight mayoral terms. (The first had been Fletcher Bowron, two decades prior.)

Former Mayor Poulson, who had lost to Yorty in a similar negative campaign, eight years earlier, when less than half of the city's voters had cast their ballots, told reporters, "The voters have approved corruption in government and racism in America. The city now has an awful black eye."

Campaign staffers were especially despondent over the election results. Many continued to work in the campaign office as a way of staying close to the cause. Others began to work for the next election. Still others remained dazed. Valerie Fields remembers that "The terrible disappointment, the racism really hurt. I remember being in my kitchen alone about three days later after the election and suddenly bursting in to tears."

How could the polls have been so wrong? What the pollsters who had predicted a Bradley had not measured in their surveys was the heavy turn-out among a new group of voters. The 1969 election witnessed the vote of a large number of people who had sat out previous elections. In the latter days of the campaign, Mayor Sam's smear tactics had finally taken hold. Motivated by fear, many people cast votes for the known commodity, Mayor Yorty.

Analysis of the returns revealed some startling reversals in voting patterns between the runoff and the primary. Though Bradley had won a two-thirds majority in the primary, the incumbent had won in ten out of fifteen districts on the second vote. Frightened by the grim picture the incumbent painted of a Bradley win, a huge number of voters who had backed other candidates in the primary went over to Yorty. Two groups who had backed Bradley in the primary—Jews and Mexican-Americans—did not deliver as well as expected in the runoff. Instead, the Jewish groups split almost evenly between Yorty and Bradley, with Bradley receiving greater support among the wealthier Jews, Yorty getting support from poorer Jews. Surprisingly, Hispanic areas, which Humphrey had won easily against Nixon less than a year before, had gone overwhelmingly for Yorty.

The Bradley team was stunned. The huge number of absentee ballots and of first-time voters who had made the effort to get to the polls to vote their fears provided painful evidence of the degree to which the city was divided. Former Pennsylvania Governor William Scranton, author of the report put out by The President's Commission On Campus Unrest, described this era as "the most divisive period in the nation's history since the Civil War." The Yorty campaign had won a stunning upset victory by a campaign calculated to set neighbor against neighbor.

It also appeared that many voters had been less than honest with pollsters on how they intended to cast their ballot. The evidence suggested that, rather than admit they were voting for Yorty, those who voted for him on racial grounds had told the poll-takers that they were voting for Bradley. (It was a phenomenon that would also characterize another political contest—Bradley's 1982 bid for Governor.)

Bradley sent Yorty a telegram acknowledging the Mayor's

victory and pledging his support in the effort to overcome the "bitterness and divisiveness" which had marked the long campaign. But even in victory, Yorty was disinclined toward reconciliation. He replied to the Bradley telegram as follows: "The attempt to form a racial coalition and conduct a partisan campaign for the nonpartisan office of Mayor was certain to be divisive. This attempt has been rejected by voters and it is time to forget recrimination and work for the best interests of our well-governed city."

Yorty and his supporters continued to attack Bradley. The Mayor reiterated that Bradley was not a bad man, just one who was supported by the wrong people—Communists and other extremists. Robert Welch of the John Birch Society announced in the group's publication that Bradley's defeat was the most important setback for the Communists in fifty years.

The dominant voices in City Hall echoed the message heard throughout the country. Division and discord overshadowed the voices of reason and reconciliation. But Tom Bradley was determined to help usher in a new era in the City of Angels, though for now he would have to resign himself to working from his seat on the City Council.

8

The Determination to Run Again

"We are delayed but not denied."
—Bishop H. H. Brookins

Even on the very night of losing, Tom Bradley's determination to continue his quest never wavered: "I decided that night that I would run again in four years." He maintained that he would learn from his defeat: "I pledged to myself that I would do whatever I needed to, to ensure that the next time I ran, people would know me for my record, for what I could provide the city." The Rev. Brookins remembers the loss as a difficult one for his friend. He urged Bradley "to become aggressive and keep the mood up, which he did. This was a critical point in his life, and his character came through untouched." For Bradley the campaign for City Hall in 1973 began on election night 1969. He had decided that in the next election, Tom Bradley would control the campaign agenda.

"The day after the election," recalls campaign strategist Warren Hollier, "he came into the headquarters. We had a nice chat and he said, 'Warren, we just have to start all over again, because we did not work strongly enough to get the people to know me.'" Jessie Mae Beavers remembers, "I walked into the headquarters and he was signing eight-by-ten photographs; I knew by the sparkle in his eye that he was going to run again, which is something that I always knew he would do." Bradley's family knew this too. As Lorraine says, "I knew he would go for it and that he would never let an opponent portray him as something he wasn't, like Yorty had." One of Bradley's closest friends summed him up as follows: "Tom holds a lot of it inside; it hurts him as much as it hurts anybody else. It's just that he is very stoic."

Bradley made the following assessment of the contribution that his candidacy had made to the political life of his city: "It was a great accomplishment. People now will be able to accept a black man's run for office as a regular occurrence. We created a better attitude for the people. . . . We all have suffered losses in the past. The black community has been disappointed on many occasions. This will just add to the list. What this means is that we are going to work even harder and longer the next time around."

The day after his defeat, Councilman Bradley began expanding his political base. In addition to engagements in the Tenth District, he informed his staff that he would now accept speaking invitations in districts throughout the city. The city's concerns would now be his. This new approach was not meant, in any way, to short-change his constituents in the Tenth District. What it did mean was that he was willing to put in more time. He was following through on the personal pledge he had made to himself the night before. The next time around, in 1973, Tom Bradley would be a known commodity.

The commitment meant longer hours. But, as Bishop Brookins comments, "Tom Bradley has always been a workaholic." Bradley's working schedule was lengthened from five to seven days a week. This extra effort required not only a supportive staff but also a family willing to make the sacrifice. And Ethel agreed that the family would make it. The Bradleys would be united in the Councilman's quest for Mayor in 1973.

In his Council work, Bradley continued to speak out against the lack of leadership from City Hall. He aggressively attacked Yorty for excessive traveling, noting that the City Council President had served as acting mayor 125 days in the 1969–1970 fiscal year, proof that Los Angeles had only a part-time Mayor in Sam Yorty. Weiner remembers, "Tom Bradley became the most active Councilman in the city." He would do whatever it took to demonstrate his commitment and vision for Los Angeles. In 1971, as a Councilman with one of the highest approval ratings from his constituents of any Council member in Los Angeles, Bradley ran unopposed for a third term.

While Bradley and others were criticizing Yorty for his stewardship of Los Angeles, the Mayor turned his attention to higher office. He said it was "possible" that he would run for State Attorney General or U.S. Senator, but to those who knew him, it seemed clear that the "Maverick" Mayor's eye was on Sacramento. Yorty wanted Ronald Reagan's job, and announced his candidacy for Governor on March 17, 1970. But there were others with similar interests. Kingmaker Jess Unruh also planned to oppose Reagan for the California governorship. Reagan himself professed to be baffled by Yorty's ambitions: "Yorty was so recently reelected as Mayor that I thought he would fulfill his contract with the people of Los Angeles."

Yorty's campaign was consistent with his past races. He attacked Reagan as an "amateur" who owed his political fortunes to his speechwriters and advisors rather than any native talent. He criticized the Governor for not being tougher on the student demonstrators and also for presiding over "the largest state tax increase in the history of California." The former attack seemed particularly inappropriate, given Reagan's reaction to the killings at Kent State University in 1970. The Governor had told reporters, "If it takes a bloodbath, let's get it over with."

In the gubernatorial primary, Unruh outdistanced Yorty 64 percent to 26 percent—the fifth straight statewide loss for Los Angeles' perennial candidate. Ronald Reagan's subsequent reelection caused many Democrats to wonder where Unruh would turn next to further his political career. Bob Kholos, who worked for Unruh in the campaign, remembered that he and the Democratic Congressman had concurred in 1969 that Tom Bradley would seek the mayoral post again in 1973. But Kholos got the impression after Unruh's gubernatorial defeat that he, too, was eyeing Yorty's job. If so, given the Speaker's connections with Democratic party machinery, he was in a position to mount a serious challenge to Bradley in the primary.

The Tenth District Councilman continued to receive approval and recognition from many organizations within the area. He was elected President of the Southern California Association of Governments from 1969 to 1971. He also served as President of the National Association of Regional Councils during these same years.

Bradley's expertise in urban affairs became more widely known in both national and international arenas. In 1972, he was the only American city official invited to join a congressional study group on European urban growth patterns. He also became the first non-mayor to be elected First Vice President of the National League of Cities in 1972, a position which led to his assuming the presidency of the organization in 1974.

Polls showed Bradley's political record was reaching a receptive audience. He emerged early as the front-runner in the mayoral race, the people's choice to unseat the incumbent. A year before the 1973 election, Bradley had achieved one of his goals. He now enjoyed 95 percent name recognition among the people of Los Angeles. In fact, his positive image of integrity was so firmly set in Southern California in 1970 that U.S. Senate hopeful John Tunney of Riverside sought Bradley's public endorsement of his candidacy to ward off the threatening well-financed campaign of Tom Hayden.

At that time, Yorty attempted to weaken Bradley's popularity through his regular diatribes against the Council, turning to personal criticism. Yorty charged that he had information from an informant who was now dead that seriously questioned the integrity of the Tenth District Councilman. The revelation was that Tom Bradley had received $2,000 in exchange for changing his vote on a service-station lease zoning matter.

Bradley recalls, "I knew this wild charge was just another of the outrageous allegations he would frequently dream up in the attempt to get me on the defensive. In the '69 campaign, I had tried to deal with each of his wild assertions as I have with other opponents, but found it simply wasn't worth getting into the gutter with him." The Councilman pointed out to the media and public that the bogus charge had been completely unfounded, that the Mayor's own version of the incident was riddled with inaccuracies.

Bradley went on the counteroffensive: "We ought to be tired of a Mayor of the city who every time he opens his mouth has an oral bowel movement." After Bradley's response, the issue was for the most part dropped from the media and consequently from the media-driven Yorty agenda of personal attacks.

Even in his third term as Mayor, Yorty had accomplished little in the way of tangible results for the city. He had not balanced a budget since his reelection in 1969. His $45,000 "slush" fund for awards, citations, and keys to the city was widely reported and criticized. It was clear from his repeated bids for state and even national office that the city was not his first priority. And his frequent helicopter rides to City Hall in 1973 made even more headlines than his drive for the Presidency in 1972. The 1972 Democratic Convention did have a very immediate personal effect on Yorty, however: "After they nominated McGovern, he was too much for me . . . too liberal. I am a Republican now."

The Mayor frequently confused the office he was in for the one that he desired. City Hall employee Eula Collins remembers, "Sam Yorty used to hold press conferences on the Vietnam War when he was the Mayor of Los Angeles. . . . He would be like Richard Nixon; he would have a map of Vietnam behind him talking about our need to stop the Communist menace."

Yorty was widely criticized for an insurance policy that he purchased for his wife from his campaign committee fund. The Mayor defended the decision at the time and had maintained its propriety through the years. He argues: "They brought up that insurance thing like it was some kind of scandal or something. It certainly was not. . . . Here I was working for the city, traveling around the world to become America's most decorated mayor, receiving death threats, and working for the city. My wife deserved some insurance if something should happen to me. After all, the same thing was being done by other mayors in other cities across the nation."

On the plus side, the Yorty record boasted eight urban renewal projects, an increase in parks and recreational centers, and new fire and police stations. But the lack of overall planning was best illustrated at the Mayor's dedication of the city's new zoo at Griffith Park. On opening day, as Yorty cut the ribbon, it was reported that animals were escaping. Someone had forgotten to put up all the necessary fences.

In the period that followed his 1969 campaign for Mayor, Bradley received "constructive criticism" from advisors and friends on what went wrong in the contest. One line of thought was that Bradley had devoted too much time to the black community—that, with such frequent appearances, he had in essence fueled the fears addressed by Yorty that he would be a black Mayor catering only to the interests of the black community. Another argument faulted the Councilman's failure to use television widely enough to communicate his record to the public. Some people felt there had been conflicts of personal ambition and ideology among the campaign staff. Of course, campaigns are like football—there is never a shortage of Monday morning quarterbacks.

Bradley welcomed the input. He listened and he discussed. Yet, as one friend says, in the final analysis, Tom Bradley "makes all of his major decisions and makes all of his own phone calls. Bradley talks to many people. He picks up the phone and dials and nobody knows who he is talking to. He gets information from a wide variety of sources. But the buck stops with him and nobody else. Anybody who thinks they tell him what to do, well, let's just say they don't know Tom Bradley."

In late 1972, Bradley's overriding goal was to assemble the best possible campaign team, a winning combination that could turn what had long been described as an "impossible dream" into reality. Several new faces joined Bradley's group of key advisors.

One of the most dynamic was Nelson Rising, a Los Angeles attorney who had helped engineer John Tunney's successful 1970 bid for the Senate, and who would be Bradley's Campaign Manager. Rising brought to the group a much-needed aggressiveness and sophistication. A brilliant strategist who understood the new role of television and television-spawned images in the political arena, he had a reputation for success in several areas. He had used his media savvy not only in the Tunney campaign, but as a consultant on *The Candidate,* a film starring Robert Redford that had explored the role of media in contemporary electoral politics. Rising had also established himself in the construction industry, and was a personal friend of Ted Kennedy. His wealth of contacts in several different worlds would prove to be an important asset to Tom Bradley's future.

Rising advised Bradley to begin his bid for City Hall early, to air commercials six weeks before the primary, positioning himself as mediator and activist leader. Bradley would inform voters of his record in the Council, and would offer specific programs for each of the city's neighborhoods.

It was Rising's suggestion that the campaign get David Garth, the nationally known media expert who had also worked on the Tunney campaign, to mastermind the public relations blitz. Bradley pondered the strategy. He particularly liked the idea of early commercials—of preempting Yorty's smear and fear attempts with issue-oriented spots that detailed his record and outlined his programs.

Given Garth's reputation as not only one of the best in the business, but also one of the most expensive, the campaign found itself financially strapped at first. It had to reach contributors early in order to finance the new strategy. Bradley remembers the obstacles faced by fundraisers at the beginning of the 1973 campaign: "There were many people who had been supportive in the last campaign who were reluctant to commit themselves this time around. They were not convinced that the chemistry had changed all that much since 1969." Yet, these people did come around, in large part because of the Councilman's persistence: "It took some persuasive talking to bring some aboard, but I was so convinced that we would do it in 1973 that I think my optimism had to have an effect."

One of those persuaded by Bradley and Bruce Corwin was one of the state's most productive fundraisers, Max Palevsky, who had worked in Senator George McGovern's 1972 presidential campaign. In the early days of the campaign, Palevsky's faith in Bradley's prospects was evident. It was a personal loan from the multi-millionaire that put David Garth to work producing the first set of commercials.

Palevsky, Rising, businessman Frederick Heim, attorney Gray Davis, and politico Paul Ziffren were instrumental, not only in raising money within the state, but also in contacting contributors throughout the country. However, along with the money came expectations, including some that ran counter to Bradley's personal style. One staffer comments, "When Max commits himself to a race, he commits his heart and soul, and he expects to run something heart and soul—it's like you take me and all of my money." The wealthy politico was bound to be frustrated by what the same staff member describes as a typical Tom Bradley campaign: "It is the most democratic situation in the world, with all the good points in the world and all the bad points; for instance, somebody who gives $5 and someone who gives $500,000 gets the same amount of influence with Bradley."

Attorney Richard Bronner, another veteran of the Tunney race, was engaged for his expertise in the day-to-day running of campaigns. Former Rhodes Scholar and attorney Stan Sanders provided key expertise and advise. Another important addition to the Bradley inner-circle was the party's former state finance chair, Ethel Narvid. Maury Weiner's grassroots expertise provided a necessary counterbalance to a media-driven campaign. And Sam Williams, who had been a long-time policy advisor of Bradley's, continued to work directly with the candidate on key issues. Fran Savitch, Dodo Meyer, Bee Canterbury Lavery, Valerie Fields, Norman Emerson, Phil Depoian, Anton Calleia, and Marshall Myers added their important perspectives. Rev. Brookins, Raye Cunningham, Bill Elkins, Masamori Kojima, Manuel Aragon, Jr., Ezunial Burts, among others, were involved in getting out the minority vote. In the 1973 effort, Stephen Reinhardt remained active, but to a lesser extent than before, due to commitments to the National Democratic Party.

The new strategy was clearly evident in Bradley's formal declaration for Mayor in December 1972. Acknowledging that his "low-profile campaign in 1969 was a mistake," Bradley told his following, "I think a much more vigorous and hard-hitting campaign is necessary. We plan to engage in that kind of campaign." Aggressively highlighting his own record as a preserver of the peace, Bradley proclaimed that the people of Encino as well as Watts had the right to expect a safe city. The mayoral hopeful highlighted his twenty-one years on the police force as ample evidence that he was the only candidate for Mayor who had faced real crime on real streets. Moreover, he announced that his police record would be open to the public for examination.

To those in attendance, it was clear that the 1973 contest would see a more outspoken Tom Bradley. As he had pledged in 1969, he was not about to let Yorty or any other candidate push him around or skew the campaign agenda with vicious accusations and half-truths. He had vowed to answer the Yorty charges with what he believed was the strongest weapon he had—the truth.

Bob Kholos remembers the speech as demonstrating "such a spark of humanity, a decency that was very rare in those days." As a veteran of the Vietnam War, Kholos was drawn to Bradley, "like many others who had been brought into Bobby Kennedy's campaign." It was, to use his words, "like being a part of history." An activist who had worked in the campaigns of Jess Unruh and Senators Wayne Morse, Harold Hughes, and George McGovern, Kholos remembers finishing up on a campaign in West Virginia in 1973. A week later he was Director of Communications working in behalf of candidate Bradley.

Following a successful Bradley fundraiser in Washington, D.C., Yorty accused the Bradley campaign of being orchestrated by the East Coast establishment. Bradley retorted that the innuendos and distortions of 1969 would not be tolerated by the public in 1973. "This election will be decided on the relevant issues facing this city," Bradley said, "and not on the tactics of my opponent." The candidate enjoyed one major advantage over his earlier attempt. In 1969, before beginning his mayoral campaign, he was known to 7 percent of the public. In 1973, 95 percent of the residents in Los Angeles knew Councilman Tom Bradley.

Even though he concurred with Rising and Garth on the importance of a media campaign using the most sophisticated polling and technical methods, Bradley also insisted on a strong grassroots campaign. Raye Cunningham, Warren Hollier, Fran Savitch, Ethel Narvid, and others who participated at this level faced a difficult challenge—the field organization was to re-register the quarter of a million citizens in Los Angeles who had been dropped from official rolls because they had failed to vote in the 1972 presidential election. Known for his desire for complete power in a campaign situation, Garth nonetheless agreed to the two-tier approach. Thousands of Bradley volunteers began to sign up for work.

The primary included more formidable candidates in 1973 than in Bradley's initial race for City Hall. In addition to Yorty, three other candidates sought the office. One perceived early on as a possible spoiler to a rubber re-match of the 1969 race was

Jess Unruh, Speaker of the State Assembly, with strong ties to the power base of the Democratic Party. Others included Tom Reddin, a popular former Police Chief of Los Angeles running on a strong law-and-order platform, and Joel Wachs, City Councilman with strong ties to the Jewish community.

With so many of the candidates vying for support among the same constituencies, it was clear that no one candidate could realistically hope to receive a majority of the votes. The primary represented a real threat to the fragile coalition that the Bradley effort had attempted to put together—the Jewish-Black-Asian-Hispanic power base that Bradley had relied on before. Reddin would drain away some of Yorty's conservative votes. Wachs could impede Bradley from including the Jewish vote in his coalition. And Unruh, who enjoyed the support of such influential black legislators as Mervyn Dymally, Leon Ralph, Bill Green, and Julian Dixon, was hoping to make inroads into Bradley's popularity within the black community.

Although a Democrat, Unruh had taken on as his Campaign Manager an up-and-coming consultant in the conservative Republican ranks, Bill Roberts, who had engineered Ronald Reagan's successful drive for Governor in 1967. But there were early signs of problems within the Unruh camp. In a disagreement over policy and finances. Roberts eventually abandoned Unruh's campaign. Bob Kholos, who had served as Press Secretary in Unruh's gubernatorial bid, defected to Bradley for the mayoral race, thus earning the nickname of Jess' Judas.

Analysis of Unruh's black support seemed to indicate it consisted largely of politicians who wanted to get back at Bradley for supporting their opposition in past elections. "What it came down to then was envy and a jealousy of the type of power and prestige that Bradley had," recalls one prominent black politician, who adds that such cleavages "have dissipated over the years." One of Unruh's most vocal black supporters, Mervyn Dymally, admitted that Bradley's lack of enthusiasm for his candidacy in an earlier election for Congress (in which Bradley had campaigned for Yvonne Brathwaite Burke) had furnished a primary motive in his decision to support Unruh. The Speaker also enjoyed support in the primary from labor and powerful AFL-CIO Executive Secretary Sig Arywitz, whose organization had backed Bradley in 1969.

In an effort to preempt much of Bradley's natural constituency, Unruh declared that he was the candidate for the mainstream: "I would have to concede the votes of the far left to Bradley, the votes of the far right to Yorty, and seek my base in the middle." Tom Reddin also tried to reach the "center majority." But, of course, Bradley would concede the middle ground to no one. Neither Jess Unruh, Sam Yorty, nor any other candidate was going to get away with portraying Bradley as an extremist this time. The record simply would not support it.

But each allegation added fuel to the fire. News reports and public sentiment proclaimed "that Bradley was all but washed up, labor had supported someone else, the Jewish community was not strongly behind him, and there were even questions in the black community." But within the Bradley campaign, Ruth Abraham, Leroy and Sylvia Weekes, Kenny Washington, Rev. H. H. Brookins, Rabbi Albert Lewis, Rev. Tom Kilgore, Rev. Charles Casassa, S.J., and others worked hard to keep the patched support together. "We got him into Canter's very early, not eating a corned beef on rye with mayo, just there to remind people of his caring and support of the Jewish community," recalls Kholos. Montana McNealy remembers that the activity in the black community was frenetic. "There were meetings in the churches and organizations, all of the concern was to ensure that the lies and distortions were met with the truth about Tom Bradley's record." To allay the fears of the law and order constituency, Bradley's record on the police force and his tough stand on crime were highlighted by his campaign pamphlets.

There were also psychological factors working on behalf of the candidate. According to Phil Depoian, "as soon as they realized it could be a re-match, the public pulled for Bradley. The public loves a rematch, especially with a strong challenger. It's just like boxing, a *Rocky* type theme. . . . The minute Yorty realized it would be a rematch, he regressed four years and immediately used the same tactics saying, 'Bradley is a revolutionary, he's a Communist, he'll ruin the city, he is anti-police, etc.' This time however, we were smarter, we knew we could beat him."

The Bradley campaign called for heavy media saturation during the primary, establishing early on the facts about his record and his platform, and creating a momentum that would carry him through the expected runoff. Hitting the race issue head on, one of Bradley's commercials had the candidate telling voters that he knew that in the last election some had voted for him and some against him because he was black. According to the Councilman, he could not and should not win the election with only black support. Bradley concluded by telling viewers that if he were elected, he would never favor one group over another. He would be a Mayor for all of Los Angeles. "It was a directness, a speech from the heart," recalls student-activist Rick Fehrenbacher, "and that helped make the difference among voters who had been frightened out of their minds in 1969."

Bradley's message was heard throughout the city. Art Gastelum, student body President of East Los Angeles College, had been a supporter of Jess Unruh prior to a candidates' debate sponsored on the campus. He admired the powerful legislator because of his dedication to equality and fairness. Yet, after hearing Bradley and "the sincerity and conviction in his speech," Gastelum switched his allegiance, and began actively campaigning for the Councilman. "That moment, that inspirational speech by Tom Bradley changed the course of my life," Gastelum recalls. Initially, he became part of the advance team with Phil Depoian. The two made sure that Bradley met the scheduled events that began before sunup and, as Gastelum remembers, "often times resulted in our catching sleep in the car, or whenever we could." It marked the beginning of a long career for Gastelum as one of Bradley's most trusted Hispanic advisors.

What was obvious to Gastelum and a growing number of other Los Angeles residents was that Sam Yorty's smear tactics would not reap their expected rewards in 1973. The country was moving away from reactionary politics, and—for once—Yorty's antennae were slow to register the change in the wind.

Unruh's efforts concentrated on weakening Bradley's major power base. He urged black voters to compare his civil rights record with Bradley's. The Speaker claimed that he had done more to improve the conditions of minorities than Bradley or anyone else running. The mild-mannered Bradley of 1969 might not even have responded to the charge, but the candidate of 1973 reacted differently. Outraged by Unruh's claims, he pointed to his record of "fairness—to all the citizens of my district and Los

Angeles," defying Unruh to produce anything more substantive on his own record. He blasted Unruh for being unqualified and uninformed about the needs of Los Angeles, pointing out that Unruh had only moved back to Los Angeles two years prior in order to run for Mayor. He accused the Speaker of being opportunistic and ruthless during his years in the legislature, and attacked the philosophy of the man who had once said that "money is the mother's milk of politics."

What was increasingly clear to the press, to the other candidates, and—most importantly—to the voters of Los Angeles was that the 1973 campaign featured a new Tom Bradley. Complementing the hard-hitting media campaign designed by Garth was the candidate's own determination to take his case to as many people as possible. Campaign worker Josephine Cooke remembers, "He walked every one of the precincts, and always looked so fresh and eager." Another worker, Jackie Calloway, commented, "The real warmth of the man comes through when you first meet him."

Bradley, the frontrunner in the polls, and Yorty, the incumbent, were the focus of most of the attacks by the other candidates. One of the attacks that received the most media coverage came from candidate and fellow Councilman Joel Wachs, who claimed that Bradley had accepted contributions from a source with "strong ties to organized crime," meaning Merv Adelson. Newspaper headlines carried the charge and the follow-up stories for days. Other candidates fueled the media's coverage, demanding specifics of the Lorimar Production Chief's role in the Bradley campaign.

Yorty claimed this was just another example of the type of people backing the Bradley candidacy—thugs, hoodlums, and the Mafia. But no proof was ever offered to substantiate the charge that Adelson had underworld connections. However, since the money, which had been offered as an unguaranteed loan, continued to divert attention away from the real issues of the campaign, Bradley agreed to return it.

Unable to dredge up any new dirt, Yorty was forced to rely on the old familiar charges that black militants were behind the Bradley effort to take over Los Angeles and that Communists had supported his candidacy in 1969. Bradley responded with a statement consistent with his long-held views on violence of any type. He took a hard line against self-proclaimed revolutionaries, or any other person who broke the law or was a threat to society. Pamphlets and television spots showing him in the police uniform he had worn for twenty-one years symbolized his enduring commitment to law and order.

The media image was backed up by many specifics. For example, Bradley outlined a neighborhood watch program, which called for community cooperation with the police department in curbing crime. He cited such past accomplishments on the Council as the establishment of an anti-crime street-lighting program in his district, which later was adopted by the entire city. And he attacked monopolies that led to inefficient use of city money, pointing to the Yellow Cab Company as one of many that enjoyed a noncompetitive contract with the city. At a time when Los Angeles was facing a budget deficit, the city needed a cost-conscious leadership that could eliminate such inequities and waste. As a well-known fiscal conservative, he could deliver that kind of leadership.

In the final analysis, Bradley's hard-hitting issue-oriented campaign worked. The primary election results showed Bradley leading the field with 35 percent and Yorty second with 29 percent. Unruh had come in a distant third with 17 percent. The rematch was now a reality.

9

Rematch—the 1973 Mayoral Campaign

"In a great city, City Hall must be a beacon to the people's aspirations, not a barrier."

—Tom Bradley

Yorty continued to harp on the same old tired themes. But this time around Bradley was prepared for Yorty's tactics, and the campaign devised a strategy to check the predictable onslaught of innuendos. Bob Kholos, who had studied Yorty extensively, describes one of the the Bradley campaign counteroffensives that he devised: "Yorty usually scheduled a noon news conference on Wednesdays, but with his schedule, they never started until around 1:00 or 2:00 P.M. We opted to schedule Bradley on Wednesday mornings for an 'Alternate News Conference' at 9:00 A.M. It was designed to put Yorty on the defensive later in the day answering Bradley's charges." According to Kholos and other members of the staff, "It worked extremely well."

Again the three-term Mayor chose to make personal attacks on Bradley's credibility. He charged that he had information that clearly revealed the "type of man Tom Bradley really is." According to Yorty, Bradley had swindled his nephews out of some property and insurance money that were rightfully theirs following the death of a brother. Bradley explained that in lieu of some personal loans owed to him, his brother, before he had died, had offered Bradley joint-tenancy of some property to help cover the debt. Furthermore, Bradley indicated that the entire financial matter had been settled out of court to the mutual satisfaction of all family members. The story generated little interest in the public debate. It was just another example of Yorty struggling to develop a credible campaign issue.

But the Mayor continued to attack. In their first debate, Yorty charged, "Your district is number one in deficient housing in the city. Your district also, of course, has the number-one problem of communicable disease. . . . if you can't do your job as Councilman, you certainly can't do the job as Mayor." Bradley responded by pointing his finger at Yorty and saying, "I just want to say to this audience that I am not responsible for one bit of that communicable disease!"

It had been four years since the last campaign. The paranoia within America was no longer at a fever pitch. Neither the city nor the country were as divided as they had been then. Paranoia no longer reigned supreme. As a result, the only message that seemed extreme was Sam Yorty's.

Everyone who had been a part of the effort in 1969 noticed a difference this time around. The crowds were much more attentive than they had been in 1969. Bradley was receiving good press, not only in the city, but throughout the nation. A *New York Times* article had covered the campaign and offered high praise for Bradley. Leroy Aarons of the *Washington Post* described Bradley as "a pained victim attempting to elucidate important issues of rapid transit, smog, and crime in the face of Yorty's 'smear' techniques." The candidate himself knew 1973 was a different year. He could tell that the voters were not buying Yorty's message. Everything was coming together. But he was determined to put in twenty-four-hour days for the remainder of the campaign. He wouldn't let victory slip away this time.

The tempo Yorty established in the 1969 campaign did not materialize in 1973. In the latter days, the polls showed Bradley ahead. Then the Mayor was put in an unfamiliar campaign position, having to defend himself against an accusation of misuse of campaign funds. Councilman Joel Wachs, an unsuccessful candidate in the primary, now endorsed Bradley, accusing Yorty of buying a life insurance policy with campaign funds. The ensuing headlines and Yorty's flip-flop on the truth of the charge left Mayor Sam vulnerable.

Bradley's media campaign, in which the challenger outspent the incumbent by nearly two to one, was working. Commenting on Bradley's success in fundraising in 1973, Yorty says, "The liberal group really turned out for Bradley in that election. Guys like Norman Lear, liberal groups like that, and there was a lot of money from some guy from Xerox [Max Palevsky]." Reflecting on his involvement in the Bradley effort, producer Norman Lear remembers: "I think Yorty is only using me as a symbol. I supported the Mayor, yes, but also many other Westside candidates in that election."

Another campaign was coming to a close. Bradley had started early, fought more aggressively, and spent more money than in the previous one. This time he had succeeded at keeping the focus on substantive issues of city government. Time would very shortly tell whether Los Angeles' citizens responded well to an issue-oriented campaign.

The initial word from the City Clerk on election night, May 29, was not good, but it was expected—Yorty was leading in absentee votes, traditionally a conservative group. Press Secretary Kholos told reporters in the ballroom that Hugh Schwartz, Bradley's pollster, had predicted the outcome on absentee ballots—though, in comparison to 1969, the gap between the two candidates was smaller.

Even with the assurances of Schwartz and others, many supporters still wondered if the absentee ballot count was an omen. Could Yorty's campaign of hate really have taken hold for a second time? Staffers noticed that Bradley, waiting for the returns to come in, seemed to be pacing more than he had in the previous election. Surely, he too had some doubts. But if he did, he never voiced them.

As the vote count trickled in, so did a sense of optimism and excitement. First, a television station predicted a Bradley victory, then came word from a wire service. As the election returns continued, any lingering doubts about the accuracy of the pollsters gave way to feelings of exuberance. History had been made—Tom Bradley, who had traveled from the cotton fields of Calvert to the government of Los Angeles, would be the city's thirty-seventh Mayor. Adjusting his tie in an oversized mirror,

Bradley had the widest grin on his face his friends could remember. "I iz da may-your!" he proclaimed to his Press Secretary in a spirit of fun.

As he looked around, there on the sofa was his mother looking up at him with that familiar smile that he had seen so many times. Except now, it was a bit broader. She came over to him, hugged her son, and said, "You hung on to your dream, Tom. And now it belongs to all of us." Her eyes glistened as she turned to Ethel and gave her daughter-in-law a wink of proud satisfaction.

This time the polls had held true. Many of Yorty's 1969 supporters deserted him in 1973, crossing over for Bradley. Others, as Mayor Sam was known to say, "went fishing" rather than to the polls. Reason won out over fear; the impossible dream had been realized. Bradley overwhelmed Yorty, winning 56 percent of the vote to the incumbent's 44 percent, a 100,000-vote margin of victory.

A special feeling seemed to hover over the Hilton. As the Mayor-elect himself put it, "The magic of the moment was everywhere that night, and it's something I will never forget as long as I live." Before he began his remarks, Bradley acknowledged a supporter by leaning over to shake her hand. He remembers: "Suddenly in every corner of the room, hands shot up in the air toward me, reaching toward the stage. It was a spontaneous act, like a symbolic reaching out and touching. It was an overwhelming emotional experience."

His mother's sense of pride was clearly evident when the new Mayor and his daughters stopped by the next morning to visit his brother Ellis, whose handicap had prevented him from attending the election night ceremonies. Ellis told his nieces, "Now the whole city can look up to someone who will never let them down." When they left, Ellis patted his brother on the back and said, "Come by again, Mayor Bradley."

For Tom Bradley, this event was truly a supreme victory. "It was the highest I have ever seen him in my life," remarks Bishop H. H. Brookins, who attributed the win to Bradley "shooting his best shot." Brookins, who had been elected Bishop of the African Methodist Episcopal Church in 1972, continues: "It was the final confirmation of Bradley being recognized by the whole community. . . . He had overcome the doubts and fears of people who had never had a black man in that position. . . . He was not only a celebrity, but also a champion. He had taken an important historical step—from one dimension to the next—in terms of leadership." State Democratic Chairman, Assemblyman John Burton told the press that Tom Bradley "was a powerful new force in California."

Reflecting on the reasons for his success in 1973, Bradley said, "Yorty failed to realize that time had not stood still. People knew me and what I stood for. His old tactics simply didn't work." Bradley credited his win to his visibility and to the city's increased maturity: "Yorty failed in 1973 to motivate the fears and hate in people. The racial campaign didn't work because people were interested in the issues, the vision of what the city could become to all people, and not scare tactics."

By contrast, Yorty attributes his loss in 1973 to "the *Times* effort to get me," as well as the fact that "Bradley had so much money." The outgoing Mayor also acknowledged that one reason might also have been that "people get tired of you."

As for the *Times,* it explained the election results in these words:

> No one can read the minds of the voters, but it would seem, from all that has been said, that three reasons account for the election of Tom Bradley.
>
> He was elected because he was trusted.
>
> He was elected because he has shown, in a career within the Police Department and in a career as a city councilman, that he is a man of action, a leader.
>
> He was elected because he knows Los Angeles, its resources, its faults, its potential.

The days after the election offered no rest for Mayor-elect Bradley. There were requests for interviews from the national press. Stories about Bradley's impossible dream appeared in *Newsweek, Time,* the *New York Times,* and the *Washington Post,* as well as in the California papers. He appeared on news shows outlining his plans to restore vision and leadership to City Hall.

There were also important meetings on the hundreds of appointments to be made by the Mayor. Who would be his key personnel aiding him in charting the city's new course? Bradley pledged to bring the best on board with him, regardless of party, race, or heritage. His would be an administration that truly represented the city's diversity. It was essential that Asians and Hispanics as well as blacks all have input into the decision-making process. Bradley was committed to seeing to it that all of the ethnicities of Los Angeles should find a voice in the city's government during his administration. Manuel Aragon, Jr., who became the city's highest ranking Mexican-American official in the city's history, came on board as a Deputy Mayor. Masamori Kojima, who had been a longtime supporter of Bradley, provided expertise from the Asian community. Jeff Matsui, who had worked with President Kennedy, joined the Bradley staff out of a sense that "Bradley, like Kennedy, had a mission." Ezunial "Eze." Burts, Bill Elkins, and Mary Henry would keep City Hall informed about black issues, as would Fran Savitch, an administrative coordinator to Weiner and also a politically astute voice of the Jewish community. Valerie Fields would continue representing the Valley and speaking out on important women's issues. Dodo Meyer would run the Mayor's office at Van Nuys as administrative coordinator for the San Fernando Valley. Bee Canterbury Lavery would serve as Chief of Protocol for the city.

The most immediate priority was to set up a transition team to facilitate the change in administrations. There was initial concern about how cooperative Yorty would be during this period. Given the heated campaigns and the fact that he had yet to concede defeat, some figured Yorty would make one last stand, a final battle before he relinquished power. But such fears proved unfounded. Jerome F. Miller, Bradley's Director of Transition, established effective links between the two staffs, developing a good working relationship that allowed for a smooth exchange of power. Those involved in making key recommendations to the new Mayor included the new Deputy Mayor and Chief of Staff, Maury Weiner, as well as Anton Calleia, Manuel Aragon, Jr., Phil Depoian, Norm Emerson, Nelson Rising, Bill Elkins, Sam Williams, Stephen Reinhardt, Ezunial Burts, Art Gastelum, and Bill Norris, among others.

Immediately after the election, Chief of Police Ed Davis requested a meeting with his new boss. Bradley appreciated the Chief's initiative. As a former cop, he knew of the division that often existed between City Hall and the Los Angeles Police Department. With the campaign charges waged by Yorty that Bradley was "anti-police" and that massive resignations would take place upon his election, the Mayor-elect valued the opportunity to begin what he hoped would be an effective working relationship with Davis. In the meeting, Davis pledged his support and cooperation. Bradley assured the Chief that he wanted to maintain a close relationship to ensure that Los Angeles had the best police force possible. Such amity would, alas, be short-lived, as Bradley sought—through personal supervision and appointment of concerned citizens such as Sam Williams to the Civilian Police Commission—to regain a measure of control on a Police Department long accustomed to behaving as an independent fiefdom.

As Bob Kholos describes the situation prevailing then, "The Police Commission under Yorty was merely a rubber stamp for the Police Chief. When Bradley took over, it began to oversee Police Department policy as the city charter mandated. . . . This is one of the reasons that Davis . . . felt he had lost power."

Another immediate task for Bradley was obtaining a pool of applicants for the 155 commissioners he would be responsible for appointing to help run the city. Bradley assembled a high-level blue-ribbon commission headed by industrialist Victor Carter and former Governor Pat Brown to make appropriate recommendations. After weeks of meetings and debates on the strengths and weaknesses of each of the candidates, the Commission narrowed down the field from twelve hundred to four hundred names for the Mayor-elect's consideration.

Bradley personally narrowed down the four hundred to 155. The initial screening pertained to overall qualities; only after he had determined, to his own satisfaction, that each of the candidates was qualified did Bradley move to the next stage. As he says, "I then culled through the applicants with several factors in mind. I sought a balance in having commissioners from throughout the city, with each race, ethnicity, and culture represented." Bradley wanted commission heads who were leaders,

Bradley sticks to the issues at a debate with incumbent Mayor Sam Yorty during the 1973 campaign. (Courtesy of Los Angeles City Hall)

Leaving their Welland Avenue home, the Bradleys go to the polls. (Bradley Family Collection)

A magical moment in Los Angeles' history . . . Tom Bradley wins the election. (Courtesy of Rick Browne)

"You hung on to your dream, Tom." Crenner congratulates her son and Ethel on election night. (Bradley Family Collection)

Wearing a bulletproof vest, Tom is sworn in by Chief Justice Earl Warren, July 1, 1973. (Photo by Harry H. Adams: Courtesy of Los Angeles City Hall)

take-charge types, with the credentials necessary to analyze a problem, talk with the people involved, and recommend viable solutions. And he wanted the best possible racial, ethnic, and cultural balance he could get.

Neither political affiliation nor support of his mayoral candidacy were factors in Bradley's selection process. Many talented commissioners who had served in the Yorty administration were eventually asked to retain their positions. Diversity of representation on the city's commissions would not only help Bradley remain true to a campaign promise, but would translate into better government; it was a means to ensure that the programs and policy of his administration would take advantage of the best that all the communities of Los Angeles had to offer.

Bradley had decided that, if he won the election, his first choice to conduct the official swearing-in ceremonies would be someone who had rendered key historical decisions that had opened the doors of opportunity to millions throughout the country—retired U.S. Chief Justice of the Supreme Court, Earl Warren. He was overjoyed when Warren accepted his invitation.

The Mayor-elect wanted the inaugural festivities not only to signal the beginning of a new era for the city, but also to "represent to the children of Los Angeles an important symbol that anything is possible if you believe in yourself, put your mind to it, and work hard."

The inaugural ceremony was different from what the city had seen in the past. Actors Lloyd Bridges and Eddie and Margo Albert served as masters of ceremonies. Parades featured the various ethnic cultures that give Los Angeles its richness. Bishop H. H. Brookins, Dr. Don R. Boyd of the Los Angeles Council of Churches, Bishop Timothy Cardinal Manning, and Rabbi Albert Lewis presided over the message that echoed the new Mayor's philosophy, illustrated best in his favorite song, "The Impossible Dream," performed by O. C. Smith, with Quincy Jones conducting the Los Angeles Philharmonic Orchestra, and the Operation Breadbasket Chorus. Florence Henderson, Vikki Carr, and Una Duvall entertained.

Bradley realized that it was important to set a tone, to provide a vision, and to outline his administration's agenda in his inaugural speech. Standard procedure with Bradley on important speeches and decisions was to receive input from a wide range of sources, and so he did with his inaugural speech. Jeff Greenfield, a noted wordsmith affiliated with David Garth, provided stylistic recommendations. Jack Tenner, Nelson Rising, Maury Weiner, Steve Reinhardt, and others suggested specific themes. But Tom Bradley prefers to write the final draft of his speeches himself, and often discards even his own work to speak extemporaneously. He listened to all suggestions and then stitched them together into a speech that bore the marks of his personal style, a speech that sounded like Tom Bradley because it was.

He delivered his inaugural address on July 1, 1973, wearing a bulletproof vest because of the numerous threats that had been made against his life. Members of the Nazi Party came dressed in black outfits and riot helmets, chanting, "White power!" and carrying "Go Back To Africa!" signs. But Bradley won out over all distractions, and the crowd was his, as he delivered a speech that was a summation of all he had stood for in the past and all he had taken upon himself to do. He praised the citizens of the city and the more than twenty thousand people who had come to witness the inauguration and parade: "Never did I lose faith that this city could live by the creed of this nation's birth. . . ."

He continued with a pledge to reunite the city: "These last few weeks have been sad for all of us who believe in the American promise. . . . But let it be said that here in Los Angeles, we began today to build the kind of government that means what it says and says what it means. Let it be said that we built the kind of government that the decent, hardworking citizens of Los Angeles respected because it respected them. . . ."

The new Mayor reaffirmed that he would "be a Mayor of all of Los Angeles." He pledged to serve the needs of the Valley as well as the Harbor area, to be a leader concerned with each and every community. The attempt was to establish early, at the very beginning of his administration, that there would be no room for favoritism or neglect during his tenure as Mayor. All communities and all people from this day forward would have a Mayor working for their interests in City Hall.

He committed his administration to maintaining law and order and to protecting the integrity of neighborhoods from the encroachment of ill-planned development. Echoing one of his campaign pledges, Bradley told the crowd gathered at City Hall that he would balance the city budget and streamline city bureaucracy. He promised to work each and every day to obtain the funds that Los Angeles was rightfully entitled to from both the state and national governments. He pointed out that Los Angeles was one of the few cities in the country without a mass-transit system, and pledged to begin work immediately on developing a system to serve the entire city. Committing his administration to putting an end to City Hall's adversary relationship with business, the new Mayor promised a public-private sector partnership that would open up new areas of employment to "all the citizens of Los Angeles, regardless of race, color, or creed."

Bradley's mediating skills were apparent in the speech. He announced the establishment of a Labor Management Board to help solve conflicts both in government and in the private sector. With the crisis of Watergate growing more severe each day, Bradley announced a policy of full financial disclosure of all staff members and called for reforms in campaign financing. With the questionable tactics of his opponent fresh in his mind, Los Angeles' new chief executive advocated the establishment of a fair campaign code for future elections. To those familiar with City Hall, the crowded agenda stood in stark contrast to the vague promises offered by Bradley's predecessor.

While the transition seemed to have gone smoothly, the new Mayor and his staff discovered upon their arrival at City Hall that all files in the offices had been shredded. They would be starting from scratch and with empty cabinets. The only key found by Wanda Moore, Bradley's executive secretary, was one with a note attached, "Here is de key to de Mayor's office, Sapphire!" Some of the new staff were outraged. Moore broke into tears.

Responding to inquiries about such events, Sam Yorty states, "I didn't do that myself, you know; I just took my papers, my personal property and files and moved out." Nonetheless Letty Herndon Brown, who had worked in Mayor Yorty's office at the end and would later be the chief scheduler for Tom Bradley, remembers, "In those last days of the Yorty administration, the shredders were on constantly."

Operating in the vacuum deliberately created by the previous administration, the new Mayor of Los Angeles was determined to move forward, to usher in a new spirit of cooperation.

10

Making History—
Mayor Tom Bradley

"I refuse to accept the idea that the 'isness' of man's present nature makes him morally incapable of reaching up for the 'oughtness' that forever confronts him."

—Martin Luther King

Although Tom Bradley sought the advice of numerous people and groups on selection of his personal staff at City Hall, it came as no surprise to those who really knew him that he alone would make the major decisions in the end. A colleague remarks, "Some people make the mistake of underestimating him in this area; they confuse his quiet approach with indecisiveness and think that he can be molded to fit others' expectations, but that is not Tom Bradley." And those who make that mistake are disabused of it sooner or later.

Stephen Reinhardt recalls one such instance: "Shortly after the 1973 election, at a meeting which included some of the major advisors, the concern turned to how the administration would be staffed." Opposition was expressed to Bradley's choice of Maury Weiner as both Chief of Staff and Deputy Mayor, and it became obvious that a number of those who were present at the meeting had their own agendas.

"One person basically said that he would put somebody in the Deputy Mayor position to run the city, while the Mayor was out cutting ribbons. . . . I looked at Tom, and he was literally turning purple, the body language was saying 'No,' " Reinhardt recalls. "But never in the course of the discussion did Bradley break in with his own viewpoint. He was merely assimilating what was happening. "After the meeting, I told Tom that I couldn't believe he had stayed silent throughout the entire meeting and that I hoped he would pick the people he wanted to in his administration." Bradley smiled and simply told Reinhardt not to worry.

When Bradley announced his appointments, it was clear that there had indeed been no reason to worry. His choices were very much his own, which did cause a breach in relations with some members of the campaign who had mistakenly thought that he would be a malleable Mayor.

Major appointments included new faces as well as Bradley supporters of many years' duration. The new Deputy Mayors were longtime aide Maury Weiner and newcomer Manuel Aragon, Jr. Anton Calleia would be the city's Chief Executive Assistant and Budget Analyst. Calleia had worked with Bradley during his years on the Council and was highly valued for his intuition on Council matters and for his knowledge of city government. Wanda Moore, Bradley's executive secretary during his Council years, whom he valued greatly for her excellent interpersonal and business communication skills, assumed the same role at City Hall.

Bob Kholos, who would stay on as Press Secretary, indicated that one of his primary goals was to curtail the *Times'* tendency to refer to Bradley as the "Black Mayor." Bradley himself, however, was capable of a sense of humor in situations where others were momentarily confounded with embarrassment. Kholos recalls one of the new Mayor's first formal appearances, at a gathering of labor leaders and workers. The speaker was awarding a special commendation to Herman "Blackie" Leavitt, who was on his right, while Bradley was on his left. According to Kholos, the speaker started his speech by saying, "Well, Blackie . . .," and then found himself speechless with the thought that this might be heard as a reference to the Mayor. After an awkward silence, Bradley began to chuckle, and then the entire audience joined in. Finally Bradley quipped, "I've been called a lot of things in my life . . . but Blackie?"

After studying the communications network within city government, Los Angeles' new Mayor concluded that there were serious structural obstacles to the kind of free flow of information he considered necessary to the forging of effective public policy. Prior to 1973, for example, there had been no formal meeting at which all the city's departmental heads were present at the same table. Bradley felt strongly that, without the free flow of ideas, there could be no coordination of policies that were representative of a coherent philosophy of government. Bradley reorganized much of city government so that its parts were enhanced. Direct communication with the Mayor himself was institutionalized as part of his administration's emphasis on the spirit of teamwork. Wanting everybody in his administration to feel that they had input into its decision-making, Bradley held regular monthly meetings with all department heads, at which they had the opportunity to exchange ideas and discuss policies with him.

He also made a commitment to cooperate with the County Board of Supervisors, which resulted early in the consolidation of beach operation and maintenance under the county, at an annual savings of one million dollars to the city. And he made it his business to eliminate the discord that had long existed between the City Council and the Mayor: "He always worked quietly behind the scenes to help reach consensus. Often he defused the conflict effectively, which all too often characterized the Council relationship," says Ninth District Councilman Gilbert Lindsay.

Mayor Bradley sent an early signal to the business community that he desired their help, that he wanted to establish a partnership between City Hall and the private sector to improve the business climate of the city. Bradley told audiences that "when the heart of the city dies, it won't be long before the suburbs go down as well." The situation called for a major effort to redevelop the downtown area, to keep and bring businesses back to the central city.

To establish the necessary working relationship with business and labor, Bradley enlisted the services of a proven leader in the business community, Fred Schnell, President of Western Operations of the Prudential Insurance Company of America, who would serve as Bradley's economic development consultant. Prudential agreed to loan Schnell to the city for one year. Schnell remarks, "Up until then, I had never been involved in politics other than voting as a private citizen," but he would prove instrumental in forging a unique public-private sector alliance that would keep Los Angeles working and growing at a time when other cities were experiencing great difficulties.

Describing the early stages of his work with Bradley, Schnell recalls, "One of the first things we did was set up an ad hoc committee of businessmen and labor leaders, a cross-section of citizens (the Economic Advisory Council). The group was informed that they had a three-month assignment to come up with recommendations to give to the Mayor and Council."

One result of their deliberations was the creation in 1975 of the City's Economic Development Office, which would coordinate the skills and expertise of all city departments as they pertain to economic development. Brad Crowe, an economist from the Yorty administration, was named its head. Originally funded with $150,000, which Bradley persuaded the City Council to grant, this office has received millions of dollars from the federal government in the years since. Under Bradley, Los Angeles' share of federal funds has gone from $81 million to $800 million.

Schnell's credibility in the business community and knowledge of problems in the city's neighborhoods proved to be an invaluable resource for Bradley, who recalls, "After the year, when the loaned executive agreement had expired, Fred was doing such an outstanding job, his experience in business had helped out to the extent that I knew I had to attempt to get him to stay on." Aware of Prudential's concern that he return and resume his duties, Schnell nonetheless took an early retirement so that he could stay on at City Hall. Bradley and Schnell enjoyed a mutual admiration and respect, which became reflected in a new spirit of cooperation between the business community and City Hall.

Once a non-adversary relationship had been established, there was an emphasis on the use of public funds—city, state, and federal—to influence the private sector to assume a more active role in the community. Schnell, a University of Illinois foundation leader, describes the prevailing philosophy at City Hall: "Whatever money we got we would use to prime the pump to get business to go into a depressed area and make it economically viable." Stafford Grady, CEO of Lloyd's Bank, singles out Schnell's involvement as a primary reason for the development of the public–private partnership: "Bradley knows that Fred Schnell speaks the businessman's language."

One of the major problems facing the new administration was that the two previous administrations had neglected to establish any precedent for tapping into the employment potential of private industry. Traditionally, the business establishment leaned toward the Republican Party. What Schnell needed to communicate was that, as he put it, "The Mayor's deal is a non-partisan approach, he is a Mayor for everybody and not a Mayor for a particular group. . . . The fact that he made the move, that he appointed someone on his staff to be the eyes and ears in the business community added to his credibility early on."

Thus began a relationship that would change the skyline and the make-up of downtown Los Angeles. Bradley's leadership, combined with the expertise of Schnell and Crowe, helped reverse the exodus from the central city area. "In '74 and '75, we had developers from Orange County running ads saying why go downtown where all the problems are, but Bradley has changed that," Schnell says. Under Bradley, the Community Redevelopment Agency has transformed downtown Los Angeles into a dynamic city core, with twelve million square feet of commercial space added, including such major developments as the Wells Fargo headquarters building, Crocker Center, Angeles Plaza senior housing, the Promenade condominium complex, the Los Angeles Bonaventure Hotel, and the Citicorp Plaza.

Through Schnell, Crowe, and others, Bradley moved quickly to open up more jobs for the city's labor pool. The Mayor's Manpower Planning Office under the direction of special assistant Jerome F. Miller created more than 6,000 jobs. Bradley's leadership in revitalizing the city produce and flower marts meant another 3,000 jobs. Under Bradley, the CETA Title I program was run efficiently; 13,600 citizens would enter the program to prepare themselves for more promising jobs. Of the 7,800 who completed the program, roughly three out of every four went on to gainful employment in the private sector.

Bradley was determined to reach beyond the traditional means for involving citizens in the decisions made at City Hall. Over fifty citizen advisory committees and special task force groups were impaneled—at no cost to the taxpayer—to study problems and arrive at the most efficient solutions. One of their most noteworthy accomplishments was Project HOPE, which mobilized millions of dollars in private capital for neighborhood conservation.

In the campaign, Bradley had promised to balance the city's budget, a pledge that was greeted with skepticism, considering the $100,000,000 deficit forecast by the outgoing administration. The City Council had already passed Yorty's $700-million budget for the upcoming fiscal year, but Bradley chose to reexamine it.

From his Council days, he knew by experience that Yorty's budgets were inflated. Working closely with Anton Calleia, Bradley combed through the figures. "We were aiming for a 10 percent cut and eventually suggested shaving the proposed budget by $12,000,000," recalled Bradley, "I think our ability to come up with such a significant amount of waste helped communicate to the public, to business, and to the press that we were serious about making good on our programs and plans." Personally, Bradley set an example of the thrift he planned to bring to City Hall. He refused to accept a $5,000 raise in salary, and vetoed increases that had been voted in for high-paid city departmental managers.

His action in the early days laid the groundwork for further development of his reputation as a fiscal conservative. He had the ability, at a time when other cities were going bankrupt, to keep the city operating efficiently within a balanced budget. In his first three years, Bradley personally inked out more than $200 million from departmental requests. In his first four years, he balanced three consecutive budgets without any new taxes. This was a remarkable accomplishment. Walter Gerken, Chairman of the Board at Pacific Mutual Life Insurance, comments, "Mayor Bradley has presided over the city during one of its greatest growth periods, particularly the rebirth of the central city. He has a high degree of fiscal responsibility but has not overlooked the need to provide social services to the residents of the city."

Each city department had its budget readjusted by the new Mayor in 1973. The LAPD's budget was reduced by less than the ten percent across-the-board cut pertaining to most departments, but relations between Bradley and Chief Ed Davis were nonetheless strained by the inroads on the Police Department budget.

The rift between the Police Chief and Bradley would widen in the years to come, often highlighted in the press—this despite the respect, grudging though it may have been, that the two men had for each other. Bradley and Davis had known each other from police academy days, and both had strong ideas about how the department should be run. Davis' view is that "one of the reasons that Bradley didn't support the department. . . . didn't tell it that he loved it and that it was doing a good job. . . . was that he remembered the policies of the department from the days when he was a cop. But those days are now gone and he needs to support the department." Bradley's succinct response to Davis' theory that the racial prejudice he had experienced on the LAPD had soured his attitude toward it was, "Hogwash!"

It is quite true, however, that Bradley made it his business to establish civilian checks on the operations of the department by appointing activists to the Police Commission. Police commissioner Sam Williams describes one of the Commission's goals: "We particularly wanted to rid the department of the nonessential spy-like information that they had on many citizens of Los Angeles." Rigid guidelines were established for the conduct of intelligence operations, including the abolition of files on the personal and political activities of law-abiding citizens and the adoption of clear and stringent rules on the use of deadly force— a particular concern of Bradley's from the times of the Watts riots in 1965.

Bradley and Davis were on a collision course, with Davis convinced that Bradley was out to weaken the Police Department, and Bradley convinced (according to Sam Williams) that Davis was too often "involved in matters that were more in line with the duties of the Mayor, and not the Chief of Police."

Bradley was very concerned about Los Angeles' lack of a mass-transit system. Population experts and demographers had predicted that, by the year 2000, the increase in Los Angeles population would be equivalent to a city the size of Houston surpassing New York City. Buses in the Wilshire corridor were already carrying 200,000 people a day, and a majority of the city's population depended on mass transit to get to work.

In his inaugural speech, elucidating on a campaign promise, Bradley had pledged to break ground on a mass-transit system "within eighteen months," though the actual text of the speech was without a specific timeframe. While his staff urged him to correct the record, Bradley refused. Delivery on the promise would become one of the most difficult tasks Bradley would face in his tenure as Mayor. Constrained by the county's failure to pass a needed tax proposal and a volatile political environment in Washington, Bradley found that he had committed himself to what many would call the impossible. Nonetheless, driven by his vision of what should be, he began to lay the necessary ground-work for what would become known as the Metro Rail Subway project, though ultimate approval for it would not come until 1985.

The Bradley administration's first step was to name Norm Emerson head of a newly formed Rapid Transit Authority, which would coordinate the efforts of all relevant city departments. The goal was to arrive at comprehensive plans for a complete mass-transit system designed to satisfy the needs of the greater Los Angeles area.

The initial plan, known on the city and county ballot as Proposition A, called for a 142-mile system that would connect Los Angeles with its neighboring communities, from Long Beach to the San Fernando Valley. Both the county and the city residents would have to vote additional sales taxes to pay for it. Bradley campaigned hard for the proposal within the city. He spelled out the system's advantages in bringing the city and county closer together and in developing the economic promise in key neighborhoods. He traveled to Sacramento, personally lobbying the legislature for support of the system.

Within the city, business and community groups attempted to organize a grassroots campaign to get the measure passed, but there was no real effort outside the city to rally support for the system. Although Bradley met with mayors and leaders of cities in the county, it was clear that outside Los Angeles, Proposition A was not generating the support needed for passage. Strong voter resistance to the increase in property taxes required to finance the system was reinforced when, just days before the issue was put to a vote, many county residents received substantially higher tax bills as a result of an already approved tax increase.

When Proposition A appeared on county ballots in November 1974, it failed to pass, although it did pass in the city. Offering his assessment of why the measure failed, Bradley points to the tax bills that arrived in many county residents' mailboxes immediately before the vote. "The fact that these people were informed only a few days before the election that their taxes were going up by as much as one-third had to have an effect on their decision," reasoned Bradley. "I think many expressed their outrage by saying no to taxes in general, by voting against the mass-transit proposal."

The proposal's defeat did not deter Bradley's enthusiasm for mass transit in Los Angeles. He immediately directed Norman Emerson and others to begin new plans, outlining several options for a more conservatively scaled rail system. To finance this starter system, Bradley would turn to another source of funds— the U.S. Department of Transportation. Finally in December 1985, a federal appropriation measure would be approved for the first 4.4-mile link of the proposed 18.6-mile line connecting downtown Los Angeles, the Wilshire Boulevard commercial corridor, Hollywood, and the San Fernando Valley. Debate over the exact routing through the potentially dangerous Fairfax District—where underground methane gas had precipitated an explosion in the summer of 1985—continued in the early part of 1986. Construction of a 23-mile Los Angeles-to-Long Beach line will serve a geographical area whose residents are highly dependent upon public transportation.

Bradley's long established reputation as an opponent to unrestricted oil drilling on the California coast was tested in the summer of 1974. The U.S. Government announced that it had granted offshore oil leases to petroleum companies for drilling along the California coast. Bradley was outraged. There had been no dialogue between Washington and Los Angeles, nor with any of the other municipalities affected.

The idea was ridden with problems. There were inadequate contingency plans for blow-outs or oil spills. The financial benefits to local governments were almost nonexistent, while the oil companies would be reaping windfall profits. Moreover, there seemed to be no sense of how these leases fit into national energy policy. Groups throughout Los Angeles and the beach communities along the coast vigorously protested, demanding to meet with the appropriate national leadership.

Bradley viewed the resulting meetings with the Department of Interior as completely worthless. The Department did not deal with any of the concerns voiced by Bradley or the citizens groups, but proceeded with its plan to issue the leases. Bradley took the case to Washington, lobbying and testifying before congressional committees. A lawsuit was filed on behalf of the California communities.

The questions Bradley and others raised did eventually find a sounding board. The Ford Administration was forced to announce that it would place the matter "under further study" before the plan continued. The oil-leasing proposal released later by the Department of Interior was more conservative in approach, with more emphasis on environmental concerns and monetary reimbursement to the communities involved.

Bradley's experience here and in the Pacific Palisades case earned him a reputation—in some quarters—as "anti-oil." But he rejected that label, insisting that he had nothing against the oil companies nor even against offshore drilling, for that matter. His concern—his opposition—was to ill-conceived policies that were not only unfair to the parties involved, but threatened one of the economic treasures of his city and state—the beaches. Indeed, Bradley would eventually find himself, years later, concurring on a drilling proposal that he felt met the criteria he had long insisted on. In 1985, he approved the amended proposal of Occidental Petroleum to drill in the Pacific Palisades.

To fulfill his campaign pledge of an open administration, Bradley has carried over from his Council days his long-established practice of conducting "Area Days" as a means of communicating directly with the citizens of Los Angeles' diverse communities. A working Mayor, concerned with solving the problems of the city, needed input from his constituents. Area Days were an important means of getting it, and they proved so successful that he has continued the practice throughout his four terms in office.

Visiting a different part of the city each time, Bradley arrives early, before people set off for work, and he stays until late in the evening. He visits schools and talks with children, tours senior centers, and tries to visit important locations that will tell him what he needs to know about that community's concerns and priorities.

The monthly Open House he instituted in the early days of his administration was an instant success. The first one at City Hall was attended by over three hundred citizens. To reach out to larger numbers of the citizens of a city that covers over 460 square miles, Bradley established full-time branches of the Mayor's office in San Pedro and West Los Angeles, and expanded the existing office in Van Nuys. Each office is overseen by an area coordinator who reports directly to an executive assistant at City Hall. Another technique Bradley used in his first year in office was a phone-in television talk show, which featured Bradley answering queries from citizens who called in.

He has designated staff persons—including Masimori Kojima. Rose Ochi, Christine Ung, Bill Elkins, Mike Angelo, and others—to serve as liaisons to the city's various ethnic communities and to handle specific issues and industries such as education and fashion. There are liaisons to the Hispanic, Korean, Filipino, Japanese, Native American, black, gay, and Chinese communities. In addition, the Mayor named regional coordinators to deal with specific areas of the city and their concerns, including San Pedro.

The personal interest the new Mayor displayed surprised many in government. Valerie Fields recalls that, when Bradley called the superintendent of schools to ask him if there was anything he would like the Mayor to see to in an upcoming trip to Washington, "He almost fell out of his chair in shock, because no elected official had ever made that kind of phone call in the past."

Pearl Baron, the Mayor's office receptionist (or "Head Gatekeeper"), points out one virtually unreported dimension of Bradley's character. "We receive calls all the time from older people who are having trouble with their water or gas bill—they don't have the money right then. Time after time I have seen Bradley contact the relevant office to ask if something can't be worked out for the person, like staggering of payments." She adds. "He loves being able to truly serve the people."

Bradley's accessibility has had its lighter moments. Raye Cunningham received a call one day from a security guard saying that "Someone named Jesus wants to see the Mayor." Obeying her boss' orders that Los Angeles' citizens should have access to City Hall, Cunningham reluctantly told the guard to send the individual up to see her. "There, he proceeded to tell me about his life as Jesus," Cunningham recalls. "He was pleased that the Mayor knew who Jesus was, and left me an address on where I could find him." A few days later, a letter came to Cunningham's attention. It read, "This is God; thank you for talking to my son." Pearl Baron reports that there have been "numerous Jesuses" as well as a couple of "Moseses" and "Muhammeds" who have come by during the Mayor's tenure. Baron adds, "We try to accommodate all the citizens."

Of course, in addition to these "leaders," Bradley also frequently confers with mayors, governors, and heads of state from throughout the country and the world. As part of his campaign to make Los Angeles the most important international city on the West Coast, a truly world-class commercial center, Bradley has actively encouraged economic and cultural ties with other nations. At present, there are seventy-one governments represented in the Los Angeles consular corps, making it the second largest in the United States. Trade offices in cities in Japan and China are now in operation, as part of Bradley's effort to stimulate trade between Los Angeles and the Pacific countries.

In the first year of his administration, Bradley's hard-working approach to the city's problems and his style of leadership began to convince even some of the skeptics who had predicted doom for Los Angeles when it elected a "black mayor." Conservative business leaders, known as "The Committee of 25," were surprised and relieved by Bradley's efforts to develop a working partnership with the city's commercial leaders. Stafford Grady comments: "Tom Bradley has made many people color blind." Early in his administration, the Mayor developed important lines of communication with this group, particularly Philip Hawley, involving them in strategic decisions concerning improvement of the city's economic promise. They would prove most resourceful when the Arab oil embargo threatened to bring Los Angeles to its knees, in one of the earliest and most serious challenges Bradley was to face.

"It hit the city particularly hard, because many of the utility departments such as water and power were dependent on oil," remembers Bradley. Particularly problematic was the fact that the Los Angeles Department of Water and Power depended on low sulfur oil, more expensive and harder to get, but required due to Los Angeles' smog problem. The crisis called for a concerted effort of the entire community to rally behind a conservation plan. Bradley immediately appointed a committee made up of nine business, community, and labor leaders, headed by Philip Hawley, CEO of the Broadway department stores. The group— the City Advisory Council—was to recommend specific conservation measures the city could take to meet what experts believed would be a long-term crisis. The Mayor's only directive to the group was that the sacrifice be spread evenly and fairly. Harold Williams, Dean of UCLA's Graduate School of Management, was chosen to coordinate activities of the committee. Asa Call, a giant in the business community and a solid Republican, worked with Bradley on the effort to contact GOP leaders in Washington, enlisting their help in developing a workable solution to the city's problems.

The City Advisory Council recommended rescheduling evening events for daylight hours, curtailing evening lighting in office buildings, and suggesting how each citizen of Los Angeles could contribute to the community effort. Business leaders predicted disaster when the committee recommended a fifty-hour work week, but the prophecies of doom were foiled. Rallied by Mayor Bradley's "Los Angeles Plan," the nation's first mandatory electricity curtailment ordinance, the community came together in a concerted effort to meet OPEC's challenge.

The response reflected well on Bradley's ability to unite the city behind him. Use of electricity at City Hall was cut by 30 percent. But more importantly, Los Angeles was the number one city in the country in conservation, with an 18 percent reduction in power use in eight weeks. It experienced none of the brownouts or the power failures that affected the rest of the country. According to Bradley, "Each and every group from the businessperson to the housewife did their part to meet our goal."

Bradley personally lobbied in Washington for adequate fuel to meet the needs of Los Angeles' millions of commuters, dependent on the freeways for their economic livelihood. At one time, according to Bob Kholos, Los Angeles had only a thirty-day supply of fuel left. But by enlisting the cooperation of leaders from throughout the community, the Mayor was able to break the stonewalling tactic that had characterized the federal government's attitude toward Los Angeles' previous requests.

Even after the embargo, Bradley continued to examine the city's potential for alternative sources of energy. One result is the Solar One project, as Bradley became the first local official in the country to create a special program for solar-generated energy. Another is the Intermountain Power Project, a 1,500-megawatt coal-fueled power plant designed to further reduce the city's dependence on foreign oil utilizing a 490-mile transmission line from Delta, Utah, to Los Angeles. Other important projects of the Bradley administration include recycling and solid waste development conversion.

In addition to developing new energy sources, Bradley's administration has remained committed to the principle of conservation. The centerpiece of this effort is the 1982 Energy L.A. Action Plan, the American Planning Association's 1983 Outstanding Planning Program Honor Award recipient. This plan was developed by the Mayor's Energy Office and adopted by the Council which is expected to decrease Los Angeles' energy use by 21 percent by 1990, saving over $500 million.

Bradley's ability to unify the city on conservation issues has been noted on several occasions. In 1977, during one of the most severe water crises in the city's history, Bradley again rallied Los Angeles to make the needed sacrifice. Bob Kholos describes his technique: "I vividly recall that, during one press conference, he indicated that he and Mrs. Bradley had devised a way of saving water by putting their plants in the shower to accomplish two tasks at once." Reinforcing Bradley's personal plea, City Hall distributed 1.25 million free water-conservation kits to residents. Again, conservation was practiced wisely by Los Angelenos. The city weathered the drought.

Sanford Sigoloff comments, "When Mayor Bradley says there is a problem, people have enough confidence in his leadership and record that they automatically listen and band together to cooperate." The drought was the impetus for City Council's adoption of the Emergency Water Conservation Plan, developed by the Mayor's blue-ribbon conservation committee.

At a Washington, D.C., reception with Senator Edward M. Kennedy and Mrs. Rose Kennedy. (Courtesy of Los Angeles City Hall)

Tom and his favorite musician, Count Basie. (Photo by Mason Dooley: Courtesy of Los Angeles City Hall)

Presenting a Certificate of Merit to the Human Relations Commission, 1975. From left, Fred Ball, Jessie Mae Beavers, Ethel Bradley, the Mayor, Vassie Wright, Maudie Cummings. (Photo by Julius Johnson: Courtesy of Los Angeles City Hall)

11

The Mayor Meets the Challenge

*"He who will not try new remedies
must expect new evils, for time is
the greatest innovator."*

—Francis Bacon

During Bradley's first term, he was faced with two labor disputes that demonstrated the need for diverse modes of transportation—specifically for mass transit—in Los Angeles. The first crippling bus strike occurred in 1974, and the second two years later.

The summer of 1974 was unusually hot in Los Angeles. But to the thousands of citizens dependent on public transportation to get to work, to the store, to the homes of friends and family, the weather was only one contributing factor to the shortness of temper that seemed to characterize the city as a whole. The major problem was the massive bus strike that threatened to paralyze the city.

Even though Bradley lacked any real authority or leverage among the parties involved, he was determined to help resolve the conflict. He had averted a threatened walk-out by drivers in an earlier dispute. But the 1974 dispute was more complicated, in part because two different unions were involved, and it resulted in work stoppage that would eventually drag on for sixty-eight days.

In the absence of the kind of comprehensive rail system that Bradley was lobbying to construct, the Rapid Transit District bus operation, one of the largest in the country, represented the entirety of mass transportation in Los Angeles. When RTD mechanics and bus drivers walked off their jobs to protest inadequate salaries and benefits, hundreds of thousands of citizens were left at bus stops throughout the city, forced to find other means of transit.

The effects of the strike were widely felt. Stranded workers arranged for rides with friends or took their cars to work. The city's freeway system, already clogged during rush hours, became even more bogged down. Accidents increased. Tempers flared, as anger was felt throughout the city's neighborhoods. It was clear to Bradley that, even though he lacked the authority to affect the parties, he had to do all within his power to prod both sides toward settling the strike immediately.

The first step was the establishment of much-needed lines of communication with the RTD management and with the membership of the two unions involved.

In a move that would be criticized by the press and by his political opponents, Bradley left for a brief vacation to Europe that had been planned for months—leaving himself open to the charge that he was away from Los Angeles at a time when he should have been on the job seeking a resolution to the gridlocked talks. Bradley defends his departure: "It was clear to everyone at the time that neither side was even near the point of seriously considering the other's position. I hoped the period while I was away would be a cooling-off period. . . . I had planned the trip for months, and at the time, my personal intervention was not of help. I stand by my decision then to go ahead with the trip." While out of the city, Bradley conversed daily with his staff on the possibility of a break in the strike.

Upon his return, he reexamined the situation, discussing it with the interested parties and with his own staff. Concluding that he had exhausted all of the local options, he then declared a seventy-two-hour moratorium to allow both parties a final opportunity to arrive at a settlement. If they did not, he would appeal to the state legislature to intervene. When the period passed with no movement from either side, Bradley made the trip to the state capitol, an unprecedented step in labor disputes. Recalling his rationale for appealing to the legislature, Bradley said, "Our hopes in this historical move was to show that we meant business, that the two sides had to find the common ground needed for a settlement. Los Angeles could not suffer through a period like this."

Going to the legislature could result in possible losses for both parties. If they could not come up with an agreement, there was the distinct possibility that the legislature could take the lead and impose a settlement that favored one side at the expense of the other. More importantly, it could set an important precedent. The legislature could be actively involved in any future strikes.

The legislature, however, was scheduled to recess for the summer in a matter of days, and senators and assemblymen, wary of getting involved in the controversy, were not inclined to go overtime to resolve the problems of Los Angeles. The session closed before the issue could be taken up by the Senate. As the legislators traveled out of Sacramento, thousands of citizens in Los Angeles remained stranded at their local bus stops.

Bradley refused to give up. He requested the assistance of the state and, if necessary, the federal government in reaching a solution. Meetings among Bradley, Governor Ronald Reagan, and L.A. County Supervisor Kenneth Hahn in Sacramento finally resulted in a plan acceptable to all parties. The strike was over.

The 1976 strike posed similar problems, but by this time both labor and management had grown to respect Bradley, and he had become seasoned in dealing with disputes of this sort.

Ray Remy who had assumed the role of Deputy Mayor in March 1976, remembers, "Each of the union heads had their job on the line, and if the Mayor had taken a high political profile, the unions would have been forced to take a position that wouldn't allow any negotiation." Here was a major test of the chief executive's mediation skills.

Bradley had no jurisdictional powers in the dispute, but he took a very strong public stand on trying to get the two sides to talk to each other. However, they were poles apart, and there was little more he could do.

Remy recalls, "We opted for the Mayor's role to be one of quiet, intense pressure aimed at keeping the communication lines open." Remy had a good relationship with the Chairman of the RTD Board, allowing for Remy to keep tabs on the progress from that angle. Bradley's strong ties with labor leader Bill

Robertson also provided important insight in getting the issue resolved. Bradley personally discussed the contested issues with the Rapid Transit District's board of directors. But, when he asked to speak directly with the workers involved, union officials balked. They opposed any direct appeals to their members. They would be the important buffer between their membership and any outside agent, including City Hall, or even the Mayor of Los Angeles himself.

The union leadership forcefully told Bradley that the proposal brought forward by management was totally unacceptable to their rank and file. When Bradley continued to be turned down in his request to speak to the workers, he switched tactics and asked that the workers be allowed to vote directly on management's proposal. Bradley remembers the logistical complexities of arranging for that vote: "The real problem was to get the membership gathered together. We had an army of volunteers who phoned every union member and told them to come to a meeting downtown, to voice their opinion on the problem."

The volunteer effort was successful. Thousands of drivers and mechanics filled the Convention Center. But union leaders had lobbied hard and successfully among the membership, and a voice vote resoundingly rejected the proposal, without even a gesture toward open discussion. The message was clear. The union was entrenched in its position. Bradley could see that the common ground necessary for a settlement was a long way off. Neither side was willing to make any move toward a settlement. It was going to be a long strike.

However, Bradley persevered in striving for common ground, returning to work behind the scenes in an effort that eventually resulted in the two sides coming together without resorting to intervention from Sacramento.

Los Angeles County Federation of Labor Executive Director Bill Robertson comments: "We don't always agree on issues, and we don't expect to, but the one thing that I can count on is that Tom Bradley will give you a fair hearing. He is extremely valuable to this community and industrial labor management relations, because he has the respect of both management and labor." Crediting Bradley's role in solving the strike, Robertson states, "He has a rare talent of immediately focusing in on the crucial issues, and he's able to placate people and tone down their tempers." Robertson cites Bradley's crucial role in heading off a garbage strike in 1976 and concludes: "We have been blessed in this community to have Tom Bradley as our Mayor, because our track-record on strikes compared to other major cities in the public and private sector has been remarkable."

Bradley's negotiating abilities would be demonstrated time and time again, though not always to the public. According to high-school educator Laurie Dix, he was responsible for averting a teacher's union strike by making one phone call to the four union presidents involved: "He got them together to agree, and the union wanted to have a press conference and give him the credit, but Bradley refused." She further explained that the Mayor told the parties involved that such a public display would damage his negotiating abilities in the future.

Putting into action his campaign pledge to guarantee equal opportunity, Mayor Bradley early committed his administration to affirmative action. It was clear from his very first executive order in July 1973, which spelled out city employment policy, that Bradley intended to ensure the city's compliance with the principles of fairness and equality. It was now city policy that "recruitment, selection, promotion, compensation benefits, training, and termination of employment of all the city of Los Angeles shall be conducted without regard to race, religion, national origin, sex, age, handicap, or sexual preference."

But the strength of any policy is measured by its enforcement, and Bradley encountered resistance from many quarters. Feedback from business leaders, for example, said that the affirmative action policy of the city was far too stringent. They complained that the standards Bradley had set for Los Angeles were higher than those set by the federal government. Far from retreating, Bradley expressed the hope that Los Angeles could then serve as an example to other cities and even Washington on equality and fairness. He remained determined to enforce the ordinance and to refuse to allow the city to do business with companies who failed to comply with the new standards for equal employment. His adamant stand on the issue put him in conflict with some of the nation's largest corporations, including the three major automobile companies, all with a long business relationship with city government. The new ordinance forbade the city to enter into business contracts with any corporation that failed to hire women and minorities in numbers comparable to their availability in the job market.

Bradley's will was tested early by the City Council. Responding to pleas from Chief of Police Ed Davis, the Council passed an emergency resolution to override the ordinance and allow the LAPD to buy needed vehicles. Bradley balked and overrode the Council's resolution. Though criticized by the Police Chief and others, the Mayor demonstrated that his administration meant business. The result was a change in hiring practices by General Motors, Chrysler, and Ford in their Los Angeles operations.

"It's something that requires constant effort," Bradley states, in commenting on his efforts to end discrimination in Los Angeles. "We're still not where we should be, but the procedures are in place to constantly monitor how we are progressing in city government, as well as within the community. At least we know we are moving in the right direction." There has been a fourteen percent increase in city employment of minorities under Tom Bradley.

Bradley's concern for minority representation in government, an issue he had been personally active in promoting since his early attempts in the 1950s on behalf of minority judges and minority city and state election candidates, remained strong. When Fourteenth District Councilman Art Snyder made an ill-fated race for State Senate in 1974, Snyder, a Republican who had criticized the Mayor on numerous occasions, suddenly found himself the recipient of unexpected support from top Bradley aide Maury Weiner and City Commissioner Bill North. Both were attempting to persuade registered Democrats to vote for the Councilman, in the hope of opening his Council seat to one of the Hispanics who made up over sixty percent of his district's population. Art Gastelum, who also worked in the campaign for Snyder, summed up the feelings regarding the candidate: "Art Snyder has always served that community well. He is an effective politician and representative of the area." Given his Senate aspirations, "we thought we could help Art and at the same time provide the opportunity to have a Hispanic voice on the Council."

It had been over twelve years since Ed Roybal had resigned his Council seat to become a U.S. Congressman. Not since then had the City Council enjoyed the personal perspective on Hispanic issues that only a member of that ethnic community could offer. For years, as both Council member and Mayor, Bradley had made no secret of his desire to remedy this void. "I maintained from my first day on the Council that there needed to be a voice for Mexican-American people, someone with the heritage and ethnic background to be a vital part of policy formation on the city level." Just as earlier attempts on Bradley's part had failed—on two separate occasions he had sought to add two seats to the Council in order to enhance the probability of Hispanic representation—so would the campaign for Snyder. Snyder lost the Senate seat, and continued to represent the Fourteenth District on the City Council.

At the conclusion of Bradley's first year as Mayor, members of the Council were asked by the media to report on their impressions of Bradley as chief executive. Only one of the twelve Councilmen, Louis Nowell, ex-Mayor Yorty's captain of the "truth squad," was critical. Nowell charged Bradley was out to "personally gain political control of the city." But even this old arch-enemy had some praise for the Mayor, saying, "He's brought more vigor and probably more concern over all the facets of our social and economic life than any mayor I've been acquainted with."

Council President John Gibson, Jr., identified Bradley as "the most aggressive Mayor I've worked with in tackling concerns of the citizens." Gibson and David Cunningham predicted that if the same hard-working habits continued, he could very well be one of, if not the best, Mayor in the city's history. Pat Russell singled out Bradley's accessibility: "County supervisors tell me they have talked more to Bradley in one year than they did with Yorty in twelve years." She added, "We have long needed an executive who acts like an executive."

The cooperative spirit of the Mayor was identified as one of his strongest assets by John Ferraro, who did offer criticism of Bradley's staff. Robert Wilkinson, on the other hand, credited the Mayor with putting together a well-organized team. Councilman Ed Edelman identified the city's success in improving relations with the state and federal government as important contributions. Bradley's diplomatic and mediational skills were singled out for praise by Ernani Bernardi and Joel Wachs, while the administration's openness to new ideas and input was highlighted by Marvin Braude, Robert J. Stevenson, and Gilbert Lindsay. Only Art Snyder declined to comment.

Citywide, Bradley was a hit. He was KNX's "Man of the Year, 1973," as the CBS radio station cited his "deep concern for the citizens of Los Angeles and his effective and innovative leadership in making the city a better place to live."

The Bradley administration's dedication to advancing the cause of women—as evidenced by the establishment of a Commission on the Status of Women, by the Volunteer Corps, and the city's Child Care Advisory Committee—was cited as a bold step. In 1974, he was awarded "Newsmaker of the Year" by the National Association of Media Women.

In 1974, after only one year in office, a poll showed Bradley to be the most popular public official in California. During the mid-year elections, Democratic National Committee Chairman Robert Strauss stated, "Any discussion of American politics must include Tom Bradley." He further added, "Bradley, by most people's estimate is one of the more interesting, more credible, more exciting men in American politics today."

One product of so much national attention was increased speculation regarding a Vice-Presidential spot for Bradley in 1976. The Mayor indicated that he had no intention of seeking the nomination, but there were nuances within his response that suggested he did not necessarily see his career culminating at City Hall. "I am simply indicating that at this point, less than one year after taking office, I think that it is premature for me to talk about, or even begin thinking about, that type of progression."

Bradley moved quickly to engineer important programs to serve the social, financial, and physical needs of those who had earlier contributed to the city's promise and who now deserved to be repaid for their efforts—Los Angeles' senior citizens. Determined to move beyond lip-service to the older, fixed-income earner, Bradley established a Mayor's Office of Aging, with a $2,000,000 budget (later formulated as the City Department of Aging). Special Assistant Emma McFarlin worked to give this constituency much-needed input into the decision-making process. Furthermore, the Mayor impaneled a Council on Aging, comprised of 150 seniors from throughout the city.

One of the most pressing problems facing seniors in a period of high inflation was decreased purchasing power of their fixed income dollars. Rent payment often consumed almost all of the monthly income check. Bradley moved quickly to procure federal and state dollars to help alleviate the senior housing shortage. His administration would add 5,000 units of subsidized housing, specifically designed for the elderly. The utility tax rebate for senior and other citizens making less than $7,500 per year also eased the challenge of stretching fixed funds to meet bills.

Outreach programs from his office included "Senior Ride," providing transportation services for medical, food, and other necessities. Advisors assisted seniors without family support in the important day-to-day decision-making functions. "Senior Line," offered in Spanish, Chinese, Japanese, Korean, Filipino, and Samoan, in addition to English, linked City Hall to the needs of this growing population. During his first term in office, Bradley established eleven multipurpose senior centers in locations throughout the metropolitan area.

Bradley had always harbored a deep concern for the safety of seniors. As a child, he remembered how his mother had depended on public transportation each day. She had walked home almost every night, and often told her young son about close calls she experienced on the street. As a police officer, after finishing his beat, Bradley had frequently accompanied seniors home from the grocery store or church to ensure their safety. Crime had been a top concern of the elderly in the Tenth District. As a Councilman he had heard and sympathized with their plight. As Mayor, he would do all he could to help provide security for this special group.

Tom Bradley's commitment to eradicating crime in Los Angeles was of vital importance to seniors. Over the first four years of his administration, he would add five hundred police officers to the streets in Los Angeles. He saw the issue very simply: "Having more police officers on the streets, thereby reducing the time it takes to respond to crime calls, is the best deterrent." This five-hundred-member addition is impressive when one considers that, during this same era, major cities in the east were being forced to sell police cars in order to remain solvent.

Bradley's police experience pushed his administration toward adopting other preventive measures to effectively curtail crime. His neighborhood watch program represented an important step, but seniors required even more specific attention, with programs designed for their particular needs. The Mayor remained determined to obtain the money needed to develop programs to disseminate information to this vulnerable group. Working with the county, Bradley sponsored yearly "Senior Safe" workshops to educate seniors how to avoid becoming victims of crime.

Recognizing the alienation of the city's youth and wanting to win them back to "the system," Bradley established the City Youth Advisory Council in early 1974. The first citizen advisory group in the nation to be composed entirely of young people, its members, who have been selected by the Mayor and the City Council, report to them on youth issues. This program has served as a model for similar efforts in cities such as Washington, D.C., and Philadelphia.

Bradley's style of leadership took some adjusting to. One aide compared Bradley to the Sphinx. Not an easy man to read, he is that rarity among politicians—a listener. Planning Commission President Dan Garcia comments, "It's interesting. The Mayor listens more than most people. He is able to grasp more of the detail and the context of the problem than most people." Alluding to what some describe as "the eerie silence" following presentation of a new idea to the Mayor, Garcia explains that the conversational hiatus is Bradley's way of assimilating information.

To attorney George David Kieffer, the deadly silence, coupled with the Mayor's stature, serves an important function: "it pulls people out more and more in a negotiating situation—people end up giving away the entire store." Another Bradley aide refers to the "magnificent, almost stony impassive quality" that Bradley displays in meetings, and Garcia describes from personal experience how unnerving it can be to those not used to his style. "For some reason, in the beginning, I felt unsure about myself with the Mayor in meetings, and one of the reasons is that he doesn't talk much. I remember that I went into one meeting with a laundry list of things to go over, there were four or five different items, and I was asking for help on commission staff, resources, and other items." Garcia presented the information to the Mayor, as Bradley sat silently in the wing-back chair across from the couch in the formal office.

Garcia continues: "When I finished, he didn't say anything; there was no direction, just silence." Thinking this was Bradley's way of dismissing him, Garcia started to get up and leave, when Bradley looked up at him and started laughing. The Mayor asked, "Dan, don't you want to know my response to your list?" Garcia reflects, "That is how he is at times; you don't know if he is paying attention, when all along he is right with you and afterwards gives you a response that not only answers your questions, but raises others." Kieffer recalls a meeting on a plane trip to San Francisco with Bradley and Phil Depoian, "I was naturally inclined to try to supply more and more details on several issues to fill the silence. . . . I realized this is a Bradley trait to pull information out of people, and this allows him to maintain an effective communication network." One is reminded of a later campaign theme designed by David Garth: "He doesn't make a lot of noise, he just gets a lot done."

One reason Bradley gets a lot done is that he never stops working. As Wanda Moore notes, "it's like he is still running the quarter-mile at UCLA—working seven days a week, fifteen to sixteen hour days—I get tired just looking at his schedule!" One member of his LAPD security force reported, "I have trouble keeping up with him. When I get home at the end of those fifteen-hour days, I'm beat. Thank God we get one day off every three days! . . . I don't know how he keeps going."

Bobby Adams, one of the officers of the LAPD in charge of the Mayor's security detail, describes his boss as "someone who just doesn't take a vacation." Adams, who has been with Bradley since the early 1970s, notes, "Whether he takes his work with him or not, he is nonetheless always working, because his mind is always going, wondering what is going on in this city. When he is out of the city or state, he's still got his folder with him. This city is his life."

On a typical day, Bradley gets up at 6:00 A.M., rides his stationary bicycle for thirty minutes while reading the *Los Angeles Times,* breakfasts with Ethel, then goes to work, often stopping off to visit brother Ellis on the way. Adams usually picks up the Mayor at the Getty House at 7:30 and takes him either to City Hall or to some city event. At day's end, "We sometimes have two or three dinners, and the key," Adams adds, alluding to Bradley's physique, "is to eat just a little bit at each one." The Mayor's favorites? "He likes steaks, fried chicken, peach cobbler, greens, rice, and gravy; he's not much on sweets, but does drink a lot of orange juice and diet soda."

What type of entertainment does Bradley prefer? Adams grins and adds, "He loves jazz—Satchmo, Count Basie, Ella Fitzgerald, likes opera, and his favorite show is *The King and I;* his favorite television show is Bill Cosby. . . . Of course, there are the Dodgers, which is Mrs. Bradley's first love, and he likes to listen to football and maybe even attend a couple of games each year." What is the one word to describe her husband? Ethel Bradley quickly responds—"Perfectionist." She adds, "The routine he follows is unbelievable. He's a workaholic and always has been. And the organization of this man is incredible. . . . Why, if I even try to put his things in another bureau drawer . . ., he'll put them right back. . . . that's Tom Bradley."

Bradley usually goes home at around 10:00 or 11:00 at night. There is not much small talk between the Mayor and Adams or the other security officers on the way home. "Time is of the essence to him," Adams explains. "He values his time, he does his work from point A to point B. He never stops." The security officer adds, "The man is driven—he has a dream and he is determined to realize it." How does this affect home life? Ethel Bradley states, "I knew a long time ago, when I married him, what he was all about. He's driven to do all he can for the city and country . . . , and I've known this from the start, and try to do all I can to help him succeed."

While at the office, "his day is full," explains Wanda Moore, his executive assistant. "He has very little time by himself, because his chair is like honey, and it draws the flies and activity around it." Lunch is usually soup and salad, eaten while Bradley pores over his paperwork. Moore continues, "He is always doing three or more things at a time. The only way he keeps up is by working a demanding schedule—and being a workaholic."

Yet even with his busy schedule, Bradley often interrupts his day to take in a particular event that seems inviting. During his first year in office, Jerry Comfort, another security agent, recalls making an unscheduled stop when the Mayor learned there was a graduation in progress at a city grammar school. Bradley walked into the ceremony and received a standing ovation from the children and their parents. Then he delivered a spontaneous speech expressing his deeply felt thoughts on youth. "You can be anything you want to be," Bradley told the smiling youngsters. "The only thing that will stop you from fulfilling your dreams is you." He added, "So go out there and dream big dreams. Work hard, study hard, and listen to your parents and teachers. Take it from me, you can be anything your heart wants you to be!"

When Bradley returned to the car, he told Comfort he had forgotten something. "I should have thanked them," Bradley said. "They all chipped in during the campaign last year, and one of the students sent me $4.21."

Comfort and Adams add that the trips to and from City Hall always find their boss "eyeing potholes in the street and making notes to give to the department when he gets into the office." Comfort concludes, "If you figure up the time he spends working, I don't think he even makes the minimum wage!"

In his commuting, Bradley also finds time for personal visits. "He keeps close tabs on all his old friends and visits them and others who have helped him out a lot, and nobody knows that." Phil Depoian remembers one December day when no one in City Hall knew where the Mayor was. Security was frantic. How could they just lose the six-foot-four Mayor? "As it turned out," Depoian adds, "he had left early and gone Christmas shopping and delivered the gifts to some children in a nearby hospital." He hadn't told anyone, and Depoian and the others learned about it only when a thank-you note arrived.

Those who know Tom Bradley are quick to single out his special warmth, but the press often reflects the mood of many who complain that the Mayor comes across as "too formal" or as "wooden." But Phil Depoian, who is commonly referred to ·as Bradley's "adopted son," because of their close relationship, thinks he understands why Bradley gives such a false impression: "When I first worked for him in the '69 campaign, I thought that too." Even some Bradley supporters called him cold, aloof, stand-offish. But after knowing Bradley for awhile, Depoian found that the Mayor opened up and could be humorous and even witty. "I couldn't understand why he was like two people, until it dawned on me one day," Depoian explained, "that he is a tremendously shy man, that people's expectations of a politician do not fit Tom Bradley." But many people around Bradley have noticed a marked change in recent years, more of a tendency to open up. Press secretary Ali Webb notes, "now he walks down the street and waves, shakes hands, and is naturally outgoing."

The setback when county voters' rejected the tax proposal to finance mass transit did not deter Bradley's efforts to improve upon the existing Los Angeles system. Los Angeles' voters had endorsed the 1974 proposal, and Bradley was determined to push forward. He lobbied in Washington, and received federal support for an expanded bus service and for the downtown "people-mover" project.

The Mayor also obtained the federal dollars needed for development of the starter section of the much needed rail-line he had proposed for Los Angeles. The city moved on its own, too. There were minibuses, Dial-A-Ride programs, and an increased emphasis on car and van pooling.

As a candidate, Bradley had pledged to represent the city's interest at the state and national capitols. His first term evidenced impressive results from such personal lobbying. In addition to improvements in transportation, Bradley reaped five times the federal funds brought in during the Yorty administration. Four-hundred-million dollars from Washington allowed Los Angeles to provide more services and assistance to its citizens.

The Mayor's Office of Small Business Assistance, set up in 1975, helped fledgling businesses make it through their difficult first years, spurring small-time commerce in deprived neighborhoods and helping to realize Bradley's pledge of equal opportunity and access. The agency helped small businesses bid and compete against larger companies in the effort to obtain contracts from the city. And the MOSBA opened up city contracts to minority and small business firms—to the tune of $7.5 million during Bradley's first term. Through the Minority and Women's Enterprise Program and the Small Local Business Program, the participation of small, minority, and women-headed firms has been enhanced. In 1982, for example, such contracts totalled over $22 million.

Working with the Council, Bradley sought to improve the availability and quality of decent housing throughout the city. The Community Redevelopment Agency sold more than $1.3 billion in tax-exempt housing revenue bonds and tax allocation bonds to aid development of 12,500 units of housing for low-, moderate-, and middle-income families. New funds from Washington provided local contractors and developers the financing needed to get started. Assistance from City Hall helped beginners make their way through the myriad of regulations.

The net results of Bradley's effort procuring public and private funds for housing construction through the Housing Unit of the City Development Department also have stimulated over $1 billion in investment representing construction or rehabilitation of over 22,700 units. Bradley's administration was pledged to simplify red tape by the establishment of a one-stop construction permit center, consolidating into one wing of City Hall the offices of Building Safety, Planning, Engineering, and other related operations necessary to obtaining a building permit.

In addition to city sponsorship at 1,200 new housing units constructed to meet the needs of seniors, other housing was designed for particular neighborhoods. For example, families displaced by the expansion of the Los Angeles International Airport were moved to South-Central Los Angeles, where financing for new housing was made available to them at below market interest rates. It marked the first new housing construction effort in the Watts area in twelve years.

The Mayor encouraged various urban renewal projects that had experienced rough times in the Pico-Union area. He became a familiar face in Washington and Sacramento, making sure that Los Angeles was getting all the assistance it was entitled to, on the state and national level.

Fred Schnell credits the respect of the private sector for the Mayor as the primary reason he was able to rally support on behalf of such projects as the Produce Mart. When Los Angeles faced the possibility of losing the produce market, which had been a vital part of the city for over seventy-five years and a source of over 8,500 jobs for a predominantly minority labor group, Bradley mobilized support for a rebuilding effort that resulted in the construction of what is now the largest produce market in the world—and an additional 1,100 jobs. "It was Bradley's vision, his ability to involve all the interested parties, that spelled the difference and saved the produce market," according to Schnell. Bradley's efforts have also helped revitalize Los Angeles' jewelry and flower markets. The International Jewelry Center, dedicated in 1979, was the first major trade center in the United States designed specifically for the jewelry industry. It consolidated scattered industry into a single downtown complex. It is because of his responsiveness to what the business community can bring to the city that men like Armand Hammer, Sanford Sigoloff, Charles Miller, Walter Gerken, Sheldon Andelson, Philip Hawley, Marvin Davis, Roy Anderson, Franklin Murphy, Thornton Bradshaw, David E. Anderson, Warren Christopher, Lew Wasserman, and other top leaders of the business community all consider Tom Bradley to be a visionary leader, nonpartisan in his commitment to realizing Los Angeles' promise, and selfless in his pursuit of the city's goals.

As Barry Erdos, Senior Vice-President and Chief Financial Officer of J. W. Robinson's stores, summed it up, "One of the major differences between Tom Bradley and other politicians is that he is not always looking for a spotlight for himself." The success of the Mayor's efforts often goes unnoticed by those unaware of his quiet but effective style—to the unending frustration of his press department.

Commenting on what some label "the inherently modest quality of the man," Art Gastelum explains, "It's so frustrating—the press office and so many of the staffers feel that our hands are tied, because we know what he does on a day-to-day basis that affects so many aspects of people's lives, but he has never let us package him with the press releases or pictures that he deserves."

Bee Canterbury Lavery calls this low-key approach "Tom Bradley's biggest fault." It is commendable, but at the same time problematic to those who want to get the message out. Gastelum recalls one of the countless times that Bradley's quiet leadership and involvement helped solve a community problem. After the mural projects at Estrada Court ran out of funding in 1974, Bradley learned of the problem when a young Hispanic student told him about it during one of his Area Day visits. "The Mayor went down to the neighborhood and talked to the kids, who told him that the major problem was the lack of paint and supplies." Gastelum remembers the first thing Bradley did upon returning to City Hall was to call Sinclair Paint. "He then returned to the neighborhood, without even telling anyone, and told the kids they would have all of the paints and the scaffolding needed to finish the project."

While short on immediate headlines, such involvement has had an impact. Carlos Chavez, teacher and director of a Department of Education Upward Bound Program in Los Angeles, devoted to enriching the potential of minority students, states, "Mayor Bradley has made a huge difference in the Chicano community. He has been a positive role model, and now the twenty-five-year-olds who remember Bradley's involvement in our neighborhoods are committed to helping join the Mayor in improving the community." State Senator Art Torres adds, "Tom Bradley has inspired many Hispanics to become involved in government."

Mayor Bradley's leadership qualities did not go unnoticed nationally. In his first term, he was designated "Man of the Year" by the Harvard Club of Southern California. During his remarks to the 160 guests at the dinner, the Mayor singled out the significance and impact of the award from Harvard alums on his relationship with his wife. Now, Bradley noted, Ethel would realize that he was important. He quipped, "You know, that behind any successful man there's a woman saying 'You ain't nothing!'" In 1974, Bradley was elected president of the National League of Cities, representing 14,883 cities, and ninety percent of the nation's urban population. The Ford administration frequently sought his advice and counsel on urban issues. Bradley testified in both Washington and the state capitol on matters affecting Los Angeles and on the need for a national urban policy. This message made an indelible impression on a Southern populist Democrat who would take over as the nation's chief executive in 1977, and would subsequently become a strong advocate of the need for a consistent national policy to deal with the nation's urban centers.

Bradley forged important international ties too. Because of California's large Hispanic population, he met with Mexican President Lopez Portillo in Tijuana in order to build better relations with California's southern neighbor. At a follow-up meeting at the Presidential Palace in Mexico City, Portillo told Bradley that he "was very pleased and very proud to see how our people are doing under your leadership outside their homeland." As head of the city with the second largest Hispanic population outside of Mexico City, Bradley would continue his close alliance with top Mexican leaders. The Mayor would even be asked to visit Tijuana during the successful campaign of Miguel de La Madrid to succeed Portillo as president.

Bradley was selected as a Co-chairman of the 1976 Democratic National Convention in New York City. In the primaries, he had supported the candidacy of Governor Jerry Brown, but at the convention itself, he remained neutral, presiding over several important meetings.

Once Carter was selected as the party's candidate, Bradley campaigned hard for the national ticket. The Mayor believed Carter was one of the few candidates who could restore credibility to a presidency badly weakened by the Watergate trauma. He was impressed by the Georgian's strong sense of values and humanistic approach to the problems facing the country. He was also looking forward to having a fellow Democrat at the controls of the national government. It stood to reason that a Democratic president would enhance and expand the networks Bradley had worked hard to create since his election as Mayor.

November brought good news for the Democrats. In an extremely close election, James Earl Carter was elected President of the United States. Carter's election thrust Bradley into the national headlines. The President-elect talked with the Los Angeles Mayor about the possibility of a HUD cabinet post.

Bradley was both honored and tempted by such an opportunity, because it would mean he would be able to shape policy at the national level. However, after several days, Bradley phoned the President-elect to say that he wanted to remove his name from further consideration.

In making his decision, Bradley had concluded that there was still too much for him to do in Los Angeles. He had never left a job incomplete, and this would be no exception. The state's largest newspaper, the *Los Angeles Times,* wrote in an editorial that Bradley "could have made a major contribution in Washington," but praised his decision to remain in Los Angeles. According to Sanford Sigoloff, "It is becoming clear to all of us in the business community that when Tom Bradley gave his word, it was golden."

A proud father and daughter Lorraine, graduation day at Pepperdine University, 1982. (Photo by Mason Dooley: Courtesy of Los Angeles City Hall)

In 1983, Tom and Ethel have an audience with Pope John Paul II. (Courtesy of Los Angeles City Hall)

Lorraine (left) and Phyllis often appear in support of their father. (Courtesy of Rick Browne)

12

Public Success and Private Sorrow

*"A child is a quicksilver fountain
spilling over with tomorrows and
tomorrows,
and that is why
she is richer than you or I."*

—Tom Bradley

Tom Bradley's poem, written to nine-year-old Nilda Oxholm of Detroit, who had sent him her third-grade American history project, captured the deep-seated faith and love he held for children. It was only an extension of his own experience. Throughout his days growing up, with his family constantly moving from one apartment to another, Crenner had instilled in all of her children the notion that there was only one true handicap for anyone in life—a negative attitude. The world awaited those who dared to reach inside and discover their true potential.

Tom hoped to pass on this spirit, not only to his two daughters, but to children everywhere. In his extensive reading, he had come across a particular quote that summed up his viewpoint. It was part of a speech by Dr. Benjamin Mays of Morehouse College. When he found himself in need of inspiration, he would turn to it.

It must be borne in mind that the tragedy in life does not lie in not reaching your goal. The tragedy lies in having no goal to reach.

It is not a calamity to die with dreams unfulfilled. But it is a calamity not to dream.

It is not a disaster to be unable to capture your ideals. But it is a disaster to have no ideal to capture.

It is not a disgrace not to reach the stars. But it is a disgrace to have no stars to reach for.

Not failure but low aim is the sin.

These words provided a special comfort for Bradley during the years of his first mayoral term. They gave him the courage to try to achieve many things that were difficult and some that seemed impossible, and his efforts were met with much success. But those words were also meaningful for his personal life as well, for any pride he might feel for his success was mellowed by personal sorrows.

Tom was pleased that his mother, Crenner Hawkins Bradley, had lived to see his election as Mayor of Los Angeles. Of their family—parents and children—only she and Tom's brother Ellis had survived the hard times to share in the joy.

It had been a hard life, one of sacrifice for both of Tom's parents. Although they had separated, Lee and Crenner had each kept the love and respect of their children. Phyllis and Lorraine had been able to know both their Grandma and Grandpa Bradley, and that had been important. Even though Crenner had played a more dominant role in their lives than Lee had, Tom was happy that his daughters had memories of Christmas, birthdays, and summer picnics with Grandpa Lee, who would come to the house on 57th Street with presents and a big hug and hearty laugh.

Lee Bradley had died in 1950 of a heart attack. Tom remembered how his father had always urged him to "keep pushing as hard as you can, Tom, 'cause that's what's gonna make it for you, son." In some ways, Lee and Crenner had been very much alike; there was the same emphasis on never giving in, never accepting defeat as anything but temporary.

For months after his father's death, Tom and Ethel had talked about how the usual sparkle in Crenner's eyes seemed to be gone. Instead there was more of a vacant stare. However, when Tom had asked his mother about it, she had said it was nothing. Yet Tom seemed to understand that reply; it was the sort of answer he would have given under the same circumstances. In that respect—the endurance of personal pain and sorrow—he and his mother were much alike. To Tom, her reply seemed to suggest that, had jobs been more plentiful when the family had moved to Los Angeles, had there not been so much strain in just getting by in those early days, his parents' lives might have been different. Bradley had then realized that, even though the two had separated long ago, the common bond between them had been much deeper than their children had ever realized.

Two of the Bradley children had not lived to share in more than Tom's early accomplishments in school and in sports. Willa Mae, who according to friends was more like Tom than any other sibling, worked as a beautician before falling ill to tuberculosis and dying in her early twenties. Lawrence, the oldest child, who had spent most of his early years working the fields as his parents had, had saved money from working as a truck driver to spend his last days rearing his family on a farm near San Bernardino. He had died of cancer in 1939. The youngest son, Howard, had died of lung disease in 1973, before Tom became Mayor.

While the entire family had always been supportive of Tom, it had been Ellis who had given the incentive in his drive for success. To Ellis, his older brother's accomplishments translated into the realities of what he (like so many others) could only dream of attaining. He had been a special person in Tom's life since childhood, and he had also become a favorite of Ethel's after their marriage. Suffering from cerebral palsy since infancy, Ellis had always looked up to his older brother as someone who had watched out for him and protected him. Ellis had been able to work at odd jobs when he was young, and he lived with Crenner, helping his mother, in her later years.

With the ebbing of his physical strength as the years wore on came a strengthening of the special bond with his older brother. Tom realized that Ellis always had felt a special pride in his achievements. Ellis had told him one day after his first political win at Polytechnic High School, "Brother, when you win, I win."

Theirs was a very special relationship, a friendship between two brothers that was so private that few, if any, of Bradley's closest advisors even knew the Mayor had a living brother. But to

Ethel and his own family, Ellis was an important contribution to Bradley's character and spirit. When staffers at City Hall were at a loss to locate the Mayor, he was usually paying a visit to Ellis.

But it was Crenner, more than anyone else in his life, who had instilled in him the faith and spirit by which he lived. So it was a great sorrow to him in 1973, not long after taking office as Mayor of Los Angeles, to receive the word that she had died of a heart attack at the age of 82. He received the news at City Hall; her doctor called and told him just as he was getting ready to pick up Ethel and drive to visit his mother at the hospital.

In the months preceding her death, Crenner had been forced to slow down her frenetic pace to some extent. There had been heart problems for years. Her doctor had advised Tom to see to it that she curbed her activities. But, for someone who had been accustomed to full-speed throughout her life, caring and cleaning for others, this was a hard prescription to follow. Besides, as she often told Tom and Ethel, it just wasn't natural to stop working. God didn't intend for her to just sit around.

As the months had passed, however, Crenner had been forced to accept the fact that she could now work only half days. Then finally, the realization came to her that her days as a maid were over. It had been a long and hard life, but it was the only life she had ever known, and it was difficult to stop.

It was also difficult for her to accept the money Tom had started leaving to pay for her rent. Since his childhood, he had been the one who had managed her money and made the major decisions. He now knew that the small amount Crenner had managed to save could pay for only some of her expenses now that she was no longer working. The first time he had explained the financial situation to her and left the money, she had said nothing, but when Tom returned the next day, she had put the money in an envelope addressed to him.

Crenner had been independent throughout her long life, and it was hard for her to suddenly change her ways. She would never accept charity or assistance from anyone—not even her own son. Tom tried continually to persuade her that it was only fair that he help her out, given all the sacrifices she had made for him. She initially resisted, angered by his insistence, but finally she agreed.

Being cooped up at home did not mean that Crenner was

"retired," however. Despite pleas from Tom and Ethel (whom she looked upon as a daughter), Crenner began her days early in the kitchen or in the sewing room and ended them with reading the Bible or exchanging stories with her neighbors. She spent her days making her famous sweet potato pie, mending and fixing, cleaning and doing chores around her apartment.

But, for Crenner, who had always had someone to care for, it wasn't enough just to look after herself. Tom's former police partner Wilbur Harris lived in the same apartment complex as Crenner, and he confessed that, for the first time in his life, he was getting fat. The reason? All of Crenner's homemade food—especially her "artisan work with meat of every kind" and her pies. Crenner had insisted that her cooking for Wilbur and having him join her for dinner was the least she could do for him, after he had worked alongside her son on the police force so many years.

On his desk in his small private office at City Hall, Bradley had one of his favorite photographs—a picture of his mother with him and Ethel that had been taken on the night of his election as Mayor. When he received the word of Crenner's death, he could not help but look at that photograph. The expression on Crenner's face, as she looked at her son, reflected the determination, perseverance, and pride she had always tried to instill in her children. She had been the anchor point, the role model, for the entire family. In her face was the struggle and hardship she had endured without complaint for the sake of her children; it was etched into the deep lines across her brow and in her cheeks. But in her dark eyes there was a deep love and compassion.

Crenner had often told Tom that it wasn't necessary to have the best in life, but only to make the best out of what you had. She had certainly exemplified that attitude. Bradley's security officer, Bobby Adams, told him that morning, on learning of Crenner's death, "You know, Mr. Mayor, for all of us who loved her, all we have to do when we miss her is to look at you." The profiles of mother and son were strikingly similar.

Crenner was gone, but her life had been an especially productive and meaningful one, and her spirit lived on. She had touched countless lives, some directly, and others through her son, in whom her spirit and faith and determination still lived.

And there was solace for Tom in the fact that his mother had lived this long. Even in his sorrow, he could not help but smile to recall the proudest day in his mother's life. To all who knew her, Crenner Bradley was a quiet and reserved woman, whose satisfaction with her son's success was more likely to be expressed by a smile or a special wink of the eye than it was to find verbal expression. However, when Bradley had been elected Los Angeles' new Mayor, Crenner had been overwhelmed. Wilbur Harris had called Tom to relate how, the day after the election, Crenner had walked up and down every street of their neighborhood, stopping everyone she passed to say, "I want to tell you that the new Mayor is my son!" The excitement of the moment had been too much for her to hold inside.

Crenner Bradley's death was only one of several personal hardships Tom Bradley would experience during this first time in office. In February 1976, Bradley reluctantly accepted the resignation of his longtime political strategist, Maury Weiner, in what many people familiar with the situation believe was a trumped up, politically motivated charge, the Deputy Mayor had been found guilty of a misdemeanor—lewd conduct in a Hollywood movie theater—even though he had maintained that he was innocent.

Weiner's departure was a stunning blow to the top leadership of the Bradley administration, and it was also, on a personal level, the loss of a dear and valuable aide and friend to Tom.

Bradley had known Weiner for over fourteen years. He considered him to be one of the most honest and ethical men he had ever met. He could not believe the charge made against Weiner, and neither could any of the staff who knew the Deputy Mayor well. Weiner and his supporters expressed confidence that the judicial system would vindicate him. However, important evidence critical to Weiner's defense was not allowed to be presented to the jury. Every effort Weiner made to get a fair and impartial airing of the case was met with roadblocks. There was suspicion by Weiner (and others) that the incident was politically engineered to embarrass Bradley.

To those who knew Weiner, his actions after the verdict were predictable. Rather than hamper the Mayor with clouds of suspicion, he resigned within twenty-four hours. After leaving city government, Weiner continued to maintain his innocence, and continues to believe that the entire episode was politically motivated. Many friends say that he thinks someone in the vice unit of the LAPD will come forward and tell the truth, because he doesn't believe that someone can live with a lie forever.

Bradley was now without the services of a trusted aide who had served him since his first run for the City Council. Visibly distraught, Bradley told staffers that Weiner's departure marked "one of the saddest days in my life." Reflecting on the incident years later, Bradley stated, "It was like the loss of a brother in my own family."

An incident such as this, in which someone's reputation is forever tarnished by damning charges is a by-product of politics that often appalls Bradley. Yet, as an administrator, he recognized that the only thing that could be done was to press on. After studying a list of possible replacements, in April 1976, Bradley made a call to the Executive Director of the Southern California Association of Governments, Ray Remy, asking the Pasadena Republican to come on board as Deputy Mayor.

Being Mayor of the country's second largest city, in command of a staff of hundreds, could not provide the answer—or the understanding—for a problem shared by millions of American parents from coast to coast. It was a tragedy that had reached into the family of Presidents and world leaders, as well as those living on the streets—how to help a daughter with a drug problem.

In 1974, less than one year into his first term, Tom and Ethel's twenty-nine-year-old daughter, Phyllis, was involved in the first of a series of incidents with the police. She was arrested for resisting arrest for a minor traffic violation. It marked the beginning of a ten-year period in which the Mayor's daughter would be involved in brushes with the law.

In 1976, she was again arrested, this time for possession of marijuana and amphetamines. In February 1978, Phyllis was arrested for shoplifting $29.29 worth of cosmetics from a drugstore. Seven months later she was arrested for a traffic violation and for possession of marijuana. In 1980, because of her earlier trouble, she was tried on felony charges for shoplifting three blouses (worth $78) from a department store. Five months later, she was given a 150-day jail term for probation violations, after tests revealed the drug PCP in her urine. In 1983, on the day the Mayor and Mrs. Bradley attended a general audience with Pope Paul II in Rome, Phyllis was involved in an automobile accident and again charged with a felony, after tests revealed she had been under the influence of drugs. Just eight days later, there would be another arrest for driving under the influence of drugs.

Phyllis' problem was one that pained her parents and her sister Lorraine. Close friends remember that, following the incidents, the usually gregarious Ethel was reclusive. She blamed herself and her husband for Phyllis' problems. Longtime friend Warren Hollier remembers that it had been a family concern for a number of years that the younger daughter had been involved with a group of people who were rather wild. To Lorraine, Phyllis' problems were rooted in a trait she had noted in her sister at an early age—the need for constant attention. But both daughters had received support and love from their parents, and Lorraine had difficulty understanding why Phyllis always seemed to need more.

As early as 1969, when Phyllis was twenty-four, both parents had worried about their daughter's choice of friends and the direction she seemed to be taking. There was also suspicion (as well as evidence, according to Hollier and other supporters) that Mayor Yorty and the Police Department planned to take advantage of Phyllis' problems in order to embarrass Bradley in his race for Mayor. However, Bradley's concern was only for the well-being of his daughter, and he did not want to see her hurt by those who might prey on her weakness for political purposes. At this time, Phyllis and her parents agreed that a change in location might help. Phyllis accepted an invitation from Warren Hollier's mother to come to visit her in Oklahoma.

However, despite what seemed like an improved outlook when she returned to California a few months later, Phyllis again set herself on the wrong course. There was speculation that her behavior was really an attempt to get the attention of her father, whose career was now taking up more and more of his time. While Ethel had grown to accept that Tom was also wedded to politics, there was evidence that Phyllis resented this growing intrusion into their personal lives. According to Lorraine, Phyllis' way of getting attention was to become periodically involved in troublesome activities, usually when her parents were out of town.

Close friends such as Hollier and Leroy Berry remember that Phyllis had been particularly close to her father when she was growing up on Welland Avenue. According to Berry, more often than not, Phyllis would be right behind her daddy, walking in his steps as he mowed lawns in the neighborhood.

When Bradley was elected to the City Council in 1963, Phyllis was nearly eighteen and living at home, sharing a bedroom with her sister Lorraine. As her father's political career flourished and Lorraine decided to attend college, Phyllis seemed unsure of what she wanted to do. There were heated debates between the sisters about Phyllis' future and the direction her life seemed to be heading. Even though they were sisters, they were growing apart. Their interests were quite different, and there were few, if any, common friends. Yet, never, in the fifteen years in which she shared a room with her sister, had Lorraine ever had any indication that drugs would become one of Phyllis' problems.

At first, to the family, it just seemed that it was taking Phyllis a little longer to figure out what she wanted to do with her life. Phyllis had been reluctant to take advice, even as a child. Whenever their mother would give strict orders to play together in the back of the house, Phyllis refused to accept Lorraine's ideas and often preferred to be by herself.

As she entered her twenties, Phyllis was more impressed by what her friends said than by the advice of her family. She seemed to be reaching out for acceptance from outside, and she would often do things, according to Lorraine, "because she thought it was the cool thing to do." It was this weakness that left her vulnerable.

Phyllis' problem became more and more rooted in a search for her own identity, a struggle to find it within the wrong peer group. The suggestion that she suffered from a neglected family life is inconsistent with the facts. Also, Lorraine argues that there is simply no truth to the notion that her sister's problems were a product of her father's political career. "Both of us enjoyed the best family life one could hope for." Furthermore, in comparing life at the Bradley home with that of their friends, Lorraine concludes, "Momma and Daddy were with us more than our friends' parents were, so the idea that she didn't get the necessary attention at home simply doesn't wash with the facts."

There is also testament from a variety of friends and colleagues to Bradley's strong sense of family. Even though his election as Mayor meant that he was really the head of what Bishop Brookins termed "an extended family," Brookins, Marilyn and Elbert Hudson, Leroy Berry, and others all recall frequent instances when Tom left an official event to attend a birthday dinner with Ethel or one of the daughters.

The fact was that Phyllis' first arrest occurred when she was twenty-nine years old—an age well beyond what one would expect from a child whose problem was rooted in a need for parental attention.

Lorraine had successfully completed college and had established herself as an excellent teacher and administrator at Louis Pasteur Junior High, then Hollywood High School. But Phyllis had experienced a less than satisfying life. While some would remark that she and her father had a striking resemblance, it was clear that, for the time being, Phyllis lacked the determination and drive that was so characteristic of Tom Bradley.

The soul searching that Tom and Ethel went through was not unlike that of other parents who have experienced the same sort of heartbreak. Press Secretary Tom Sullivan remembers that, on days after Phyllis' incidents, there would be a special sadness in the Mayor's eyes. Security officers Jerry Comfort and Bobby Adams comment that, even though Bradley refused to talk about it, it was obvious how much pain he was feeling inside. There were times when friends found Ethel worrying about what she could do to help Phyllis.

Of course the first question that both parents asked themselves was where had they gone wrong. To Bradley, there was the recognition that his forty-five years of public service had placed an enormous responsibility on Ethel for keeping the family together. Ethel was the bedrock committed to doing whatever she could to make it easier for him to do his job. The understanding and love that she had demonstrated—often after she had told him frankly that she didn't agree with a decision—had always been a constant source of support. She had sacrificed much in terms of a private life, but had done so with the understanding that her husband was compelled, even destined, to "do his thing."

But Phyllis' problems struck deeper. It was a hurt that only a parent could feel. Reflecting on this pain, Bradley recalls, "As a father I can tell you that nothing hurts any worse than for your own child to be involved in events like these." Explaining the sense of helplessness that often comes over a parent in this kind of situation, Bradley, like so many other parents, singles out the need to show immediate support and love. As father and mother, he and Ethel attempted to convey to their daughter that her problem was one in which the entire family would pull together to help solve. Tom reasoned that it was crucial to arrest Phyllis' drift toward failure, and they had to do anything they could to demonstrate hope and support from her family.

But even after showing support and a willingness to help, Bradley could not escape doing what almost every parent does in these circumstances—to question his own success and failure as a parent. Commenting on this, Bradley states, "It is hard to say what went wrong there, and believe me, any father or mother will ask themselves that, day in and day out—why, with two lovely daughters that you love so dearly, who have been brought up under the same roof, one seems to have had the problems that Phyllis has gone through."

Bradley recalls his prescription for dealing with the problem: "In my own situation, I remember that the first thing I did after Phyllis was home was to go into her room and to tell her that I wanted her to know that her mother and sister and I loved her very much and that we would do whatever we could to help her through this."

Identifying this reassurance of love and support as critical, Bradley recalls a family meeting in which he, Ethel, and Lorraine told Phyllis that they would be there for her and that she could count on them to help her in any way they could. It was an emotional meeting, with everyone a little nervous, but it was important to establish that support at the very beginning.

Because of his own background and experience, Bradley could go one step beyond the usual parental assistance. Even before Phyllis' problems, he had long been devoted to community rehabilitation programs to pick up where the family's support ends. His commitment was a product of his own experience growing up. He remembered his days in junior high school and at Polytechnic High, when he had seen so many kids waste their lives with drugs, because there had been no one to help. As a policeman, he had also seen the tragedy of drugs. Now this menace had even touched his own family.

Bradley knew how important rehabilitation programs were for those with the courage to recognize they had a problem, and the willingness to take the necessary first step toward a new life. It was a crucial step that could not be taken until the loved one was convinced that he or she did need help. It would prove to be a long, difficult, and painful ten-year struggle before Phyllis would become convinced.

Phyllis' problems were particularly hard for Ethel to accept. Possibly because of his police background, Tom was able more easily to accept the fact that Phyllis had a problem. It was also apparent to the family's closest friends, who conjectured about how this might affect Tom's political career (and there were those who thought that the political differences between the LAPD Chief and the Mayor increased the chances for Phyllis to be arrested), Tom Bradley's one and only concern was the well-being of his daughter. In the numerous times the family gathered to offer help, there was never any discussion of the ramifications of Phyllis' problems on her father's career.

Ethel was more reluctant, initially, to believe that her daughter needed help. She believed and defended Phyllis' stories that she had done nothing wrong, that she had merely been set up by the police. Given Ethel's own experiences, it seemed to fit that some of Bradley's political opponents would stoop to anything to get at the Mayor. And now they were after Phyllis. But after awhile, Ethel had to accept the fact that Phyllis' stories of innocence were merely lies calculated to excuse her troubled behavior. It was a revelation especially hard for Ethel. Lorraine remembers, "It cut deep and left an awful wound in Momma."

The rest of the Bradley family—Ethel, Tom, and Lorraine—were forced to realize that, for the time being, all of their support and all of the rehabilitation programs simply were of no help to Phyllis. The reason was painfully simple. Phyllis still denied that there was a problem, and so continued to be involved in periodic drug-related incidents.

Tom's efforts turned toward attempting to convince Ethel that guilt was not the answer to Phyllis' problems. He admitted that the home environment should be reexamined in cases where the problem occurs during the formative years. However, in cases such as their daughter's, factors beyond the reach of parents often play a crucial role. He explained: "By the time a child is eighteen or over, they have long since developed particular peer groups, and the family is only one influence. . . . Phyllis' problem began much later in her life, when we were only one of the many influences, and for us to have simply turned inward and blamed ourselves would have been to ignore the outside influences, which I believe were very important, and had to be attended to."

The grit and determination of the family to help Phyllis with her problem has been evident throughout the years. But until their younger daughter realized she needed help, there was little they could do but offer their love and support, as well as their prayers for her well-being and for the time when she would be prepared to cope with her problem.

At times, Phyllis gave indications that she was on the right track, that the corner had been turned. But then there would be another incident, another setback. Her condition could be described by one of Tom's favorite phrases, which his children had heard over and over as they were growing up—"Words without deeds have no real meaning."

After the years of hope greeted with disappointment, there was evidence in 1985 that the years of support, long talks, and attempts to provide an alternative to drugs was paying off. Tom, Ethel, and Lorraine, as well as family friends, noticed a dramatic change in Phyllis' outlook on life. Suddenly she seemed interested in making something of herself; she seemed eager to put her past behind her, to make amends with those she had hurt. Lorraine attributed it to the six-month period Phyllis had spent in county jail, after the long ten-year string of arrests. There was also the fact that she had come close to being killed in the last one—a 1983 automobile accident in San Pedro, in which she had been driving under the influence of drugs.

In early 1985, Phyllis called her sister and parents, asking if they could get together. She had something she wanted to tell them. The family met at Getty House, hopeful that it might be the signal of a new beginning, but aware that there were still pitfalls for what had become Phyllis' problem.

In an emotional and difficult speech, Phyllis admitted to her family that she had a drug problem. She asked for their support and guidance in enrolling in a first-rate drug-rehabilitation program.

It was a happy moment for everyone. Tom believed that this time his daughter had demonstrated what had been lacking before—the perseverance and determination to put her past behind her, to move forward. She had taken her first important step toward a more satisfying and productive life.

There was further evidence that Phyllis had indeed made a dramatic turn for the better. She moved out of the city to an eastern suburb, taking the advice of her family and counselor to establish new friends and a fresh start. Since then, she has been employed steadily as a computer operator at a university and has contributed significantly to a minority studies program.

Deep within Tom and Ethel Bradley is a faith that their daughter is moving forward toward realizing her own potential, and toward making a contribution to society as a survivor who has met the drug challenge head-on and won.

13

Seeking a Mandate to Continue

*"Leadership and learning are in-
dispensable to each other."*
—John F. Kennedy

In mid-December 1976, Alan Robbins, a thirty-three-year-old
Democratic State Senator from the San Fernando Valley, announced his candidacy for Mayor of Los Angeles. Surrounded by
a staff made up primarily of Republicans with strong ties to
former Mayor Yorty, Robbins declared that his campaign would
steer clear of the racial overtones of the 1973 contest. However,
as the campaign progressed, the evidence suggested that, like
Yorty, Robbins would make race a vital part of his campaign
strategy. This was inevitable in a campaign that took as one of its
main issues the controversial policy of school busing. Robbins
charged that Bradley had not been straightforward with the citizens of Los Angeles about his position on busing, although he
could have voiced the community's opposition to busing "more
easily than almost any other Mayor because he's black."

As the campaign got under way, Robbins continued to hit
hard at the busing issue, charging that Bradley's avoidance of the
topic had added to the problem. Robbins highlighted the School
Board's position against mandatory busing, and the public's dis-
satisfaction with the policy. He endorsed candidates for the
School Board who ran on an anti-busing platform and constantly
charged that Bradley was evading the issue.

However, Bradley had already come out strongly against
"massive crosstown busing," explaining that it would strain the
city's budget and be "an emotionally draining experience." He

With Charlton
Heston on National
Film Day in Los
Angeles, 1973.
(Photo by Mason
Dooley: Courtesy of
Los Angeles City
Hall

Bradley welcomes Their Majesties, Emperor and Empress
Hirohito of Japan, October 10, 1975. (Photo by Conrad
Mercurio: Courtesy of Los Angeles City Hall)

did, nonetheless, indicate that if the courts ultimately ruled that busing should be the policy to achieve integration, he would "exert moral leadership to ensure peaceful compliance with the order." That said, Bradley failed to see the legitimacy or the relevance of busing as the central issue in the mayoral campaign.

Another suggestive theme was Robbins' assertion that the Mayor had not been supportive of the Police Department. In an effort to call attention to his own supposed "tough stand on crime," Robbins announced that he would distribute 750,000 red rape whistles throughout the campaign as symbols of his anti-crime record.

Robbins emphasized that, as State Senator, he had sponsored legislation in Sacramento calling for tougher punishment of rapists. While several of the Mayor's advisors criticized the whistle handout as a move with inflammatory racist overtones, Robbins defended himself saying, "I used the whistles to remind voters that I authored the first legislation in the nation that protected the rights of victims of forceable rape. . . . I could not imagine what the racial angle would be if there was one, because I also used them in my 1974 reelection campaign, and my opponent in that was a white male attorney named Jack Ellis." Despite Robbins' claim to being tough on crime, the California Peace Officers Association rated Senator Robbins as 45 on a scale of 100, a below average ranking in the California State Senate.

It was clear that Robbins, like Yorty, would seek to aggravate rather than minimize the cleavages within the city. In his campaign speeches, Robbins charged that Bradley had catered only to the downtown business interests. He told audiences that Bradley was the "Rolls Royce Mayor," who had ignored the San Fernando Valley, treating it and other parts of the city as "stepchildren," during his first term. Furthermore, Bradley, according to Robbins, was a candidate of the elite, rather than the common man. If elected, Robbins promised to take City Hall away from the special interests. He wanted to get a fair share of city expenditures, commissioners, and land-use planning for the rest of the city.

The State Senator went on to attack Bradley's aggressive support of the downtown redevelopment project, which the City Council had approved in 1975. Robbins called the project "welfare for the rich" and accused Bradley of "stuffing his pockets with campaign contributions" from those businesses who would benefit from the plan.

Bradley responded to that charge in an uncharacteristically abrasive tone; he called Robbins "an unmitigated liar" and indicated that the charge was "further evidence of what people who know him best say about Senator Robbins. . . . The fact that he's the biggest spender in the history of the State Senate gives him no justification for these kinds of charges." This would be one of the harshest rebuttals the Mayor would unleash in the campaign, as he fought to prevent Robbins from putting him on the defensive.

In fact, the 255-block rehabilitation project under attack by Robbins was one of Bradley's proudest achievements. It was an invaluable contribution to the economic promise of Los Angeles' central city area and a substantial enlargement of its tax base. Mayoral advisor Hal Kwalwasser states, "He was out in front in getting the business community involved in changing the face of the City of Los Angeles, trying to recapture suburban areas."

"The Mayor thinks that the way to get things done," Bill Robertson adds, "is to involve labor, industry, and government; it's similar to the spirit that FDR engendered after World War II." In the twenty years preceding the plan, few buildings had been constructed in downtown Los Angeles, and businesses continued to relocate in suburban areas. The result was a loss, not only of jobs and commerce, but of important tax dollars needed to keep the city operating within a balanced budget. Walter Gerken comments, "Bradley has a good sense of economic realities and works well with the business community. Under his leadership, Los Angeles has become the financial center of the West."

Robbins' proclivity for exceeding the bounds of good taste in his political diatribes was perhaps most clearly demonstrated when he compared Mayor Bradley with Adolph Hitler. Responding to a Bradley brochure that asked voters in the Valley, "What Has Alan Robbins Really Done For The Area?," the State Senator remarked, "I want to tell you, for Tom Bradley to put out a campaign brochure bragging about what he has done for the Valley is about akin to Adolph Hitler putting out a campaign brochure of what he did for the Jews and Gypsies." Bradley Campaign Director David Mixner labeled the remark, "appalling bad taste." Members of the community expressed outrage. A few days later, Robbins apologized for the statement. It was the mark of a candidate who realized that his campaign was going nowhere.

In a Yorty like vein, Robbins raised topics that subtly played to the race issue. Depending on the audience and situation, the veiled allusions to Bradley's race were part and parcel of Robbins' comments on busing, crime, and funding of projects in minority neighborhoods. An "Us *vs.* Them" philosophy seemed to be at the root of the Senator's much-criticized idea that the Valley should secede from the City of Los Angeles.

The underlying racism of this theme was noted by many journalists covering the campaign. Kenneth Reich wrote in the *Los Angeles Times* that "the persistent thrust, the clear hope of much of Bradley's opposition is that the predominantly white Los Angeles electorate will not believe a black is as safely conservative as a white."

To the Mayor, such speculation contributed little to the public debate on the real issues. But over the years he had grown to accept, if reluctantly, the media's obsessive analysis of how race would affect voters.

"It's something I have always had to live with," remarks Bradley. "On my part I try to keep the emphasis on the pertinent issues, to downplay anything like that, because it is not relevant to the decision-making process." The Mayor further explains, "I have never made a decision based on race, sex, or ethnicity, and I don't believe the vast majority of the public do either."

In addition to Robbins, there was early speculation that Arthur Snyder, the City Councilman from the predominantly Chicano district on the city's northeast side, might also oppose Bradley. As reported in the *New York Times,* the Councilman maintained that "race is not an issue at all" in the election, but then went on to charge that Bradley's administration had done very little to improve the quality of life for Mexican-Americans, and to claim that Bradley was elected in 1973 primarily because voters "wanted to prove to themselves and to the world that it was possible for a black to be elected in a city where blacks are a small minority." Snyder eventually decided against entering the race in the face of the Mayor's high approval rating.

There were still other candidates vying for the mayoral post in the 1977 election. The City Clerk reported that thirty-three had filed declarations of intentions to run for the office. Fifteen eventually appeared on the ballot. John Mareulis, of the *Valley News,* reported that some of those running included, "Calypso Joe, Ani Ya Gin Nei Mie Choo, Mark 'Nobody' Philger and, in addition to Senator Robbins, another 'Alan Robbins' from Encino."

Also indicating to the City Clerk's office that she intended to run was perennial mayoral candidate Eileen Anderson, known for the spring green bathing suit she wore in performing her dance routines on streetcorners in the downtown area. Her platform emphasized the construction of large tunnels through the Santa Monica Mountains to be equipped with fans to clear out Los Angeles' smog. Bradley's human resources and urban programs director, Grace Montanez Davis, who replaced Deputy Mayor Manuel Aragon Jr., who chose to enter private business in August 1975, remembers mentioning to Bradley that "something should be done about Anderson's wild dance routines that seemed to be characterized by fewer and fewer clothing accessories. . . . He just looked at me, before I could even finish my sentence, and said, 'I like Eileen!' I knew then, from the tone of his voice, that that dance routine of Anderson's was here to stay."

Aside from Robbins and Bradley, the candidate receiving the most attention was Howard Jarvis, whose candidacy was based primarily on a stand against excessive property taxes. Jarvis, known for his anti-tax stands, also took aim at city employee salaries, which he labeled as too high. He connected education with "Mafia rackets," calling for deep budget cuts.

Addressing the tax and salary issues, Bradley pointed to his record as proof of his abilities as a financial manager. He had already set a personal example by refusing to accept a $5,000 increase in the Mayor's salary. He had vetoed salary increases for the highly-paid city departmental managers. Additionally, Bradley's successful fight for a ten percent cut in the city's 1976 property-tax rate—two years before Proposition 13, California's controversial tax-slashing initiative—and his record of balanced budgets seemed sufficient to nullify the challenger's accusation. Bradley's tightfisted approach to government had made the crucial difference in keeping Los Angeles fiscally fit. As Wanda Moore said, "The man certainly is not a big-spending liberal; the real truth is that he is just downright cheap!"

As Mayor, Bradley still preferred the old-fashioned way of paying with cash, shunning the use of credit cards, even in his travels. Practicality and durability were traits he stressed to his daughters, advising against paying more money just for unnecessary frills. On his trips, Bradley traveled in coach, always concerned about frequent-flyer programs that could save the city a bit more money.

The Mayor's frugal ways were well known at City Hall. Craig Lawson, Research Director on the Mayor's staff, recalls one incident that clearly illustrates Bradley's attitude about spending city money. One hot Saturday in late August, Lawson had gone to his office at City Hall to catch up on some work and noticed that Bradley was in, as was often the case on weekends. Lawson had some research to show Bradley, so he called and asked if he might see him for a few minutes. "When I entered the outer office, which was like an oven, I noticed a suit of clothes all nicely laid out on the visitor's chair." Upon entering the small inner office where the Mayor does his work, Lawson was amazed to see "Tom Bradley, who is known for his meticulous and formal dress, sitting there in his T-shirt and boxer shorts." Normally the most carefully dressed of men (he would win a Men's Fashion Association American Image Award in 1985), Bradley had sacrificed his usual decorousness to his belief that the air conditioners at City Hall should not run on weekends!

In the speech declaring his candidacy for a second term, Bradley honed in on what he labeled "the kind of enlightened stinginess" that had allowed him to "produce balanced budgets for three consecutive years without new taxes." He reminded his constituents that his administration had heard their cries for tax reform—thus the ten percent reduction in property taxes. The Mayor pledged to "continue to streamline government, to make it work better for all of us, for less money."

In 1977, Sam Yorty kibbitzed from the sidelines, attempting to help defeat Bradley. Hosting a weekly television show aired in the Los Angeles area, the former Mayor reminded listeners that Bradley, in 1973, had attacked his extensive travel away from Los Angeles. According to Yorty, whose guest just happened to be Alan Robbins, the records revealed that Mayor Bradley had been out of the city more frequently than Mayor Sam had been.

Bradley's staff members were quick to point out the flaws in the claim. The important issue was not the number of days absent, but the activity that took place during those days away from Los Angeles. Bradley's press secretary Tom Sullivan explained: "When this Mayor goes out of town it is usually to Sacramento or Washington to testify or lobby in behalf of the city's interest. With Yorty, the record shows he mainly traveled for pleasure."

Bradley's international travel had also been very firmly grounded in his goals and aspirations for Los Angeles—specifically, his intention of making her a truly international city. As Los Angeles' chief executive, he had worked hard to increase trade and further the city's reputation as the "Gateway to the Pacific Rim." According to Bee Canterbury Lavery, with the exception of Washington, D.C., Los Angeles was the American city most visited by foreign dignitaries.

Heads of state from throughout Europe, Asia, and Africa met with Bradley during their visits to America. With each visit came invitations for Bradley to travel abroad. The Mayor had visited countries throughout the world, in each instance adding to the city's economic potential by promoting Los Angeles as a tourist destination and aggressively selling its port and airport facilities. Agreements were often reached for increased trade and cooperation as a result of Bradley's contacts with foreign leaders. By July 1985, when Bradley met with the president of China, he had hosted the leaders of virtually every foreign nation with which the United States had diplomatic relations.

The extensive harbor revitalization that occurred under Bradley's administration had further enhanced the city's international status. In contrast to the equal sharing of trade between Los Angeles, Seattle, and San Francisco in the 1970s, Los Angeles now boasted the number-one port on the Pacific Coast in dollar volume of international trade, more than Seattle and San Francisco combined. Serving as the nation's window to Asia (an increasingly important role, given the fact that over sixty percent of the world's population lives along the vast Pacific rim), the Los Angeles Customs District account would grow by over $50 billion in trade, an increase from $8.4 billion in 1974. This increase was to result in creating 800,000 new directly related jobs.

The Los Angeles area ranks fourteenth among countries of the world in trade, exceeding the whole of Australia, Mexico, and Sweden.

According to the Bradley campaign, the bottom line of all of these impressive facts and figures was more jobs for more Los Angelenos. Rather than being defensive about it, Bradley pointed with pride to his traveling.

The Bradley campaign staff included many of the same strategists who had provided a winning combination in 1973. Nelson Rising was again one of the chief strategists. Maureen Kindel, a former fundraiser for the Los Angeles Music Center, joined Fran Savitch, Phil Depoian, and Dodo Meyer, three of the Mayor's most trusted aides, in providing input for the reelection bid, serving as a link to involving many GOP women's groups. Kindel served as the campaign's Finance Chairman. Savitch and Depoian were important strategists. National Democratic advisor David Mixner, who had worked in McCarthy's presidential campaign in 1969, and in Senator John Tunney's unsuccessful bid for reelection in 1976, was named Bradley's Campaign Manager. Jay Berman became the press spokesman.

Absent from the campaign team was 1973 fundraiser Max Palevsky, who publicly indicated he would not be a part of the reelection effort. A Democratic political insider remarks, "Max has always wanted to control candidates, and it was clear that he couldn't do that with Tom Bradley; only Bradley controls Bradley." There was widespread speculation concerning Palevsky's decision. Nelson Rising told Kenneth Reich of the *Los Angeles Times* that Palevsky "had not been one to put a lot of energy and enthusiasm behind incumbents."

The *Times* reported that colleagues who had worked with Palevsky in his past campaign efforts, including the presidential bids of George McGovern and Jimmy Carter, concluded that the wealthly politico "wished to exert more control over candidates than the candidates or their workers liked." What emerged was that, while the principal fundraiser for the $1,277,000 spent in getting Tom Bradley elected in 1973 would eventually endorse the Mayor, he would not play an active role in the reelection effort.

Bradley enjoyed the endorsements of Governor Jerry Brown, Senator Alan Cranston, and the AFL–CIO's 650,000-member organization in his reelection bid. Bill Robertson and Jerry Cremins, of the county labor organization, praised Bradley's "excellence in office, under trying economic circumstances." The only union group that withheld its support was the firefighters, unhappy with Bradley's cut in staffing of city departments and agencies and his program to recruit female firefighters.

The majority of City Council members also fell in line behind Bradley. Councilman Joel Wachs announced the formation of a "truth squad" to refute what he termed were "gross misrepresentations" and "half-truths" waged by Robbins. Furthermore, Wachs pointed out that, while Bradley had worked to ease the burden of the taxpayer, Robbins was the author of bills that would have "cost California taxpayers $600 million." With surrogates refuting many of Robbins' claims, the Mayor was able to keep above much of the verbal fray.

City Council President John S. Gibson, Jr., who represented the San Pedro area, pledged his support in a move that torpedoed Robbins' efforts to take advantage of what his campaign perceived to be that area's disenchantment with the Mayor's leadership. Councilman Art Snyder, who at one time entertained the notion of opposing Bradley, eventually endorsed the Mayor. In campaigning for Bradley, Snyder faulted Robbins for the lack of any concrete programs to match those of the incumbent, and he predicted a big turn-out in the Hispanic community for Bradley.

In charge of the 1977 fundraising operation was Irene Tritschler, who had worked for Bradley in 1973, at the beginning of her fundraising career. She has worked in each of the Bradley campaigns since then, and she also served as the state Coordinator for the 1984 Democratic presidential bid. "I liked the man instantly," Tritschler said, in remembering her first meeting with

Bradley in 1973. "It wasn't what he said, because he hadn't said anything yet when I realized it. . . . I guess it was his presence; there is almost an instant respect for him."

The successful fundraiser further adds that Bradley has an unbelievable number of second- and third-time givers. One unexpected source of support has been Republicans: "They look at the skyline and realize that Bradley has made that possible, and kept this city operating in the black. I have not found any one group that really doesn't support him; he is immensely popular in the Asian, Hispanic, and Jewish communities."

As the primary election approached, it was reported that Bradley's campaign had raised nearly $900,000, more than six times that collected by Robbins. His contributors ranged from Jacqueline Kennedy Onassis to third-grader Cyrus Polk in South-Central Los Angeles.

The popularity Bradley enjoyed among the Japanese, both in California and in Japan itself, was unusual. According to Japanese government leaders, with the exception of the President of the United States and Senator Edward Kennedy, Tom Bradley is the most widely known American in their country, as he is in Japan's Pacific neighbors. He has won the affection of his Japanese constituents partly through his accessibility. As mayoral aide Jeff Matsui comments, "The Japanese community is not used to having an elected official on the Mayor's level meet with them on a regular basis." Bradley enhanced his standing in Los Angeles' Japanese community when he hosted a state visited by the Emperor of Japan in 1975, which engendered a strong sense of pride in the city's huge Japanese-American population.

The growing Asian community in Los Angeles reflects the changing demographics of America's second largest city. As City Councilman Michael Woo pointed out in 1985, "In 1970 there were only eight thousand Koreans in Los Angeles, now there are over 100,000 which translates into problems for housing, employment, and assimilation." The ability of Bradley to bring the many different groups together is especially noteworthy, given the divergent backgrounds. As local leader Masimori Kojima says, "You know your history—the Cambodians don't love the Vietnamese, and the Chinese and Koreans remember that Japan has

At the 49th Annual Academy Awards Ceremony, March 30, 1977. (Courtesy of Long Photography)

Backstage at the Greek Theater with Harry Belafonte, July 17, 1979. (Photo by Jason Respini, Bradley Family Collection)

Henry Kissinger, the Mayor, and Los Angeles Supervisor Kenneth Hahn at the World Affairs Council, 1976. (Courtesy of Los Angeles City Hall)

not always been such a friendly neighbor." The melting-pot experience has been enriched by a commonly respected Mayor. And Los Angeles has been very fortunate in that respect, since nearly a fifth of its population is foreign-born—about triple the U.S. average.

After being criticized by Robbins and the press for not being more active in the campaign, Bradley cited his daily responsibilities at City Hall as a reason. According to Campaign Director Rising, "The people of Los Angeles would rather see their Mayor running the government effectively instead of out campaigning."

However, candidate Bradley did find some time to campaign. In his appearances before groups and organizations, the Mayor emphasized his administration's fiscal "stinginess," and he highlighted the accomplishments of his years in office. Bradley cited the drop in the city's crime rate as a result of the additional officers that his administration had put on the streets. In asking voters for their support, he cautioned that now "was not a time for untested approaches, for irresponsible answers to complex problems."

This was an era when experts were questioning whether cities could survive. Indeed, cities across the United States were in financial chaos; New York was on the verge of bankruptcy, dependent on the federal government for a bailout; and other municipalities were torn apart by racial unrest or labor strikes. Yet Los Angeles, under Tom Bradley, had forged a path toward a healthy, vital future and was enjoying financial solvency.

The Bradley campaign proudly highlighted the Mayor's record on jobs as evidence of his leadership. The City Economic Development Office (CEDO) had been extremely successful in improving the city's business climate. Furthermore, it had actively worked, not only to lure new businesses into the Los Angeles area, but also to maintain those already operating.

The CEDO had made the difference in keeping a tuna cannery from leaving the San Pedro area. The result was 1,200 jobs saved for the people of Los Angeles. Delivering on his promise to revitalize the Harbor area, Bradley had worked to convert Fort MacArthur from a military installation into a recreational area, a project that meant two thousand additional jobs. The Bradley campaign stressed examples such as these as it took its message to the people.

During the course of the campaign, Bradley received some unexpected recognition from Washington. President Jimmy Carter appointed Bradley to be on a nine-member board to recommend a new FBI Director. Furthermore, a fundraiser for his reelection was sponsored by such leaders as former Vice-President Hubert H. Humphrey, Senator Edward M. Kennedy, and others. While in the capitol, Bradley conferred with HUD Secretary Patricia Harris to discuss the federal government's urban programs as they related to Los Angeles.

Locally, the national recognition was played up by Robbins as further examples of Bradley's coziness with the effete establishment, and yet another reason why Los Angeles needed new leadership. The State Senator accused Bradley of going to the East Coast "image makers" to help him in his reelection effort.

In the primary, Bradley enjoyed the endorsements of the city's major newspapers, the *Los Angeles Times* and the *Herald Examiner,* as well as ethnic and neighborhood papers throughout the area, including the *Los Angeles Sentinel* and *La Opinion.* The polls were also with him, showing him with a sixty-percent share of the vote, more than enough to win reelection without a runoff. He had support in virtually every neighborhood of the city. Even in the Valley, which was Robbins own backyard and home to forty percent of the voters, Bradley was ahead. He enjoyed the support of a majority of Republican, Democratic, and independent voters.

Veteran political pundits concluded that Robbins' divisive message was not finding a receptive audience. In a city where blacks constitute less than fifteen percent of the 2.8-million population, and a sometimes subtle, sometimes strident appeal to racism had been made, over three-fourths of the citizens of Los Angeles gave Bradley high marks as Mayor in a poll by the *Los Angeles Times.*

There was conjecture that Robbins had realized the strong odds against his own candidacy from the beginning, and had made this race for the sake of increased recognition, possibly leading up to another run for the city's top spot in 1981.

The City of Los Angeles gave Tom Bradley the ringing endorsement he wanted at the polls. He was reelected with almost 60 percent of the vote. Robbins came in second with 27.5 percent, and Howard Jarvis was a distant third at 10 percent. The victory was deeply pleasing to Bradley. He believed that he had made a good start in delivering on his 1973 promises, on his commitment to making Los Angeles the world-class city it ought to be, and now it was obvious that his constituents agreed. The 1977 election had been a referendum on policies rather than race.

Following a jubilant victory celebration at the Los Angeles Hilton, which included a surprise appearance by Governor Jerry Brown, Bradley held a morning press conference. He began the address, not by mentioning his opponent's name, but by blowing one of thousands of the rape whistles that Robbins had given out during the campaign. He told reporters that it signaled the end to racially motivated campaigns. The election returns revealed that Bradley had won fourteen of the fifteen city districts, losing to Robbins in only one district in the Valley.

Even though the busing issue had not translated into a victory for Robbins, his candidacy did serve as a symbol for those opposed to that means of achieving intergration. The *Christian Science Monitor* reported that up to 80 percent of those who voted for Robbins were actually voting against mandatory busing. In addition, the controversial issue also had an effect on the Los Angeles School Board elections. Two candidates who had favored the policy, Howard Miller and Robert L. Docter, were forced into a runoff, where they eventually lost their seats to anti-busing candidates.

Robbins feels the race he ran in 1977 did produce significant changes in City Hall. Looking back, Robbins said, "Mayor Bradley has appointed more commissioners from the Valley since my election and he has shown more attention to the needs of the Valley." Reflecting on the relationship that he has had with Bradley over the years, Robbins adds, "During the campaign in 1977, I tried to get mad at him, but I couldn't. . . . It is very hard for anyone to stay mad at Tom Bradley or continue to dislike him over a period of time, with the exception of Sam Yorty. Since the election, Tom and I wound up friends, and I would describe us today as good friends because we work very closely on issues of mutual concern to the community. I have endorsed Tom for reelection, and he has endorsed me, because we both are interested in a better Valley and a better Los Angeles."

Bradley's win focused increased attention on his political future. The press reminded him that he had publicly stated that he would not seek a third term as Mayor. Was he planning on running for Senate in 1982, or would he go for the gubernatorial spot, which Jerry Brown was expected to vacate that same year? His response was succinct. His plans were to serve out the mandate that he had been given by the people of Los Angeles. It was a job that consumed almost every hour of his day. He was ready to get on with it.

Bradley took the oath of office for his second term from another history-making figure from the judicial branch. Rose Bird, the newly appointed Chief Justice of the California Supreme Court and the first woman to occupy the position, presided over the swearing-in ceremonies. In an uncharacteristically long forty-five-minute speech, preceded by Aretha Franklin's singing of "The Impossible Dream," the Mayor proposed a major overhaul of city government.

Declaring that "the structure of government suffers from a bad case of obsolescence," Bradley committed himself to making changes in individual departments and in the city charter itself—within the "existing structure and funds available." He maintained that the existing system contributed to "needless waste and duplication," and cited the overlap of city and county paramedic programs as one example of the kind of inefficiency that better-coordinated planning could eliminate. A better-managed city government could make all the difference in a time of limited resources. With the Mayor of his hometown of Calvert, Texas, looking on, Bradley asked the support of the people of Los Angeles so that "we can build a brighter future, even while living within limits. . . . We can, in fact, achieve excellence without extravagance."

The Mayor also acknowledged the tension within the community, resulting from an issue that his principal opponent had attempted to exploit in the election—busing: "In this city, then, let us resolve here and now to devote our energies to peaceful and responsible compliance with any final order for integration in the school district." Though it was obvious throughout the city that there was "anxiety attached to the court-ordered integration in our schools," Bradley pledged to lead the city through emotionally trying times. He called upon all citizens on both sides of the issue to display "dignity and genuine respect for each other," to keep in mind "that the safety and education of our children are of paramount concern to us. . . . We must not fail them."

Mayor Bradley's Select Committee for the 1984 Olympics, From left, John Argue, David Wolper, John Ferraro, the Mayor, Rod Rood, Howard Allen, Peter Ueberroth, (Courtesy of Los Angeles City Hall)

From left, Councilman John Ferraro, Secretary-Treasurer of the Los Angeles County Federation of Labor, AFL-CIO, Bill Robertson, Supervisor Kenneth Hahn, Los Angeles Raiders owner Al Davis, Tom Bradley make a team effort pact for Olympic success at the Los Angeles Memorial Coliseum, 1980. (Courtesy of Board of Supervisors, LA County)

14

The Olympic Dream

*"Some men see things as they are
and say why. I dream things that
never were and say why not."*
—Robert F. Kennedy

One of the most disturbing statistics to Bradley, as he began his second term, was the large number of young people in Los Angeles and throughout the country who were turning to crime. There were many voices calling for stiffer penalties and tougher sentences. As a former police officer, Bradley agreed that steps had to be taken in that direction. But what was lacking in the shallow, quick-fix solutions proposed by politicians in election years was a careful examination of the causes. Why were more and more young people finding themselves on the wrong side of the law?

Many youngsters growing up in the squalor of the nation's ghettos saw no other way out. Crime became their means for survival. Lacking the familial support needed to instill the value of an education, thousands dropped out of school and took to the streets. They became street-wise, but talent- and skill-short. It was only a matter of time before they had their initial brush with the law—usually from stealing food or clothing. After that, the crimes would become more serious. For many, it became the only career they would know. Bradley was well aware of the syndrome. Many of those he had played with as a kid had gone down the same road, ending up with nothing but a jail record.

In 1977, roughly one out of every two young blacks and Hispanics in Los Angeles were unemployed. They lacked the skills needed in the ever changing job market. If the problem were not addressed with specific policies and programs designed to meet the needs of this group, many would be lost to lives of crime. Bradley was convinced that Los Angeles could not afford to waste this most precious resource.

Through Operation HEAVY, a program instituted at no cost to the taxpayers, shortly before Bradley's reelection, City Hall, the Police Department, and the schools of Los Angeles began a coordinated effort to provide juveniles with counseling, job training and placement, and recreation, as an alternative to police and probation procedures. Bradley realized that this alone would not solve the problem, but he directed Rose Ochi and Jamesetta Hawthorne, of the Criminal Justice Office, to devote their efforts to see that it could be an important first step in offering the city's youth a viable alternative to crime. Hawthorne remembers, "In its first year, HEAVY worked with 2,700 young people, and it has helped over ten thousand others since then."

The Mayor's summer youth program, SPEEDY, also helped make a difference. Thirty-five thousand disadvantaged students found jobs during the 1977 summer recess. Programs such as these "that contribute to the city's most valuable resource—it's youth—are exactly what every city across America should be doing more of," comments former *Los Angeles Herald-Examiner* publisher, Francis Dale. "Los Angeles needs to do all it can in this area of training and development." HEAVY and SPEEDY were good beginnings, but Bradley remained determined to make things even better during his next four years.

Shortly after taking the oath of office for his second term, the Mayor and Mrs. Bradley moved from their home of twenty-seven years—the six-room house on Welland in Leimert Park—to Hancock Park and the three-story, fourteen-room French colonial brick house donated to the city as the official mayoral residence by Getty Oil. A former residence of Actor John Barrymore and actress Dolores Costello, Getty House, as it would be referred to in honor of the benefactor, marked the culmination of an eleven-year search, instituted by Mayor Yorty, for a suitable mayoral residence. Equipped with two large dining rooms, a library, and kitchen on the first floor, and private living quarters upstairs, the new residence seemed perfectly suited for the entertainment and official functions expected of Los Angeles' first family. But what the Bradleys, especially Ethel, did not expect was the impending controversy concerning the house's furnishings.

"It all started when the Yorty faction on the residence committee tried to keep the Bradleys from moving in," recalls Jessie Mae Beavers. Following numerous delays due to "decorating and painting," required by the residence committee, "our photographer at the *Sentinel* did a portrait of the Bradley family, and Ethel decided to hang it on the first floor, along with a few other personal items." That was enough to enrage some of the mayoral residence committee members. They went public with their complaints. And if that were not enough, they even decided to correct the problem. Beavers continues, "Rather than attempt to calmly deal with the situation, they marched into the house, took down the portrait, and told Ethel to keep all of the family's personal effects upstairs."

Beavers remembers her close friend's reaction to the situation: "Ethel was outraged by such pettiness." Yet she was also aware that "some opponents and critics would try to get at the Mayor by provoking her in such instances." The Bradleys' older daughter agrees: "She has always been a perfect hostess, but has faced problems from the start on assuming her rightful role as first lady of the city." After providing several examples of how the press has aggravated the problem, Lorraine states, "they have perpetuated the myth that she isn't able to handle this function, which is ridiculous; Momma was a successful businesswoman and went to City College and has always been a real leader."

Critics also seemed to forget that Ethel Bradley had long been involved in community affairs and was from a family of interior decorators. She and Tom had hosted numerous Kappa and political dinners, and she had continued to be a social leader during the Council days. Visitors to their house on Welland remembered the Louis XIV furniture, the Waterford crystal, and the Lennox china that Ethel had for such special occasions. Those were items, according to her children, that only came out for use when the Bradleys were entertaining. To those who knew her, Ethel was nothing short of a "class act."

In the attempt to explain the motive for such attitudes and

behavior, Lorraine adds, "I tend to agree with others who think that it is some people's way of saying, 'okay, we can accept a black Mayor, but we don't have to accept a black first lady.'" She admits that there has been more acceptance with time, but she emphasizes that "earlier on, criticism of Momma was used by some to attack and get at Daddy."

Jessie Mae Beavers is quick to refute any suggestion that Mrs. Bradley does not enjoy her public role: "Those people who say that Ethel does not like her position should realize this is a defense mechanism, because I personally know that, when he was elected, she had great enthusiasm for stepping into the role as first lady."

How has the strain affected the family? "Sure it hurts," remarks Lorraine. "It has caused problems, but Momma and Daddy know that the attacks on her are really meant to tear him down, and I can assure you that we are not going to let that happen, or for him to get sidetracked from accomplishing his job." Beavers adds, "Ethel is strong, but only human and she has decided at times to bow out rather than stand up for herself and in doing so let it hurt him."

In Ethel Bradley's own words, "The Mayor and I understand the dynamics, and I am resolved to the fact that I will never get the recognition that others might. . . . That is the way it is and will be, and I have learned to live with it." To those long-time friends of the Bradleys, inherent in their relationship is a unique understanding of the demands of such a public life. An old friend describes it as follows, "They have steeled themselves for such attacks, and have a special bond between them that allows them to understand and put up with such distortions."

The 1978 state races in November witnessed the reelection of Governor Jerry Brown. It was widely believed that Brown, who had earlier run a spirited last-minute campaign for the presidency and embarrassed Jimmy Carter in some key states during the latter days of the 1976 primaries, might make another try for the White House in 1980. Many Democrats throughout the country were going public with their growing disillusionment with Jimmy Carter's presidency. Brown and Senator Edward Kennedy had both toyed with the idea of opposing the incumbent in the 1980 primaries.

An April 1979 *Times* poll of Los Angeles residents showed that President Carter had an approval rating of 49 percent, Governor Brown 60 percent, and Mayor Bradley 76 percent. Although he was then less that halfway through his second mayoral term, there was already talk of a Tom Bradley-for-Governor movement in 1982. The *Times* reported that Bradley took in $150,000 at a fundraiser that May, and that the money might be earmarked for something other than a run for a third mayoral term. Bradley told supporters at the dinner, "I won't tell you what [the answer] is going to be because I don't know. I think I can tell you what the answer is *not* going to be. You don't bring 1,600 people to the Century Plaza to raise a war chest if you plan to retire from politics. So my friends, guess a little while longer. The best is yet to come."

As citizens wondered about the Mayor's plans, the media zeroed in on the element that was always thought to help sell papers. A *Times* story read, "A key question about a Bradley statewide candidacy would be his race. . . . Bradley, one of the nation's best-known black politicians, has shown strength in elections and polls among a broad cross-section of Los Angeles residents." But, everyone wondered, could Bradley or any black candidate have a wide enough appeal among the state's heterogeneous constituency to actually be elected? Furthermore, could anyone beat a 130-year history in which no Mayor of Los Angeles had ever been elected to higher office?

The state's Democratic Party leadership was engaged in reviewing the list of hopefuls, in the hope of consolidating support around the candidate with the best chance at keeping the statehouse in Democratic hands. Talk throughout the state centered on Tom Bradley as the most likely candidate for Governor, or even U.S. Senator.

Republican Senator Sam Hayakawa, "Sleeping Sam" as he had been labeled by the press, had been a disappointment even to ardent Republicans. As Senator he had been lackluster, his performance belying the provocative speeches he had been famous for as President of San Francisco State University during the student protests of the 1960s. There was no vision or excitement. Many Californians openly regretted turning out the talented John Tunney in the last election. There was a general feeling that California needed a new Senator. But which job would Bradley go after? The Mayor's response was typical. In response to reporters' questions, Bradley explained that he had just been reelected Mayor. He was far too busy running the city and keeping a balanced budget to be concerned with electoral possibilities three years hence.

Beginning in 1978, one problem loomed on the political horizon that had the potential to counteract any serious discussion of the gubernatorial and senate races in 1982. In June 1978, California voters exercised their constitutional muscle by voting on Proposition 13, the property tax reform initiative. This represented the first step in a tax revolt that would be felt nationwide, and would present a significant challenge, not only to Bradley, but to policy-makers throughout the country.

While providing relief for the homeowner, the proposition had serious ramifications for city and county governments. With fewer dollars paid into the state treasury, there would be a reduced amount available for public services on the local level. Bradley and his budgetary staff went to work immediately on the effort to comply with the provision.

In the attempt to meet the financial emergency. Bradley proposed to cut $206.5 million from the city's $1.05 billion budget for the 1978–79 fiscal year. But this first cut was not enough. Proposition 13 translated into a $234-million loss in revenue for Los Angeles. There were press predictions of up to 8,300 city workers, including 1,080 police officers, losing their jobs because of the cuts. The one pledge made by Bradley was that all departments would be fairly treated, that no department would remain untouched. With regret, the Mayor noted that, because of the seniority system (last hired, first fired) minorities and women would be laid off in disproportionately high numbers.

Even before the proposition's passage, Bradley had persuaded the heads of the city's forty-one departments to submit revised budgets. The Police Department, under Chief Daryl

Gates, who had taken over when Ed Davis retired in 1977, had agreed to a seventeen-percent cut in funds for 1978–79 and to layoffs in the department. But, after the announcement of the cutbacks, in the wake of the initiative, Gates resisted. Instead he publicly offered his own modified budget. Under this proposal, there would be no reduction in the police personnel. The department would meet the financial crunch by delaying the pay raises that were due according to the union contract.

However, the Chief's recommendation was not popular even within his own department, and the union was flabbergasted that Gates had bargained away the pay-raise without even a mention to its leaders or membership. There was considerable speculation that Gates had his own political aspirations and was grandstanding to a public fearful of the results of having fewer cops on the beat. But the discord within the department overshadowed any political advantage for the Chief.

The initial public concern over Bradley cutbacks subsided when the Mayor announced that his personnel reductions were earmarked for office jobs, not for officers on patrol on city streets. Ultimately, because of Bradley's fiscal and managerial abilities, the Police Department has been strengthened, not weakened, under his administration. Through pension reform, the hiring of civilians for purely administrative positions, and streamlining of the command structure, the city was able to put more police officers on the street, even when the total number of police staff was reduced by seventy-four employees (to 10,227) because of Proposition 13.

Bradley went to the City Council to give an unprecedented speech on the revised budget he had submitted. In trying to assuage those who objected to the cuts, he had the difficult task of carrying out the people's mandate (as he said, "the people's message was clear") by defending serious reductions that he himself regretted. After all, the cutbacks and firings were not "Bradley's lay offs"; they were Proposition 13's. However, since the cuts had to be made, the reductions that he was proposing represented a consensus reached in discussions between himself and each departmental head; as such, they were what they mutually considered to be the best solution to a difficult situation.

The cuts in the budget had been very difficult for Bradley to make, and not everyone on the City Council agreed with them, but ultimately the budget did pass.

During the summer months, Bradley renewed his long-standing opposition to drilling in the Pacific Palisades by vetoing an ordinance that would have permitted Occidental Petroleum to move ahead on its project. He also called for the state to release gas-tax revenues to help pay for some of the $175-million budget cuts.

It may have been Bradley's concern for the youth of Los Angeles and his memories of what the Olympics of 1932 had meant to his own impoverished boyhood that made him so determined to bring the Olympic Games to Los Angeles for 1984, despite the possible political consequence to himself. In 1978, the mandate from the public seemed to focus entirely on cost-cutting, but Bradley had already set in motion the machinery for the 1984 Olympics. The years 1977 and 1978 were ones of intense behind-the-scenes struggle for Tom Bradley, who was determined to get the Olympics for Los Angeles, despite those who predicted it could only mean disaster.

In 1932, when Tom was fourteen years old, Los Angeles had hosted the Games of the Tenth Olympiad. The Olympic Village was only a dozen blocks away from his home, and the events taking place there piqued young Bradley's curiosity. He knew that he could not afford the $11 children's season admission ticket to all events at the Coliseum. The price might as well have been $1,000 a day in the height of the Depression. So Bradley peered through the fence at the Stadium, which looked to him like pictures he had seen of the ancient coliseums in Greece and Rome.

After the Games began, Bradley caught glimpses of the athletes who had come from around the world. Each day he read about the events, as he was delivering the *Record* on his paper route. When his track heroes were scheduled to compete, Tom Bradley, like so many other youngsters of that day, scaled the fence and took in a couple of hours of the Games. He was lucky enough to see one of the best events. "The one-hundred-meter dash turned out to be the most exciting event of the entire

Olympics," Bradley recalled. "That was the one where Eddie Tolan beat Ralph Metcalfe, who was the favorite." The memory of Eddie Tolan's historic one-hundred-meter dash never left Tom Bradley.

The Games were full of great accomplishments that Bradley remembered fondly. Who could forget Mildred "Babe" Didrikson's world records in the hurdles and the javelin throw and in the high jump? And then there was Buster Crabbe winning the only Olympic gold medal in swimming not taken by the Japanese team.

Four years later, in 1936, Tom Bradley had again been fascinated by the Games, this time listening to the competition reported by radio from Berlin. There was such a feeling of pride when his hero and role model, Jesse Owens, broke the color barrier and exposed the Nazi lie of Aryan superiority. That Olympics had served as a flame of hope to millions, among them the future Mayor of Los Angeles. They inspired him to believe that, given the chance, the true heroes would prevail. And they showed him that the Olympics could, if only for a short time, bring people together, making them forget their prejudices as they celebrated human excellence.

In 1928, California's voters had approved a one-million-dollar bond issue to fund the 1932 Los Angeles Olympics. Most of the money had gone to enlarge and renovate the stadium located near young Tom Bradley's home. Named the Los Angeles Memorial Coliseum, it was capable of seating 105,000 people. The twelve-thousand-seat Olympic Swim Stadium was also built, and the Olympic Auditorium. But after all this construction was paid for, when the Olympics were over and the bond repaid in full, the state found itself with a surplus of funds. Establishing a precedent that would not be repeated until the Games returned to Los Angeles in 1984, when it would be greatly improved upon, the 1932 Olympics were an economic success. A one-million-dollar profit was realized, and it was especially appreciated in the midst of the worldwide depression. Historian Andrew Strenk reports that over sixty conventions were held in the city to coincide with the Games, helping local businesses to reap $50 million during the two-week period.

But the benefits were not just monetary. Four-hundred-thousand visitors to the 1932 Olympics spread word that Los Angeles was one of the fastest growing centers of commerce, sports, and entertainment in the world, thus conferring international recognition on a city that had been so little known that many members of the International Olympic Committee had been uncertain of its location when it had first put in its bid for the 1932 Games. In fact, some IOC members wondered aloud if Los Angeles was a suburb of New York. So successful were the Games that, in 1939, a group of citizens formed the Southern California Committee for the Olympic Games (SCCOG), which would later prove to be the cornerstone of Mayor Tom Bradley's campaign to bring the Olympics back to Los Angeles. For years, they worked with city officials in an effort to do what only two other cities (Paris and London) had done—host the Games for a second time.

Mayors Bowron, Poulson, and Yorty all renewed the city's efforts to bring the Games back. But it would be under Tom Bradley's leadership that the Olympic flame would shine brightly over a capacity crowd at the Los Angeles Coliseum in 1984.

In 1974, less than a year after Bradley had begun his first term in office as Mayor, the city made a bid for the 1980 Games, a move just to put its name in contention for future games. (By then it seemed virtually certain that the USSR had secured the 1980 Olympics.) But Mayor Bradley wanted to set the stage for a serious bid for 1984. Anton Calleia recalls that, prior to the Los Angeles presentation in Vienna, a Russian representative asked him, "Why are you trying to spoil it for us?" Visibly upset, the Soviet official recalled how past bids by the Yorty administration had included "extravagant promises" and "delegates traveling all over the world spending dollars left and right." Calleia continues, "I told him that such antics were not Tom Bradley's style." The Soviet counterpart remained openly suspicious and retorted, "The last time you spent a lot of money; this time we will not be outspent!"

And there was immediate evidence. After the meeting, the Los Angeles delegation noticed while crowded on the Vienna streetcar returning to their hotel that the Russian counterparts sped by in sleek black limousines.

Although the Los Angeles bid for 1980 was rejected, it was done in an atmosphere of great cordiality, which offered hope

that a future bid would be looked upon with favor. Those returning home from the 1974 meeting with the International Olympic
Committee believed Los Angeles was closer to bringing the
Games back to the Coliseum than it had been at any time since
the Games were first held there. Attorney John Argue, president
of the SCCOG (and whose father had founded the SCCOG in
1939) remembers, "They liked Bradley, and the U.S. delegation
could sense it. He was sincere, and has a real spirit that reflects
the Olympics. He just hit it off with them from the very beginning."

Bradley strongly believed in the potential benefits of the
Olympics for Los Angeles, but he was also aware of the financial
quagmire that had trapped all other host cities under the IOC's
public-funding ruling. The Games themselves had always made
money, but the construction costs incurred in providing adequate
facilities had caused astronomical deficits. Taxpayers had had to
foot the bill for the $800,000 deficit in Munich in 1972. A much
more spectacular deficit appeared on the Olympics balance sheet
in 1976, when extravagant building costs and mismanagement
culminated in a $1-billion debt for Montreal. Reports were that
the 1980 Moscow Olympics would cost over $10 billion. Now
Bradley was trying to bring the Games to Los Angeles at a time
of growing public protest over high taxes.

Since the public would not stand for an increase in taxes,
Bradley knew that the only way he could sell the Olympics to
Los Angeles' citizens was to guarantee them that they would not
be taxed to pay for the Games. Money wasn't the only problem,
however.

There were rumors that the Olympics would result in an
influx of terrorists coming to Los Angeles, and fears of a repeat
of the 1972 Munich tragedy. Others opposed to the Games coming to Los Angeles cited the terrible traffic congestion that could
result. There were even those who warned of national security
threats—waves of Communists infiltrating Southern California
and fanning out throughout the United States. Anton Calleia
remembers, "Even on the Mayor's own staff there were those
who strongly opposed Bradley pursuing the Games, [who]
thought that it was politically a very damaging issue." But
Bradley resisted their advice. He saw the Olympics as a gold

mine, when no one else recognized it as such. He would do everything possible to turn the Olympic dream into a reality. Ethel Bradley remembers that, from taking office in 1973, her husband had been convinced that the Olympics would bring tremendous benefits to the city.

For the three years following the 1974 meeting in Austria, Bradley worked quietly behind the scenes building support for the Olympics. Knowing that the concern over finances was the major stumbling block, he maintained that Los Angeles would not construct the extremely expensive complexes that had over-burdened other cities. According to Bradley, "Los Angeles [needs] only a velodrome, archery range, and swimming pool." All other events could be held on existing facilities. The Mayor stressed that the Olympics should focus on world-class athletes, not "new buildings and extravagant frills."

This represented a bold departure from tradition. All previous Games had been publicly funded, but the 1984 Olympics in Los Angeles would be privately funded. And, Bradley was sure, they would more than cover costs.

All who had had previous contact with the IOC recognized the delicacy required to get the IOC to agree to place ultimate financial responsibility in private hands, rather than for the host city to assume the burden of all costs. What was called for was careful negotiating. Calleia remembers, "The IOC sees itself like the College of Cardinals, or like the knights of the Round Table. They can be very difficult to deal with." But the Mayor was always certain an agreement could be worked out for a privately financed Olympics. "We can stage the Games our way and set an example for the rest of the world," he persistently claimed. Bradley realized that the careful negotiating required to chal-lenge such tradition would be a true measure of his leadership and ability to involve the right people.

By 1977, over one hundred influential persons from the sports, political, and business communities had joined in the effort to work out a viable proposal, and the IOC was said to be open to hearing a proposal that would involve private financing.

The tax-weary Los Angeles public, however, was still du-bious, despite Bradley's reputation for fiscal prowess. In his first year in office, he had saved the city millions through his reexamination of the Yorty budget. Still, the 1972 and the 1976 Games had demonstrated that the Olympics, while noble in spirit, were financially disastrous for their hosts.

There was even talk of the demise of the Olympic Games because of the financial burden. Unlike past multi-city competitions, only two cities (Los Angeles and Teheran) were actively seeking the 1984 games. The 1980 Moscow Games were possible only because of heavy subsidization by the government, which recognized the propaganda uses of hosting the Olympics. By contrast, the federal government of the United States had already let it be known that financial support for the 1984 Games would not come from Washington. Los Angeles was on its own.

Another major hurdle for Bradley was the struggle to obtain City Council endorsement of the Olympic proposal, since one of the requirements of the IOC was a signed contract with the host city. Getting the Council to back the Games was no easy task, given the divergent constituencies and political agendas of each of the Council's fifteen members. All of Bradley's persuasive skills would be called upon, with the outcome unclear until the final vote.

The Council received the Mayor's proposal for the 1984 Olympics in the spring of 1977. In it Bradley tried to assuage some of the Council's financial concerns by calling attention to a "spartan approach" to the Games in Los Angeles. Argue, Calleia, and others presented arguments to the Council on behalf of Bradley's proposal. The proponents maintained that every effort would be made to secure federal and state support of the Games.

But there were many questions still to be answered concerning the financing of the Olympics, and the Council was persistent in raising them. One of the most astute critics was then City Controller, Ira Reiner, who today recalls their adversarial relationship: "As Controller, I had to raise concerns about the potential cost to the city of hosting the Olympics. I wasn't against the Games; I was merely against building state-of-the-art facilities at taxpayers' expense. . . . Although [Bradley and I] were at great odds at the time, he deserves the primary credit for bringing the Games to L.A. . . . it was Tom Bradley's determination that brought them here."

Despite the criticism by new Councilman Bob Ronka, Zev

The Olympics contract signing at the White House with Councilman John Ferraro and IOC President Lord Killanin, October 1978. (Courtesy of Los Angeles City Hall)

Ethel Bradley enjoying the garden at her new home, Getty House. (Bradley Family Collection)

At a dedication of the Los Angeles Children's Museum, 1979. (Courtesy of Los Angeles City Hall)

Yaroslavsky, Ernani Bernardi, and Joy Picus, City Council President John Ferraro maintained his long-standing support for the Games. Ultimately the City Council did give its approval that year in a unanimous vote, but another more crucial vote on the issue would be required in 1978, after the IOC had accepted Los Angeles' terms for hosting the Games.

Shortly after Bradley's reelection in April 1977, the Mayor began to consolidate the efforts to bring the Games to Los Angeles. For awhile many other American cities—Atlanta, Boston, Chicago, New Orleans, and New York—were vying for USOC approval of proposals to make the official United States bid before the International Olympic Committee.

As deadline for final bids approached, it was apparent that only two cities were still in the running—New York and Los Angeles—each representing not only different ends of the country, but also philosophies for hosting the Games. At the meeting in Colorado Springs, New York outspent the Los Angeles Committee ten-dollars to one. The "Big Apple's" proposal was along traditional lines—city financing, new grandiose facilities to surpass previous Olympics, and a projected $200–300 million deficit. Furthermore, the New York delegation had the support not only of the Mayor of the largest city in the country, but also the backing of the Governor and various other state and national politicians.

Los Angeles' proposal was much different, more in line with the reality of the times and echoing California Governor Jerry Brown's realization that we were living in an "era of limits." The City of Angels bid carried with it a new commercial theme—the Games would be privately funded, with a projected surplus.

After carefully surveying the situation and noting that the USOC seemed to be impressed with New York's glitzy approach, Bradley concluded the West Coast delegation needed further assistance. "We needed support from the Governor, and that's exactly what Los Angeles got." Anton Calleia contacted Gray Davis, Governor Brown's Chief of Staff and former Finance Director for Bradley's 1973 mayoral campaign, who called Governor Brown, who was in Santa Barbara. Brown agreed to fly immediately by private jet to Colorado Springs. He and Mayor

Bradley took charge with the other members in presenting Los Angeles' case to the USOC. It paid off.

Don Miller, Executive Director of the USOC from 1973 to 1985, had this to say about Bradley's efforts on behalf of the Olympics: "Personally, I can't speak more highly of any public official in this country than I can of Tom Bradley. Myself as well as the entire USOC knew L.A. could do the best job, primarily because of Mayor Bradley's dedication. He was very influential in ensuring the success of the Games at all stages of the process— no detail was too small for him to consider and work out."

Although Bradley won over the USOC, Los Angeles was still divided in its feelings about hosting the Olympics when Bradley, accompanied by a team composed of both supporters and skeptics, went off to Athens in May of 1978 in hopes of hammering out an agreement with the IOC that would be acceptable to all. A public-opinion poll taken around that time showed 59 percent of Los Angeles County voters opposed hosting the Games.

Stopping off in Berlin to meet with German trade leaders prior to attending the IOC meeting, Bradley learned from Calleia that IOC President Lord Killanin desired a private meeting with him concerning the financial responsibility issue, before the official IOC activities at the Acropolis that evening. The problem was that Bradley's flight was scheduled to arrive from West Germany only one hour before the Acropolis meeting. It looked like a logistical impossibility.

Calleia explained the problem to Bee Canterbury Lavery, who immediately departed for the airport to await Bradley's arrival. That late, scorching hot afternoon, traffic throughout Athens was at a standstill. And the hopes of a Bradley-Killanin meeting looked bleak.

A distraught Lavery jumped out of the stalled limousine, telling a police officer there was an important man stranded at the airport "who can save the Olympics for the world." She attempted to explain the nature of the meeting between Bradley and Lord Killanin. It seemed to Lavery that the police officer only understood one word—"Olympics"—but luckily that was enough to induce his cooperation.

Bradley stepped out of the plane, to be greeted by his Chief of

Protocol, motioning him away from the long lines of Customs and into a special Greek armored vehicle that escorted their limousine out of the airport. Lavery remembers Bradley turning to her on the way to the hotel to say, "Bee, I think you are overdoing it a bit this time!"

"I don't know how we made it back alive," Lavery remembers. "We must have broken every speed limit, run every light, and almost hit every car, but we made it." Bradley and Killanin met privately and discussed the sticky issue of financial responsibility.

At the general meeting, much to Bradley's surprise, the IOC renewed its demand that the city and country accept the complete financial responsibility of the Games. There would be no letter of exception to Rule 4, the one concerning financial responsibility, which Bradley had understood from IOC Executive Director Monique Berlioux would be publicly announced. The city was expected to obtain some kind of insurance against financial loss! It was a clear obstacle to Bradley and to those who hoped to bring the Olympics to Los Angeles. While they did agree to pursue such a policy, all knew it would not really be possible. They were merely biding for more time. However, on the question of financial liability, the Mayor refused to budge: "We had as an absolute condition of accepting the Games the requirement that our taxpayers not be held liable for any budget deficit. We were convinced that we could put on the Games without a deficit, but we also believed that it was essential to assure our taxpayers that they would not foot the Olympic-size bill that other cities had incurred."

After the meeting in Athens, Bradley decided on another tack in his efforts to procure the 1984 Games. To negotiate the IOC's adamant stand on financial responsibility, the chief executive turned to the private sector. He brought together a team of civic and business leaders to form the nucleus of an Organizing Committee (LAOC), to put together a proposal for a self-supporting Olympics and to negotiate with the IOC. Besides appointing SCCOG President Argue, committee members were Rodney Rood, special assistant to the Chairman of Atlantic Richfield; Howard Allen, President of the Los Angeles Area Chamber of Commerce and Chairman and Chief Executive Officer of Southern California

Edison Company; Justin Dart, industrialist and close friend of Ronald Reagan; David Wolper, film producer; Bill Robertson, labor leader; and Paul Ziffren, a prominent attorney and Democrat.

Tom Sullivan told the press that the LAOC's new offer of a privately financed Olympics to the IOC in Montreal in late June constituted the "city's last offer." According to Sullivan, if the proposal (which called for financial responsibility to rest with private interests rather than the city) was refused, "it's over."

On July 18, it seemed to be just that. Bradley received a cable from Lord Killanin informing him that the IOC had rejected the proposal for private rather than public financial responsibility. In a calculated strategic move, the Mayor then told the press that he had recommended to the City Council that Los Angeles withdraw its bid. As he explained at a press conference, he now felt that he had exhausted all possible options for arriving at a proposal mutually agreeable to the IOC and the citizens of Los Angeles.

The Council, especially those who had opposed the Olympic proposal all along, moved quickly to carry out the Mayor's decision. But just as it seemed that a 1984 Los Angeles Olympics was dead, there was a last-minute reprieve. One day after the initial denial, Bradley received another cable from Lord Killanin extending the city's deadline for a decision, and indicating the willingness of the IOC to meet again with the Los Angeles committee on the matter of financial responsibility. Furthermore, Anton Calleia, the Mayor's budgetary expert and official liaison for Bradley in the Olympic negotiations, heard from an IOC member that the international committee was willing to go along with the Los Angeles proposal if the private organizing committee was appointed by officials in public office. In a staring match with Tom Bradley, the IOC had blinked.

Over the weeks of the deadline extension, from July 31 to August 21, 1978, Bradley lobbied hard to change the financially important Rule 4. Throughout July, Bradley conducted intense telephone negotiations between President Robert J. Kane and Executive Director Don Miller of the USOC and IOC leaders Lord Killanin and Madame Berlioux, and John Argue of the LAOC. These negotiations centered on the precise language of the contracts that specified the liability to be assumed by the organizing committee and the USOC. The City of Los Angeles would not be financially liable.

There was widespread skepticism about the chances that the IOC would accept the offer, since Bradley was still insisting on private financing. And, as Councilman Ernani Bernardi stated to Bill Boyarsky of the *Los Angeles Times,* if the IOC would not approve of prudent cost-control measures, "the IOC had better find another pigeon." Meanwhile Councilmen Bernardi and Bob Ronka proposed that the question be put to the voters in November.

The Council, with fears of a financial fiasco, wished to ensure that there would be no financial liability for the city. Placing Charter Amendment N on the November 1978 ballot was the logical answer. If it passed, it would guarantee that the Olympic Games would not be financed by city government funds. The Los Angeles electorate backed it overwhelmingly (by 74 percent), sending a message to the politicians that the taxpayers would not pay for an Olympic party for the world. The Charter amendment borrowed language from a cost-control ordinance authored by Ferraro.

The LAPD also voiced the concern that the Olympics might prove to be beyond its capability in preserving the peace. Bradley received a letter from President Jimmy Carter on September 19, 1978, pledging the federal government's cooperation in providing adequate security for the Games. Conspicuously absent, however, was any mention of the federal funding that the city was counting on to help defray the financial costs to be incurred.

Although the IOC Executive Board was presented Los Angeles' proposal in late August, it was not formally announced that the entire General Assembly had approved it (by a vote of 74 to 3) until October 8, 1978. And on October 12, the City Council was scheduled to take a vote on the IOC contract. Bradley's struggle with his own Council was as serious a challenge as his negotiations with the IOC. As the *Los Angeles Times* said, Bradley's efforts to get an Olympic package passed by the City Council would amount to "a test of Bradley's political ability and his relationship with the Council." The next three days were among the toughest in Bradley's public career.

Councilman Marvin Braude, who terms himself an ardent Bradley supporter, singles out the night of October 11 as one of the most critical in his twenty-year tenure on the Council. Of the fifteen Council members, Braude was the only undecided vote; the Council was deadlocked at seven to seven. Forfeiting his world series tickets for the evening, Mayor Bradley invited Braude to Getty House. "I remember that Tom had called me and asked me to come to his house on a Sunday, and we talked about it. He never lobbied me before as he did so strongly that day. Although I was strongly influenced, I was already leaning in the direction of voting for the Olympics, because I felt that, in a civilized society, if you can't have an international Olympics in Los Angeles, you can't have it anywhere in the world. I could not vote against it out of fear."

In a squeaker, the Council approved the IOC contract the next day, with Braude's vote securing the necessary majority of eight.

What had once seemed like an impossible dream became a reality in the Roosevelt Room of the White House on October 20, 1978. There, Bradley and Lord Killanin signed the contract formally awarding the 1984 Games to Los Angeles. Other important Olympic supporters were in attendance at the ceremony— SCCOG President John Argue, IOC Director Monique Berlioux, Los Angeles Mayoral Aide Anton Calleia, City Council President John Ferraro, USOC President Robert Kane, USOC Executive Director Don Miller, and White House Staffer Jack Watson, Jr. At the same moment, the Los Angeles Coliseum torch, which had blazoned over the Olympics of 1932, was once again lit to commemorate the occasion. To Bradley, it was not only a victory for Los Angeles, but a tribute to the United States to host the Olympics.

In November 1978, the Mayor submitted a proposal requesting federal funding and the help of the Army Corp of Engineers in the construction of particular Olympic sites on federal flood control land in the San Fernando Valley. He formed an interdepartmental city committee to submit plans and to help coordinate the municipal efforts with those of the private organizing committee. He also appointed Deputy Mayor Ray Remy as his Olympic liaison.

In early 1979, the LAOC was expanded by over fifty new members, to become the LAOOC, Los Angeles Olympic Organizing Committee; it elected John Argue as Founding Chairman and Paul Ziffren as Founding Secretary.

During this inital phase of organizing the Olympic event, the newly formed LAOOC was jockeying with the USOC directors for control over the Games. In December 1978, a basic agreement was consummated with the USOC at Colorado Springs. Bill Robertson, who had been responsible for much of the support of organized labor to bring the bid to fruition, proved to have indispensable negotiating skills. A decision was reached in which the LAOOC controlled three-quarters (fifty-five appointments) of the positions on the Board of Directors and Executive Board of the Organizing Committee, with the USOC controlling the remainder. The LAOOC would receive 40 percent of the potential financial surplus.

On March 1, 1979, the final contract was signed by Count de Beaumont of France, head of the IOC's Finance Commission, IOC Director Monique Berlioux, USOC leaders Robert Kane and Don F. Miller, and John Argue and Rodney Rood of the LAOOC for the City of Los Angeles.

Though Argue was offered the Presidency of the LAOOC to cap his six-year struggle to bring the Olympics to Los Angeles, he declined the offer. A nationwide search for a director was conducted by Korn/Ferry International. Ultimately, from a field of candidates, which had included General Alexander Haig, National Football Commissioner Pete Roselle, and Ed Steidle, Chairman of the May Company, they finally chose Peter Ueberroth, whose entrepreneurial spirit was deemed the essential ingredient for the successful management of these "Spartan" Games. Paul Ziffren was elected chairman of the LAOOC by the Executive Board. The choices were confirmed on March 26, 1979, less than two thousand days before the opening of the Olympic Games on July 28, 1984. In February 1980, Harry Usher, then an attorney with Ueberroth's company, was brought aboard as the Executive Vice-President/General Manager of the Olympics. Six months after the Mayor's request for federal funding, there was still no official word from the White House, even after a meeting with President Carter that included Remy, Bradley, and Ueberroth.

Television would be a major source of funds. David Wolper negotiated a mammoth contract with ABC—$225 million, three times the amount paid by NBC for the Moscow Olympics. Wolper comments, "I formed an advisory committee of people in business, from sports, the networks, and others that knew the business. It was a given that we here in the entertainment capital of the world who knew the players for over thirty years would understand the television negotiating process better than the IOC. We could get a better deal." To remove from consideration those without serious intentions, Wolper required that each bid be accompanied by a $750,000 check. "This allowed the LAOOC to carry on operations," Wolper explained. With negotiations taking place at his home, Wolper and his committee received bids. After the negotiations had been completed and signed by ABC and the LAOOC in Nagoya, Japan, in September 1979, Bradley joined the committee at Wolper's home for a celebration. It represented another departure from the IOC's long-standing rules. A private body had negotiated the television rights for the Olympics.

The early 1980s would see the LAOOC embarked on a for-midable task—finding the private donations for the necessary funding of the Games. The License Committee, led by Card Walker, negotiated multi-million dollar contracts with blue-chip corporations. Official sponsors, from an auto maker to a travel company, emerged, with each spending at least $4 million for the Olympic logo of official sponsorship. These included Buick, McDonalds, American Express, First Interstate Bank, ARCO, Levi Strauss, and Fuji, among others. Ira Reiner, acting in his new capacity as City Attorney, with Tom Bradley's support, negotiated with the LAOOC to obtain the best financial package for the city, although according to Reiner, "they wanted to give the city as little money as possible."

15

Laying the Groundwork for Governor

> *"Hands are the heart's land-scape."*
>
> —Pope John Paul II

With the 1981 mayoral primary election approaching, a citizens committee of Democrats and Republicans, led by Century City attorney Peter D. Kelley and Donald G. Livingston of Carter Hawley Hale Stores, urged Bradley "to seriously consider running for a third term." Bradley recognized that many of the plans and projects he had begun for Los Angeles necessitated his continued attention. Equally clear to the Mayor was that, unlike Yorty's second term, which was characterized by drift and a lack of direction, the Bradley team's partnership with business was still on a productive track.

Bradley, who was on everybody's list as a front-runner for the Democratic nomination for Governor, stepped up his citywide appearances. There were indications that the 1981 election would be a rematch of the 1973 race. Seventy-one-year-old Sam Yorty was thinking about running again for Mayor in November 1980, despite his poor showing in the June Republican Primary for U.S. Senate. He had already charged that the increase in crime within the city was due to Bradley's appointment of minorities and women, or—as Yorty identified it—the "quota" system. There were others who entertained the idea of challenging Bradley, including LAPD Chief Daryl Gates and City Controller Ira Rei-

Mayor Bradley declares January 13, 1981, "Ronald Reagan Day" in Los Angeles. (Courtesy of Los Angeles City Hall)

Gregory Peck, Lew Wasserman, Bradley, and Warren Christopher at a gubernatorial fundraiser. (Courtesy of Rick Browne)

ner. But Bradley enjoyed such a high approval rating that the bets among political insiders was that he was unbeatable. Ultimately, only Yorty decided to take on the challenge, declaring his candidacy in January 1981.

In retrospect, Yorty says that he opposed Bradley in 1981 "because I thought he needed some opposition, and I got more votes then than anybody since without any party affiliation under my name. . . . One of the reasons that I ran was because of his anti-Police Commission. The Police don't even dare make an honest mistake under the Bradley administration, because they will be criticized, and as a result I think they are more reluctant to take a chance. Policemen have to make decisions on the spur of the moment. When they make an honest mistake, you have to back them up and Bradley's Police Commission never has." Yorty's feeling about the Police Commissioners appointed by Bradley is shared by former Police Chief Ed Davis, who retired from the force in 1977 and is now a conservative GOP State Senator. Davis says, "Bradley appointed a bunch of liberals to the Police Commission. The liberals were out to fight rather than work with the department." Though long-time antagonists, Bradley and Davis have at least a grudging respect for each other—unlike the unmitigated antagonism between Bradley and Yorty.

Press Secretary Tom Sullivan served as surrogate speaker during the early days of the campaign, when Bradley chose not to dignify Yorty's words with a response. He asserted that Bradley's pro-police bias had resulted in a police budget that had more than doubled during his seven years in office. During those years, funds devoted to police protection had averaged forty percent of the total city budget.

Yorty ran true to form, attacking Bradley for "lack of leadership," for his close alliance with "the Downtown crowd," and, as usual, for his race. A couple of weeks before the April election, Yorty told the Venice Chamber of Commerce that "black people are really racist," a claim he supported by saying that "they vote for black people because they are black."

With the big guns like David Garth coming in from New York to design television commercials for Bradley, it might have seemed that the Bradley camp took serious heed of the Yorty challenge. But a more likely explanation was that the 1981 campaign, under the direction of Bill Heckman, was intended to be a dress rehearsal for the gubernatorial race Bradley was expected to make in 1982.

With Yorty always on the attack, there were those within the Bradley campaign who urged the Mayor to adopt a more aggressive campaign schedule to be sure of matching his 59-percent victory margin of 1977. Yet Bradley made few campaign appearances, choosing instead to go about performing his mayoral duties, remaining above the fray. He did, however, make a lot of speeches, after Yorty made the mistake of challenging Bradley to cite one good thing that he had done for the city in his seven years as Mayor. It was a challenge Bradley couldn't resist answering, an opening to cite his impressive record of accomplishments.

In speeches throughout the city, Bradley stressed his administration's success at putting more police officers on Los Angeles' streets. He emphasized his fiscal record of offering balanced budgets throughout his tenure. He pointed with pride to the creation of jobs and the redevelopment that had occurred throughout the city, and to the cooperative spirit that now characterized the city's diverse neighborhoods. He mentioned the thirty new community centers for seniors and facilities for the handicapped built during his administrations.

There were literally dozens of substantive accomplishments Bradley could point to. One of the most significant was the transformation of the Port of Los Angeles, which was then in progress, thanks to a five-year $500-million modernization plan, financed primarily by Harbor revenues, not tax dollars. Net income to the Port increased from $5.9 million, when Bradley took office in 1973, to $42.8 million in 1981–82.

The City Loan Development Program, under the leadership of Adrian Dove, which stimulates private investment in business through loans of public money, had been responsible for creating thousands of new jobs since the program's inception in 1979. The Community Development Department had helped thousands of young families of moderate means to buy homes at a time when skyrocketing mortgage rates would have made it virtually impossible without the innovative financing techniques worked out by the CDD. The Vermont-Slauson Neighborhood Shopping Center, which opened in 1981, was the first major economic development in the South-Central district of the city in sixteen years, and it created nine hundred jobs.

Yorty continued to try to aggravate racial tensions by bringing up the issue that Alan Robbins had embraced in 1977—busing. The Olympics were also brought into the contest, with Yorty charging that "Bradley had lied to the people of the Valley" about his plans to construct facilities for the Games in the Sepulveda Basin area despite the opposition of local residents. And, as usual, he accused the *Los Angeles Times* of being a "Bradley stooge."

The Bradley campaign chose to ignore Yorty's racist charges and discuss real issues, pointing out how federal cuts in programs were having a severe impact on the employment of unskilled workers and pledging to work with private enterprise to help alleviate rising unemployment and federal cuts emanating from Washington. Bill Robertson announced the Los Angeles County Federation of Labor's endorsement of Bradley's reelection bid. Jerry Cremins of the Building Trades Union added his powerful support. This overshadowed the endorsement of Yorty by the firefighters and utilities unions who were upset by the Mayor's position against pay increases for their members.

During the campaign, former Vice-President Walter F. Mondale, a strong contender for the party's 1984 presidential nomination, dropped by City Hall, pledging his support to Bradley. The Mondale-Bradley friendship had a long history. The Mayor had delivered the nominating speeches for the Vice-President at both the 1976 and 1980 Democratic National Conventions, and would later give the speech nominating him for President in 1984.

A mid-March poll by the *Los Angeles Times* revealed that Bradley enjoyed an 85 percent approval rating statewide. Reporter Bill Boyarsky analyzed the findings in regard to the possibility of a Bradley gubernatorial bid. The demographics of those who did not support a Bradley candidacy would prove prophetic of the gubernatorial election results of 1982. There was less support for Bradley on the part of "law-and-order oriented voters who are pro-police, anti-gun control, pro-death penalty and who are hostile to the courts." Boyarsky noted that the findings suggested the Mayor could be in trouble from a candidate "capable of mounting a major law-and-order campaign." The *Times* article also raised the race issue: "Political strategists have speculated that the fact that Bradley is black with a reputation as a Democratic liberal could hurt him in a statewide race against a well-financed conservative Republican candidate."

Meanwhile the Bradley campaign designed a hard-hitting media spot explaining Bradley's record on crime. Acknowledging that "every big city has a crime problem," Bradley told the viewing audience that "Here in Los Angeles we are doing something about it." Recalling his own days on the police force, he said, "If you're a cop walking a beat, you know what the fear of crime does to families in the neighborhoods. During my twenty-one years on the police force, I saw that fear first-hand." Extolling the Bradley record in fiscal matters and in preserving the peace, the spot concluded, "That's why in spite of my fight to control city spending, I've doubled the police budgets and now my new anti-crime program will mean more police on the streets, tough new efforts to stop gang violence, and mandatory sentences for violent offenders."

Bradley commercials proved to be a major part of the last-minute blitz by the incumbent. The *Times* reported that over $289,000 was paid to the Garth Agency in New York in March out of the $630,000 raised by the Bradley reelection campaign. The media campaign and low-key approach paid off handsomely for Bradley. On primary election day he received over 64 percent of the vote, thus eliminating the need for a runoff and giving him an even greater margin than the 59 percent he had enjoyed in 1977. Pressed for details of how his smashing victory would affect his decision on running for Governor, Tom Sullivan told reporters that the city's budget was at the top of the Mayor's list of post-election concerns. But to Democrats across the state, it was clear that Tom Bradley had positioned himself for a run for the statehouse. Pictured on the front page of the *Los Angeles Times* with Governor Jerry Brown, who had walked into the celebration unexpectedly and grabbed his hand in a symbol of triumph, Bradley told reporters that he "needed a few days to savor this victory."

Victory night was deeply gratifying to Bradley, and proved satisfying to the First Lady of Los Angeles as well. Watching the

Dodgers game rather than the election returns in the Mayor's suite, Ethel celebrated not only four more years at City Hall but a win for Dodger Blue over San Francisco. Yorty proved to be as salty in defeat as he had been throughout the election, telling supporters, "It looks like the man bought a pretty good election."

Yorty was complaining that the minority vote had done him in. ("You have seventeen percent blacks in the city and they vote ninety percent and the whites only vote forty percent.") But in fact, Bradley had carried the mainly white Valley for the first time in his four mayoral contests. His 50.4 percent margin there represented a five-percentage-point increase over the 1977 totals. The *Times* analysis highlighted the potential significance of this statistic in a gubernatorial race: "The Valley is largely white and the fact that Bradley carried it will fortify arguments that, despite being black, he would be a potent candidate for Governor next year."

While Los Angeles was busy with a mayoral campaign and its two-hundredth-birthday celebration, the rest of the state continued to speculate on probable candidates for Jerry Brown's job in 1982. By April 1981, Republican candidates had over $3 million in their campaign coffers. The Republican race looked as if it would be between Lieutenant Governor Mike Curb, considered the Golden Boy of the GOP, and Attorney General George Deukmejian, a cautious law-and-order candidate and favorite of the Republican outsiders. Curb had been running for Governor since assuming his office in Sacramento in 1978. The former record executive and self-made millionaire had received national attention by issuing controversial directives while assuming the gubernatorial duties when Jerry Brown was out of the state. His strategy was to try to force Deukmejian out of the running early in the campaign. Another GOP gubernatorial hopeful was San Diego Mayor Pete Wilson, though he would later decide to concentrate on a run for U.S. Senate.

On the Democratic side, the odds-on favorite was Tom Bradley. Yet, there was conjecture that former U.S. Senator John V. Tunney, State Treasurer Jess Unruh, and Controller Ken Cory might also try for the top spot. Bradley Campaign Chairman Nelson Rising noted that he was particularly pleased by polls showing his candidate convincingly beating all three GOP hopefuls, the smallest margin of victory being eleven percent.

Publicly, Bradley continued to describe himself as only a "possible" candidate. There were reports in June that an initial campaign committee would be formed following the Mayor's inaugural. The polls were encouraging, the attention flattering, but it was essential to lay the necessary groundwork with the state's Democratic leaders prior to any announcement. Finally, in January of 1982, Bradley made it official, saying he would run for Governor because "I want to revive the promise and opportunity of the American Dream." His announcement was covered by *Life* magazine, which summed up his record as Mayor in these words: "As mayor, he has cut taxes, revitalized the downtown business district, brought the police under civilian control, produced nine consecutive balanced budgets, set Los Angeles on the road to mass transit and currently enjoys, in a city where the black population is less than one-fifth, an approval rating of some 85 percent."

The intensity of the battle between the Curb and Deukmejian forces was reflected by both GOP candidates breaking all records in campaign expenditures for a primary. In the first six months of the campaign, Curb spent $3.1 million as compared to Deukmejian's $2.6 million. Curb wrapped himself in traditional conservative political garb by calling for cuts in social welfare and for the recall of the "liberal Rose Bird" as Chief Justice, while attacking Deukmejian as a do-nothing career politician who had voted for pay raises for himself and his cronies. The Deukmejian campaign's cornerstone was its emphasis on his political experience and maturity in comparison to Curb, who had been elected to his first political office as Lieutenant Governor.

While polls showed Curb maintaining his lead over the Attorney General, Deukmejian Campaign Manager Bill Roberts told the press that the election would be turned around by a new series of attack ads and a mailer to be sent out the weekend before the primary.

Three-hundred-thousand dollars worth of attack spots in behalf of Deukmejian's candidacy hit the airwaves in those final days. One of the thirty-second spots produced by Carl Haglund raised the question of Republican loyalty, pointing out that Mike Curb had not registered to vote until he was twenty-nine years old. In the spot, the Attorney General told voters, "Mike Curb's smear campaign deliberately misleads Republican voters." He further explains, "Curb has a lot of nerve attacking me when he didn't care enough about our state or nation to vote. He says for eight years he was too busy. Too busy to vote for Ronald Reagan or any Republican." Another Deukmejian spot warned voters, "There are a lot of things you don't know about Mike Curb." The hard-hitting style served as a preview of what the Democratic candidate might expect in the general election.

There was little controversy on the Democratic ticket. The Garth, Friedman, and Morris advertising spots focused on educating the state's voters about the positions and programs of Tom Bradley. The $1-million Bradley media blitz during the primary dwarfed the expenditures of his principal opponents, State Senate Floor Majority Leader John Garamendi and former California Health and Welfare Secretary Mario Obledo, who had spent less than $800,000 combined. The photogenic Garamendi had increased his visibility statewide and strengthened his position for a future statewide campaign. Obledo, a popular Hispanic leader and one of the first in the state's history to mount a statewide campaign for the top spot, represented the promise of the future for Hispanic leadership in Sacramento. But neither Garamendi nor Obledo were able to mount a serious challenge to the well-oiled Bradley effort.

The results of the June 9 primary demonstrated the strength of Bradley's ability to attract voters on a statewide basis. Bradley captured 67 percent of the vote. State Senator John Garamendi was a distant second with 24 percent and Mario Obledo garnered 5 percent.

On the Republican side, Lieutenant Governor Mike Curb, the odds-on favorite to win the GOP nomination (by ten percentage points, according to the last pre-election poll), had been upset by Attorney General George "Duke" Deukmejian by a six-point margin, 51 to 45. But in his victory, Deukmejian faced charges by

Mayor Bradley welcomes Japanese Prime Minister Yasushiro Nakasone to Los Angeles' 200th birthday celebration. (Courtesy of Los Angeles City Hall)

On a trade mission to Israel with Prime Minister Menachem Begin. (Courtesy of Los Angeles City hall)

L.A.'s star pitcher throwing the first ball at Dodger Stadium. (Bradley Family Collection)

the Curb campaign that he had engaged in "smear tactics" during the last weekend of the campaign, part of a long history of questionable tactics he had used.

Bradley was determined to wage an open campaign, to keep the discussion focused on who was best suited to lead the state into the next century, to enhance the hope and promise of the California dream. With that in mind, the Democratic candidate proposed that both gubernatorial candidates sign a "fair campaign code" agreement. He presented his proposal to George Deukmejian the day after winning the primary.

The Deukmejian campaign balked at signing the agreement. Yes, they wanted a clean campaign, based on the issues, maintained Bill Roberts, but Bradley's proposal was unacceptable. Roberts cited one section of the proposal as a particular stumbling block. The code called for each side to make available to the opposition all commercials and brochures twenty-four hours before they were to be shown or disseminated. Nelson Rising maintained the proposed code would impede any smear effort or questionable strategy. Furthermore, it could help ensure that the campaign's focus remained on pertinent issues facing the state's next chief executive.

According to Roberts, giving an opponent information like that had little to do with a fair campaign code. Why would the Deukmejian organization provide Bradley or anyone else with a preview of their campaign strategy? To do so would give the opponent the time needed to construct a response or counterargument to an issue that might have been weeks or even months in researching? Timing and the element of surprise were important factors in campaigning.

Roberts certainly was not going to agree to anything that did the homework for his opponent. No, the Deukmejian campaign would not agree to showing its cards or previewing the issues it planned to raise against the candidate they referred to as Los Angeles' "ceremonial Mayor." The decision had nothing to do with fairness. It was a matter of common political sense, and anyone who was out to win would realize it.

If winning was the only real criterion, Roberts carried impressive credentials and a strong record. He had engineered many successful campaigns that had produced winning candidates in past elections. Roberts and Stuart Spencer had crafted the campaign strategy that catapulted an activist actor into the Governor's mansion in Sacramento in 1967. Among his colleagues, Roberts was known as a master at formulating the winning combination, albeit sometimes at the expense of commonly accepted ethical standards.

The Bradley team opted to launch its campaign before the traditional Labor Day speeches, hoping to establish the campaign agenda by seizing the initiative. The Deukmejian effort, on the other hand, seemed content to maintain a low profile during the summer months, despite the eight-point edge Bradley had in the polls after the primary.

Bradley sought to establish the state's sagging economy as the number-one issue of the campaign. "Given the fact that more people were in unemployment lines than at any time since the Great Depression, I wanted to highlight how I thought we could work to put the hope and promise back into the California dream." He directed his staff to develop position papers and program proposals for getting the California economy back on track and Californians back to work. Speeches and commercials highlighting the problem—that California workers were getting "pinkslips instead of paychecks"—were prevalent during the summer months.

Given Bradley's success in managing the state's largest city, the campaign hoped to position him as the only candidate qualified to put California back on the road to economic recovery. Nine years of running the City of Los Angeles without increasing taxes (in fact, under the stringent economics imposed by Proposition 13) made for a very impressive record.

In contrast with Bradley's positive approach of outlining detailed programs and proposals on numerous issues directly linked to the economy, the Deukmejian campaign opted for a negative tack, charging that Bradley was a "big-spending liberal." Bill Roberts repeated the "ceremonial Mayor" charge and told reporters there had not been "a hell of a lot of progress in Los Angeles during his nine years as Mayor."

Defending his record and his own proposals to revitalize the economy, Bradley criticized the Deukmejian campaign for its lack of specifics. He characterized his opponent as a "politician who preaches the politics of patience," while over "four thousand Californians each day are joining the unemployment lines." And, when relevant, he did not hesitate to criticize national policy, even though his campaign polls showed that many of his supporters expressed approval of President Reagan.

For example, in one of Bradley's first major speeches of the campaign, given at the California Building Trades Convention in late June, he recalled Deukmejian's support of a Reagan veto of the 1982 Mortgage Assistance Bill. The bill, which enjoyed strong bipartisan support in Congress, could have provided immediate relief for workers in the depressed California housing market, as well as financial relief to homebuyers. Its veto further depressed the California housing industry.

Polls after the June primary suggested that, in addition to the economy, crime was a major concern of California voters. George Deukmejian was expected to make it a cornerstone of his campaign. But the Bradley team wasn't ready to concede the law-and-order voters to Deukmejian.

Dodo Meyer recalls, "We thought that Tom Bradley's record spoke for itself on this issue—he spent twenty-one years on the police force and was the only candidate running to have faced real crime on real streets." Meyer was joined by other key campaign personnel in her belief that stressing this aspect of Bradley's life in public service would help dispel concern over Bradley's race among the statewide voters.

An article in the *Los Angeles Times* seemed to offer encouraging support for this perspective. Professor Charles Henry, a noted political scientist from Berkeley, addressed what the *Times* called the election's "hidden issue"—"Bradley had preempted the traditional grounds, the subtle grounds, that the race issue be raised on, namely, law and order." Henry believed Bradley's early commercials, which stressed his tough stands on crime, effectively explained his impressive record to voters unfamiliar with his past. Henry concluded, "He's a former Los Angeles police officer, and I think that's been a tremendous assistance to him in his entire political career."

Several Bradley supporters wanted to believe Henry's optimistic assessment. They concurred that Bradley's record would speak for itself, that his police work and nine years as Mayor of a city with a diverse heterogeneous constituency provided credible evidence for even the most skeptical voter.

Still, George Deukmejian's tough campaigns of the past had been fraught with questionable tactics, charges of smears, and last-minute mailers. The recent primary was a case in point. And in 1978, in the election for Attorney General, Yvonne Brathwaite Burke had charged that Deukmejian's campaign against her had had numerous racial overtones, expressed in a kind of code. For instance, particular commercials proclaimed Duke's opposition to busing, welfare, and other social programs—all issues associated in the public's mind with minorities.

Such tactics were standard operating procedure for Bradley's various political opponents. They had been cornerstones of his challengers' campaigns in his four mayoral elections. But, with the exception of 1969, he had successfully countered such appeals to racism. So Bradley did not believe race would be a significant issue in the 1982 campaign. He had always publicly and privately held that Californians would make their decision based on the strength of the records and programs of the candidates. He stressed that this was 1982, not 1969. In this day and age, the facts would surely overpower any fears.

After the June primary, using a technique that most of Bradley's opponents over the years had tried, Bill Roberts assured reporters and the press that "Bradley's race would not be an issue" in the upcoming campaign—thereby ensuring that the public was reminded (in case it had forgotten) that Bradley was black.

After the Roberts pronouncement, newspapers throughout the state dutifully fell into step and reported that the Deukmejian campaign had pledged that "race would not be an issue" in the gubernatorial contest. In the story carrying Roberts' statement, and in articles that ran throughout the campaign, the fact of Bradley's race rarely went unmentioned. In the *Los Angeles Times* and other papers, the "non-issue" was generally highlighted in coverage that ran along the lines of "In his bid to become the nation's first black Governor, Tom Bradley. . . ."

Phil Depoian claims that the Deukmejian campaign's efforts to keep the race issue in the media headlines were part of a deliberate political strategy: "There's no doubt that they looked at these references to the Mayor's race as effective in the effort to skirt discussion and debate on the real issues. . . . As long as they could keep the public and the journalists' minds off the real issues and the records, they could hope to benefit by playing to people's stereotypes and fears." In response, Bill Roberts has denied these assertions, indicating that "The media are the ones that were preoccupied with that issue, and I only responded to their questions."

But the effort to counter the general constituency's focus on the race issue produced the reverse problem within the black community. According to Bishop H. H. Brookins, "Because Mayor Bradley let some of his campaign staff pull him away from his grassroots approach to campaigning, to go more with a media effort, many blacks believed that he was neglecting them and they didn't get excited about the campaign." Leroy Berry adds, "The field operation favored statistics over direct contact, and this hurt Tom."

This was a feeling shared by many Bradley enthusiasts throughout the state, and not just black supporters. They wanted to help and offered their services, but did not feel welcome by the Mayor's gubernatorial campaign staff. Many persisted in their efforts and eventually were brought into the campaign. Still others were disappointed by what they believed was a campaign style that ran counter to the candidate. Merced supporter Rick Rank states, "The field operation tended to favor computer printouts over the phone call, and that doesn't work here, nor anywhere else." Tom Bradley was known for his direct contact with the people. Yet the grassroots effort, the Mayor's style of politics, seemed to be missing from the overall campaign agenda.

One disenchanted supporter in 1982 was Kerman Maddox, Chief of Staff to Assemblywoman Maxine Waters, who would later help engineer Bradley's 1985 reelection effort in the black community. He recalls, "We didn't see the Mayor down in the community enough, and I think that was a mistake." Maddox echoed a commonly heard complaint in the campaign, "I called the headquarters and told them, look I don't want money, just the opportunity to help out. . . . No one returned my calls, and when I finally went in to see Raye Cunningham about it, I was told that the campaign staff had already made decisions, and as a result, many of us, including the black leadership, felt we were locked out of the campaign."

Similar stories echoed throughout the state's diverse constituencies. Deputy Mayor Grace Montanez Davis faulted the overall strategy, "I think the top Bradley campaign strategists thought the minority communities were givens, and spent most of the effort working on getting out the vote in the other areas." The result would be apathetic minority vote, which affected the final vote tab in November.

There were serious problems with the grassroots effort in 1982. As Florence Burns, a Bradley supporter in San Francisco, remembers, "The field organization ignored the north and the traditional powers in the area. The viewpoint was that phone banks and computers could take the place of old-fashioned grassroots." Art Gastelum adds, "The challenge was to combine the two approaches—the new technology with the Mayor's proven grassroots approach. But I am not sure that the campaign ever realized this or took the suggestions seriously until it was too late."

16

A Dream for California

*"I'll be one Governor who will
make a difference."*

—Tom Bradley

The Bradley campaign staff reflected this divided approach. Tom Sullivan recalls that some of Bradley's longtime associates wanted to run the statewide campaign according to their proven blueprint for mayoral campaigns. But other people argued that the state's size demanded a more sophisticated approach. It was, as one staffer put it, "a different breed of cat." The new technology of telephone and computer banks was recommended by Joe Trippi, brought on board to run the field operation.

With Nelson Rising functioning as the campaign Chairman and operating out of his Glendale office, the campaign's state headquarters on Wilshire was presided over by Phil Depoian, who, as General Campaign manager, spent most of his time traveling with Bradley. Jules Radcliff, a Century City attorney, who had served as general counsel to the mayoral campaign in 1981, had come on board in April as Deputy Campaign Manager to oversee the day-to-day activities at the Wilshire Boulevard general headquarters. Radcliff explains his increased visibility as reflective of the recognition that "the system of management had not kept pace with the staff's growth and responsibility in running a statewide campaign." There had been key changes after the primary. Gene Moskovitch replaced Dwayne Peterson as Issues Coordinator. Bill Heckman, Bradley's 1981 mayoral re-election Campaign Manager, who had held the position of Field Coordinator, had also left the campaign due to differences with top personnel.

Supporter Zulene Payne and Senator Edward M. Kennedy at a Bradley for Governor fundraiser at the Century Plaza Hotel, 1982. (Photo by Rick Browne: Courtesy of Zulene Payne

1982 MAPA Convention, from left, Bradley, U.S. Congressman Ed Roybal, partially hidden State Assemblywoman Gloria Molina, State Assemblyman Richard Alatorre. (Courtesy of Los Angeles City Hall)

Because of what one insider called "a lot of strong person-alities and egos," tension during the last two months among the Bradley campaign staff was high. Tom Sullivan notes, "it really came down to the struggle between the old guard, who thought they had more credibility, and the new members on the campaign, who were quick to point out flaws and offer input."

A key Bradley strategist notes, "There was a need to have a real administrator at the top, and we lacked that. Instead of correcting the problem, the Rising campaign tried a patch job, of bringing in an administrative type person, Jules Radcliff, who also had interest in policy, and the result was two different directions in the campaign." As the campaign picked up steam, so did the conflict between the camps. Raye Cunningham, states, "The big mistake was the fighting from the top of the fort, because we never knew who was really in charge." The result was "two different elements in the campaign office, Phil and Jules who rarely talked to each other, and didn't want anybody else to either." Tom Sullivan notes, "It came down at times to a battle of turf, of who does what . . ., things that Nelson and Phil should have straightened out." From Radcliff's perspective, "There's a natural and expected degree of creative tension, and I believe that during my months there, we were humming along, a sort of synergistic effect." Still, to other staffers, such conflicts seemed dysfunctional.

Efforts would be made throughout the campaign to make peace, but there were also numerous power plays among the key players. The scheduling responsibility was handed to longtime Bradley aide Letty Herndon Brown, while Virginia "Jinx" Ring and Helen Magee would aid in the fundraising effort. Letty Herndon Brown recalls, "There was too much self-interest and bad-mouthing going on between supporters of Depoian and his long-time opponents, headed by Radcliff, about the direction of the campaign." Tom Sullivan adds, "There was an absence of any real teamwork and the one trait that is always stressed in a Tom Bradley campaign—loyalty." The overall result was that, by election day, such strains had fragmented the campaign staff, putting them on what Sandra Farrar described as "a dual-track campaign with two different leaders."

Offering his own perspective, Phil Depoian states, "There

seemed to be an effort about three or four weeks out by Nelson to have Jules be more of an administrator, to exercise more control at the campaign office." Adding that he didn't think during that period of time that he spent more than "four minutes at the general headquarters" due to his schedule of traveling with Bradley, Depoian adds, "I said to myself, what sense does this make, four weeks from the election, to start changing things around?"

Radcliff, who for all practical purposes left the campaign in October due to medical reasons, states, "I had fulfilled my commitment made to Nelson and Sam, and personally am not aware of any major changes at that time by Nelson or anyone; for the most part, by then, we were on automatic pilot." Though such disagreement and disarray could hardly fail to damage the campaign efforts, Meg Gilbert, on loan from California Labor, remembers that the common belief was that, "despite the campaign and the lack of coordination, Tom Bradley would still win on his personal merits alone." Mike Gage, Campaign Manager for Lieutenant Governor candidate Leo McCarthy, recalls, "From our perspective, we had no idea who was in charge at the Bradley headquarters."

Deputy Mayor Ray Remy, who in his own words, "consciously stayed out of the organizational issues of the campaign," but who did serve as an important touchstone and practical critic for public statements, speeches, and policies, was aware of such conflicts early in the campaign. Remy recalls talking to Bradley about the differences in the staff, and notes the reason why the candidate did not deal with the issue immediately: "Tom Bradley is about the best executive and administrator in the country, but he is uncomfortable in dealing with people close to him, in terms of their strengths and weaknesses. . . . It stems from his strong streak of loyalty; it's very hard for him to do something to someone who he perceives has been loyal to him."

One early concern of the Bradley campaign was an initiative that would appear on the November ballot, calling for handgun registration. Nelson Rising's political experience told him this would be an emotional measure and would serve as a lightning rod in bringing many conservatives to the polls who might otherwise not bother to vote. Rising urged Bradley to oppose the measure because of its political ramifications.

There were others within the Bradley campaign who urged the Mayor to take no position. Such an approach would be politically expedient. Bradley would not be identified with the controversial measure.

Yet, during his years on the police force, Bradley had seen too many citizens and colleagues murdered by the cheap Saturday-night-special handguns that this measure would specifically help to control. Opponents of the measure, including George Deuk-mejian, charged the initiative ran counter to constitutional rights of citizens to bear arms. Supporters of the initiative argued that it represented a first step in controlling violence and senseless murders. With crime as a major issue on the campaign agenda, the initiative became a focal point of the 1984 campaign. It was a hot potato that few Bradley advisors wanted their candidate to handle. Yet those who really knew his character, such as Ray Remy, were in no doubt about the position that Tom Bradley would take. His decision to publicly support the initiative would have a dire effect in the upcoming race.

In retrospect, Duane Garrett, a campaign Co-chairman of Bradley's gubernatorial effort, identifies the handgun measure as the single most important factor in the election's eventual outcome. "Tom's principled stand on that matter simply was not understood by people who have an almost pathological attachment to their handguns." According to the prominent San Francisco attorney, who played a major role in fundraising, "Some people who never voted before came out and voted for the first time against the measure—and consequently against Bradley. Had the gun initiative not been on the ballot, I think it would have been a totally different election."

Beginning major speaking appearances and commercials a full two months before his opponent, Bradley launched his "issue-oriented" campaign throughout the state. In early August, the campaign experimented with an approach designed to communicate to Californians that Bradley was the only candidate with progams to get the state working again—the weekly Saturday morning radio address.

Emphasizing the economic issue, the radio speeches outlined proposals and programs designed to create jobs for the "1.3 million Californians out of work, and to preserve job security among those working." The speeches were laden with specifics of how each problem affected California. The housing speech discussed the depressed housing market and its effect on "275,000 Californians now getting pinkslips instead of earning paychecks." In calling for a better business climate and an "end to the regulation glut," Bradley told listeners, "We've got to send the message loud and clear that California wants business because business means jobs, and jobs mean taking our citizens out of the unemployment lines and putting them back to work." He had already created jobs for 200,000 in the city of Los Angeles; now he wanted to put the same skills to work for hundreds of thousands of citizens throughout the state.

Even the crime speech, following a detailed account of various "tough, no nonsense measures to take the terror of crime out of our lives," contained recommendations reflecting Bradley's conviction that the problem had economic roots. "If we are to find a long-term, long-lasting solution to the crime problem," Bradley stated, "we must also restore vitality to California's economy and put Californians back to work." In an obvious reference to his opponent's lack of experience in economic matters, Bradley told voters, "Any candidate ill-equipped or unable to put California back to work will also be unable to put a dent in the epidemic of crime.

Imbedded within the Bradley rhetoric were symbols and images of what the Mayor called the California dream, the essence of which was illustrated in his campaign stock speech:

> I remember when my parents moved to California, when I was six and my mother told me we were going to a place where it didn't matter what your name was or where you lived. She told me California was a special place where people judged you on what you did, and nothing else. So I worked hard and studied hard. I've

always believed California is a very special place. I know what it's meant to me. It's a place where if you work hard, if you treat people like you want to be treated, you can set your goals high and not only dream dreams, but you and your children can then go out and realize them.

Pressed by reporters to comment on the "historical significance" of the election, Bradley, in an uncharacteristic reference to his race, summed up the essence of his California dream metaphor: "Young people of every race, creed, and color—I want them to know if they work hard, they can achieve. They can look at Tom Bradley and say, 'If he can do it, so can I.'"

On numerous other occasions, Bradley displayed a less serious reaction to reporters' queries on the "historical significance" of the election. He noted that it could indeed be a moment for the history books—if elected, he would be the tallest chief executive in the state's history.

One early tactic of the Deukmejian campaign was to link Bradley to Governor Jerry Brown, the Democratic nominee in a Senate race against San Diego Mayor Pete Wilson. The GOP candidate told reporters, "We're going to be asking him what he is going to do differently than Jerry Brown; Tom Bradley has expressly praised Jerry Brown's appointments to the courts . . . , and that's going to be a very important issue." Bradley responded by saying, "If he wanted to debate Jerry Brown, he's running for the wrong office. I'm not Jerry Brown. I'm Tom Bradley, and I'm promoting what I plan to do for this state. People make the distinction. They know I will function differently."

While polls revealed that only one out of ten voters believed Brown and Bradley were similar in their approaches to government, Deukmejian continued to make the charge. Bradley also pointed out another difference between himself and the outgoing Governor. When asked whether, if elected, he would continue Brown's tradition of driving an old Plymouth to work, Bradley gestured towards his lanky frame and joked to reporters, "I can't fit in a Plymouth." Deputy campaign manager Jules Radcliff remembers, "The polls in August and early September showed we were right on track, and our objective was to keep up this pace throughout the campaign."

While President Reagan was not the focus of a specific attack by the Bradley campaign, one member of his Administration was—the controversial Secretary of the Interior, James Watt. Citing his own leadership in protecting "California's most precious resource—our coastline," Bradley criticized Deukmejian's support of Watt's oil-leasing proposal to open up the entire California coastline for drilling. He further attacked Deukmejian's policies on the environment by decrying the Attorney General's disbanding of the state's environmental legal unit. Bradley charged these actions were proof that, with Deukmejian as Governor, "the entire California coastline would be up for sale."

The widespread opposition to oil drilling on the California coast went beyond the traditional environmental groups. Concerns voiced in beach communities from Eureka to Imperial and from the state's tourist industry prompted the Democratic candidate to emphasize the "stark differences" between himself and Deukmejian on environmental issues.

Research by Bradley workers Debra Dentler, Monica Guttman, Sandra Farrar, and Rosemary Girellini into the Attorney General's record on legislation affecting women identified questionable bills that Deukmejian had supported while in the legislature. Farrar and Guttman provided the speechwriting team with the facts it would need to create what would be a major speech.

The topic had been discussed in the campaign's "kitchen cabinet" meeting for weeks. Fran Savitch, Valerie Fields, Dodo Meyer, Bee Canterbury Lavery, and Maureen Kindel had long favored the development of a message specifically tailored to the women of the state. They wanted Bradley television and radio commercials to address this issue head on. While Deukmejian was running a spot on "the number-one fear of California women—rape," they wanted to counter these scare tactics with a message that addressed other, more substantive concerns of women. Bradley had, after all, been a champion of women's rights for years. In 1975, he had appointed the first commission on the status of women to address issues of equal opportunity, and under his administration there had been an overall 25 percent increase in city jobs held by women, with twice as many women holding top jobs at City Hall, compared to ten years before.

In the radio address that Bradley finally made, he attacked his opponent's "record of callousness and indifference to the needs of women." Bradley listed the votes his opponent had cast against the best interests of women—"against a bill to provide leaves of absence for women suffering from disabilities caused by pregnancy, miscarriage, and childbirth; against Equal Worker's Compensation for women in areas of law enforcement; against a bill to study opening up employment opportunities for women in the California Highway Patrol; against fairness in our community property laws; against a bill signed into law by Governor Reagan which prohibits charging rape victims for the cost of medical examinations required to prosecute the rapist. I strongly disagree with Mr. Deukmejian on every one of these issues."

The Democratic candidate's record on the issue stood in "stark contrast—thirty-eight years of service to the community . . . legislation, programs, ordinances, and appointments that open up opportunities and expand women's participation in society." Concurrently, the campaign began work on a radio and television spot featuring college students Valerie Cain, Trish Deghi, Valerie Smith, Laura Segal, and other women talking about the "proven record" of Tom Bradley.

With crime the touchstone of his campaign, Deukmejian ("the crime fighter for California") charged Bradley had "reduced the fiscal support of the police department," at a time when "crime was up in Los Angeles". The Bradley campaign disputed the claim, explaining once again, as it had in the recent race against Yorty, that while office workers had been cut, cops on the beat had been increased. Deukmejian attempted to bolster his case against Bradley by obtaining endorsements from law-enforcement officers who had worked with the Mayor in Los Angeles. In one campaign commercial, former Los Angeles Police Chief Ed Davis told voters, "I worked in Mayor Bradley's Los Angeles and I worked with Attorney General George Deukmejian, and I know why most police officers support George Deukmejian. His actions speak louder than Bradley's words."

The former Police Chief's public endorsement of his opponent did not surprise Bradley. The relationship between the Mayor and the former Los Angeles Police Chief had been strained for a number of years before the Chief retired in 1978 to enter state politics. Davis had resented Bradley's refusal to issue blanket approval of his proposed budgets for the Police Department. He had also resented City Hall criticism of the department's handling of various incidents involving what the Mayor believed to be abuse of power by police officers.

Bradley responded to Davis' endorsement by recalling an incident that illustrated the extravagant shopping lists of the former Police Chief: "When Ed Davis asked for a submarine, I turned him down . . . , a tank, I turned him down. . . . He also wanted an airplane to interdict narcotics smugglers." The Bradley campaign subsequently announced an endorsement by the Police Chief of Deukmejian's hometown of Long Beach as further evidence of Bradley's record against crime.

The Deukmejian campaign called for defeat of the three "liberal" Supreme Court Justices who would be on the November ballot for confirmation. The Attorney General blamed the court, especially the Brown-appointed Chief Justice, Rose Bird, for not being tough enough on criminals. Attempting to tap into the public's concern with crime, Deukmejian singled out the Justices, Jerry Brown, and Tom Bradley as the "liberal team" responsible for crime's chokehold in California. The GOP candidate also pledged that, if elected, he would actively seek to change the philosophical make-up of the court, a promise criticized by Bradley as an attempt to politicize or pack the state Supreme Court. The Mayor reaffirmed his own position that the courts should retain their independence from the executive branch, regardless of who won the election.

Although Bradley outlined a six-point "tough no-nonsense approach to crime," pointing to his record as proof that he was the "only candidate who had faced real crime on real streets in real neighborhoods," the GOP platform remained vague. Deukmejian continued to hammer away at generalizations, trying to stereotype Bradley's political philosophy: "He's an absolutely honest and dedicated liberal, and what he believes are those funny things that liberals believe about crime."

Polls in September showed Bradley with a lead of as much as

eighteen points. But among those who supported Deukmejian, almost one-fourth singled out his stand on crime as the primary reason. In comparison, less than one out of ten citizens who favored Bradley identified the Mayor's position on crime as the motivating force for their support.

Following the traditional Labor Day opening of the campaign, the candidates' efforts centered on putting more commercials in living rooms throughout the state. Cowboy star Slim Pickens told viewers, "My daddy told me there were two things you never could trust, a skunk or a politician. Well, I can tell you there's one guy you can trust who's running for Governor, and that's George Deukmejian." Concurrent with the Pickens advertisement were radio and television commercials emphasizing Deukmejian's major campaign themes: "Bradley has cut the police force while the crime rate has increased in Los Angeles." Another crime-related commercial highlighted "the crime increase in Los Angeles," and concluded, "Bradley and Brown are a great pair—both the same, all talk and no action." The Pickens ad, with the subtle racism of the skunk reference, signaled to the Bradley campaign that the non-issue, Bradley's race, would again be an issue during the campaign's final eight weeks.

David Garth and Hank Morris had prepared some counter-commercials to air if the situation required it. Amid considerable debate, the Bradley team decided to run the counter-spots, and the result was what came to be referred to as the Watergate commercial. It told viewers, "Ten years after Watergate, you can reject the politics of negativism and vote for Tom Bradley." Bill Roberts charged the commercial was "shabby and unfair." Rejecting the contention that the commercial was designed to counter the negative campaign waged against Bradley, Roberts maintained his candidate's commercials were "informative" and "issue-oriented."

On September 28, the *Los Angeles Times* reported that the Bradley campaign spot, which was an attempt to counter the "highly negative" Deukmejian commercials, had elicited protests "not only from the opposition, but also the League of Women Voters." The Bradley commercial, citing Deukmejian's refusal to sign the code of ethics suggested by Bradley, had mentioned the League of Women Voters' endorsement of the code. But as a group committed to the principle of nonpartisanship, the League requested that its name be removed from the commercial. The public outcry reinforced the feeling among some Bradley supporters, including top staffers, that the commercial had lowered the Bradley campaign to the level of the opposition.

A combative tone characterized the first televised debate between the two candidates in Sacramento, on September 29. Early in the debate, when Deukmejian again tried to identify Bradley with Cesar Chavez, the farmworkers, and Jerry Brown, Bradley charged that Deukmejian was distorting the record, attempting to "put words in my mouth."

Enumerating what he believed to be inconsistencies between campaign rhetoric and the actual record, Bradley turned to Deukmejian, pointed his finger at him, and asked him to explain why his campaign continued to portray Bradley as the candidate who favored higher taxes, when as a State Senator, in 1967, Deukmejian had carried the Reagan bill for the largest tax increase in the state's history. He had steered it through the Assembly, speaking and lobbying in its behalf more strenuously than anyone else. Bradley stated, "You're going to have to face up to these questions. I'm a good guy, but if you distort my record, you've got to answer to me." He told his opponent, "You've got to be consistent my friend."

Deukmejian took the opportunity to bring up the disputed "Watergate commercial," stating, "They are using Watergate for only one purpose—to distort, to mislead, to try to smear me with the worst political act of this decade." Bradley responded by maintaining that the reference to Watergate was not directed at Deukmejian personally, but to a period in which people were turned off by the negative tactics used by some public officials.

Near the close of the debate, William Endicott of the *Los Angeles Times* introduced a new topic into the campaign, asking Deukmejian if he concurred with a published statement made by his campaign manager, Bill Roberts, that "he would lie to win a race." A visibly shaken Deukmejian replied, "I have never heard him make such a statement."

Though the initial response of the Republican campaign was

that the quote had been taken out of context, the full citation (from an interview with Roberts in a publication entitled *Book of America*) reads: "I'm opposed to putting a lot of rules and restrictions on campaigning. I think I ought to have the right to lie to you if I think it will help me win. I think you have the right to detect my lie and vote 'no' when you go in the polling booth."

The Bradley campaign, according to Depoian, hoped that Roberts' statement would "serve as a clear signal to the public of the type of people running the GOP effort." The message was out in Roberts' own words: He would do anything to win an election.

But Bradley's Watergate commercial seemed to be attracting much more attention in the press than Roberts' declaration that he would lie in a campaign in order to win. The commercial was highlighted as a possible "turning point in the campaign in an October 1 *Los Angeles Times* story headlined "Negative Trend Seen In Race For Governor." Quoting Seymour Lipset, political scientist at Stanford University, that both candidates "clearly don't want to fight on issues, so they're fighting over personalities," the *Times* article noted, "With a few exceptions, the Bradley campaign until that point had concentrated heavily on issues and resisted the temptation to lash out at Deukmejian."

With four weeks until election day and Bradley still enjoying a comfortable lead, both campaigns announced a major assault of the airwaves in the effort to reach the California population. Each campaign would spend over $200,000 on commercials for the second week in October. Then suddenly another incident sparked the ongoing dispute about campaign ethics: the Deukmejian campaign previewed several previously unaired Bradley commercials to reporters.

The Bradley campaign demanded to know how the opposition had acquired the spots. Deukmejian's campaign refused to reveal its sources. Charging that his opponent had "surreptitiously" obtained the commercials, Bradley was quoted in the *Times:* "And now, with this illegal securing of my commercials before they have been scheduled to run, people must ask, is this the kind of mentality we're going to be faced with if he becomes Governor?"

The Mayor continued to highlight the incident as a perfect demonstration of the philosophy of his opponent's Campaign

Manager, an example of what Roberts would do to win an election. It amounted to nothing short of theft. And yet Deukmejian did not repudiate Roberts. An October 7 *Los Angeles Times* campaign story was headlined, "Deukmejian Would Lie To Win—Bradley," and quoted Bradley telling supporters that the Attorney General "is prepared to say anything and do anything . . . to win."

Statewide polls continued to show Bradley enjoying a significant lead over his opponent. But during the first weekend of October, Bill Roberts publicly stated that latent racism within the California voting public could decide the outcome of the election, now less than four weeks away.

Roberts' comments on the race issue's impact received banner headlines throughout the state. An October 6 *Los Angeles Times* story was headlined "Deukmejian Side; Bias Closes Gap, Hidden Anti-Black Vote 'Fact Of Life.' " In addressing a query by a *Times* reporter, Roberts told the press, "You will not get the truth from people regarding the race issue. . . . If we are down only five points or less in the polls by election time, we're going to win. . . . It's just a fact of life." Deukmejian's Campaign Manager identified the race issue as the reason why he disregarded the polls: "If people are going to vote that way, they certainly are not going to announce it for a survey [poll] taker." While continuing to focus attention on the issue, Roberts nonetheless publicly negated any attempt by his candidate to use Bradley's race as a means of attracting support, "We're not getting involved in the issue at all, and I think George Deukmejian already has pretty well repudiated racist voting."

Roberts' remarks dominated political discussion for the next five days. Papers throughout the state speculated on the potential impact of his statement on the election. When asked if he took the statement as an insult, Bradley stated, "It's an insult—not to me, but to all the people of California—to suggest that in 1982 people will vote for Governor based on something other than the merits of the candidates."

Once again the campaign agenda had been turned around. Discussion centered on the propriety of the Roberts statement. Had it been a slip of the tongue? Was it a calculated move to turn the media and public attention away from other issues and back to the fact that one candidate was black? Was the Deukmejian campaign openly courting the racist vote?

Superior Court Judge Jack Tenner adds, "To speculate what was in Bill Roberts' mind or Deukmejian's doesn't matter, because it is the effect that counts, and race was now an issue." Former U.S. Senator John Tunney states, "If you go up and down the state saying that something is not an issue, such as race, it finally becomes an issue in the public's mind." Former Governor Pat Brown concludes, "Let's make this perfectly clear. The whole thing was planned from the beginning by Roberts and Deukmejian."

Some journalists echoed these sentiments. In his *Los Angeles Herald Examiner* column, entitled, "Duke's Campaign Didn't Slip With Race Remark," David Israel charged that the entire Roberts event had been part of the GOP master "scam," a type of "voodoo politics." He chastized Deukmejian for the underhanded approach, concluding that the Attorney General was not only "going to benefit by the racist vote . . . , he is campaigning for it." The *Herald* writer concluded that that tack was the "only chance" Deukmejian had to "win the election."

The October 9 edition of the *Los Angeles Times* carried Deukmejian's reaction to his campaign manager's statement. Repeating Roberts' words once again, in a page-one story, the article reported that the statement had "caught Deukmejian completely by surprise," but that he had called Roberts, and they had "had a very serious discussion." Stating that he would not "relate our verbatim conversation," Deukmejian attempted to offer a context for Roberts' controversial statements: "sometimes he [Roberts] looks at these issues, he looks at them as a professional, as sort of theorizing, and yet there are other practical aspects to issues like this and discussions about such issues." Deukmejian told the reporter that "race is not relevant to this campaign" and that Roberts had repeatedly advised the campaign staff that references to Bradley's race were not to be permitted. The Attorney General added, "We're not counting on anything like that [the anti-black bias] in the campaign."

In campaign appearances, and in response to reporters' persistent questions, Deukmejian continued to get mileage out of the incident by repeatedly denying the significance of the issue his own campaign manager had publicly raised. Press coverage also remained focused on it, as reporters debated the GOP Campaign Manager's future, some speculating that Roberts would leave the campaign soon.

17

Vision vs. Reruns

"Race is not an issue."
—George Deukmejian

The question in the Bradley campaign was how to get the campaign back on track, back to a discussion of substantive issues affecting the future of California. Kerman Maddox comments, "The feeling in the black community was that Tom Bradley had been slapped and people wanted him to react, but then, that would have only played into Deukmejian's hands even more by keeping the issue alive." There was discussion of a speech or commercial to address the issue.

Personally, Bradley made the choice to ignore it: "I didn't see any reason to address that type of appeal, and I think the majority of citizens of California also rejected it."

Bradley attempted to keep the campaign on the positive track, again citing his record in Los Angeles and his plans for the state. In mid-October, several business leaders announced the formation of "Bi-Partisan Business Committee for Bradley" at a news conference featuring some of the most distinguished business names in the United States—Philip Hawley, Sanford Sigoloff, Walter Gerken, and Stafford Grady. The Bradley campaign hoped the endorsements would again return the discussion to the issues of who was best suited to lead California in a new decade. It felt confident that such support demonstrated Bradley's superior credentials in the economic area, and among a constituency commonly identified with the Republican Party. Grady, the Chairman of the Board of Lloyd's Bank, expresses the common theme of those gathered: "The integrity and leadership of Tom Bradley—his ability to mediate solutions among sides that often seem unwilling to budge in their positions—has been the chief ingredient of the economic success in Los Angeles; we were eager for his leadership to be put to work throughout the state."

But while the campaign was moving on, the media was not. Many journalists remained stuck on the Roberts incident. By week's end and after a full seven days of stories on the episode and aftermath, Deukmejian announced the departure of Roberts. The headline in the *Los Angeles Times* read: "Head of Deukmejian Drive Quits After Racial Remark." Quoted in the article, Deukmejian discounted the notion that this late campaign shake-up would have a negative impact on his election chances. The Attorney General noted that "my own surveys show there is a shift taking place, that Bradley is beginning to lose support, [because of] a growing number of persons undecided in the campaign." The Republican hopeful offered supporters an optimistic outlook, "We're going to go on and we are going to win. We're in the last three weeks, the most critical period, the period we've been pointing for." Evening tracking polls showed some Bradley supporters now reported as undecided. No one could say for sure whether they had been affected by the previous week's events and their press coverage.

A *Los Angeles Times* poll reported on October 17 that for the first time in the campaign, Deukmejian had narrowed Bradley's lead, cutting it to 7 percent. It was the first solid evidence that the "hidden anti-black" allegation was paying off for the GOP candidate. Explaining the gain, *Times* writer William Endicott commented, "Deukmejian's gain on Bradley in the governor's contest appears attributable in large part to the Attorney General's ability to draw back into his campaign a large number of conservative voters who were uncommitted earlier or favored Bradley." The article further stated that "those voters who showed an anti-black sentiment in response to such questions as whether government had paid too much attention to blacks and other minority groups go heavily to Deukmejian." Yet the Democratic candidate's own polls, according to Jules Radcliff, showed the Mayor holding on to his lead.

An Associated Press story in mid-October also found "bias

against candidates who were of other racial or ethnic descents—Chinese 8 percent, Hispanic 6 percent, Jewish 4 percent. Interestingly, the Field Poll reported 12 percent of the voters polled were disinclined to vote for a candidate of Armenian descent. This was double the number who admitted they would not vote for a black candidate. Yet analysis of the election coverage reveals very little attention paid to Deukmejian's background in comparison to the wide coverage and interest in Bradley's race.

The association of race with crime in the public's mind was much discussed in the media, especially during the speculation on what effect Roberts' "hidden anti-black vote" comment would have. Headlined, "Crime And Fear Will Play Role In Balloting For Governor," an October 12 *Times* article read: "They are there as the Nov. 2 election approaches—Californians with dogs growling in their yards and bars on their windows. And they seem ready to express some of that fear in their votes. . . . People say they are trusting their instincts more than the rhetoric, (and several) brought up race when asked how crime would affect their vote for governor this year. . . . One Sacramento woman, a white residing in an integrated neighborhood, said she had come to equate blacks with crime, 'and I'm sorry, I just don't think Bradley (who is black) would be tough on criminals.' "

Expressing the use of symbolic issues in political discourse, which he felt the Deukmejian campaign expertly manipulated, Judge Jack Tenner states, "No one uses 'nigger,' but they will say, 'I'm against busing . . ., I'm against crime. . . . I'm against taxpayers' welfare money being used for abortions.' " The end product is the same, according to San Jose State media professor Phil Wander: "When you add it all up, the bottom line is race and racism, and Deukmejian's team catered to this appeal." Advertising professor and consultant Robert A. Baukus asserts that, once the race issue is addressed "in the mediated reality of the coverage, it becomes a part of the public's campaign agenda." *Herald Examiner* publisher Francis Dale, a former chairman of President Richard Nixon's campaign, has stated, "No matter when you raise it, if you simply hint at it, it will take off and run, and you can't control it anymore."

Deukmejian commercials airing at this time continued to insinuate that Bradley was "soft on crime." In one spot, Slim

Pickens told voters why he moved his family out of Los Angeles: "We feared for our safety, because Bradley cut the size of the police force." In a television ad, a cab driver warned a visitor in a ride to a downtown Los Angeles hotel to "be sure and lock your doors, because Bradley cut the police force and crime is up."

Other Deukmejian radio spots on the crime issue opened with the rhetorical question: "Do you support the 'victims bill of rights?' If you said yes, then your position matches with Attorney General George Deukmejian, who believes that laws must protect victims of crime, not just the accused. . . . Do you support a reduction of the police force? If you said yes, then you agree with Mayor Bradley, who cut hundreds of officers from L.A.'s police force while the crime rate increased."

The charges about Bradley's reduction in the police force continued unabated, although the Bradley campaign continued to explain that the cuts mentioned in the Deukmejian ads were of office personnel, not patrol officers. Tom Sullivan gave the numbers: "Although six hundred positions have been trimmed from the Police Department during Bradley's nine years as Mayor, the number of officers actually on street patrol has risen by 365."

The announced change in leadership within the opposition's campaign did not persuade Bradley or his staff that there would be a change in Deukmejian's tactics. As Bradley said, "It's easy to change campaign managers . . ., but the question is, will the nature of George Deukmejian's campaign change? The Deukmejian campaign seemed to make a smooth transition to new leadership after Roberts' departure. New commercials crafted by a new media team, headed by Sal Russo and Doug Watts, were aired. They were more impressive than those of the past. Meanwhile, the media continued to harp on the race issue. Many within the Bradley team shared the feeling expressed by field staffer John David—"uneasy . . . , that's the best way to put it."

Two weeks before the election, longtime Bradley advisor and friend Sam Williams told a group of top staffers at the Bradley state headquarters in Los Angeles to re-double their work. He reminded them how, in 1969, the polls had shown Bradley to be ahead, even up to the day of the election—that in that election, like the present one, "other issues" had been introduced into the campaign, and that the fear and scare tactics had won out over reason on election day, despite what the polls had predicted. Campaign Manager Nelson Rising told the Bradley troops it would require everybody's help in 1982 to make the difference. With the candidate looking on, Rising told the staff "to rededicate themselves, to give 200 percent during the final weeks to guarantee the victory all of California deserved on November 2." The strategy, according to Rising, would be to keep the record before the public to fight the tactics of insinuation and fear-mongering with the facts.

But the inner office conflicts were also taking their toll on the Bradley effort during the last two weeks. There were in essence two press offices vying for control. Tom Sullivan issued official statements, but at other times Joe Trippi, Alan Katz and Blair Levin contacted the press on the Bradley positions. Letty Herndon Brown and other staffers worked out their own network with Bradley to ensure that he was given key information and provided speeches on time. Ervin Fang, an assistant speechwriter, remembers, "I think the height of ineptitude was when I walked in and found several members of the staff looking at a state government jobs book and arguing over which job they wanted after the election. . . . I just walked to the office, did my work, and stayed away from there." But even with the discord, prospects looked good for the Democratic candidate. "It was like he would win it in spite of what was happening at the headquarters," recalls Tom Sullivan.

The Bradley campaign continued to emphasize their candidate's past record of working with business and labor to improve the business climate in Los Angeles, while highlighting Deukmejian's lack of experience in the area. In one commercial featuring only a stopwatch, an off-camera announcer asks voters, "I'll give you ten seconds to name one job George Deukmejian ever created." When the watch has ticked off ten seconds, the announcer adds, "Time's up. Tom Bradley created 200,000 new jobs while Mayor of Los Angeles."

In a year that had witnessed more small businesses folding than any other since the Great Depression, Bradley proposed a revitalization plan to help the budding entrepreneur. He pointed out that 95 percent of all the businesses in California were run by fewer than fifty people. He proposed that state regulations, which had strangled the vitality of many beginning business, be tiered to allow the new businesses to have the opportunity to get on their feet. He was still trying to return the debate to the issues, primarily the economic challenge that had to be met with a specific agenda.

Bradley again charged his opponent's campaign's promises were short on specifics. The Mayor's message was that California deserved to have a Governor who would "spell out specific programs" so that voters could determine who really was most capable of governing the Golden State.

Bradley's specific proposals on the state's problems prompted Deukmejian to charge that "Bradley is camouflaging himself as a Republican by speaking out against crime and for private-sector jobs while ignoring traditional Democratic issues such as the need for more social programs." The GOP candidate raised the question. "Isn't it a little strange that he is talking about issues . . . conservatives and Republicans talk about usually?"

No matter what Bradley said, however, he couldn't seem to get the press to focus on anything besides race. *Los Angeles Times* articles profiling Bradley on October 21 and 22 carried such headlines as "Tom Bradley as Candidate: 'Colorblind' Man's Bid to Make History"; "Bradley: Bid for New Niche in History"; "Bradley: An Effort to Make History"; "Bradley: Seeks Place in History"; "Bradley: Grandson of Slaves Pursues a Place in History—A Manager, Not a Crusading Idealogue"; "Bradley: A Manager Who Avoids Symbolic Crusades, Losing Battles"; "Bradley: A Fascination With Details of Government."

During the last two weeks of the campaign, Deukmejian as much as admitted that he preferred to unleash charges rather than support them. In a joint appearance at an economic conference in Orange County on October 21, the GOP hopeful charged that Bradley "would rather raise taxes, than cut social programs." Asked for specifics or evidence to support his assertion, the Attorney General admitted he had no hard facts to support his contention. Nonetheless, he told the press he would continue to make the charge, because "I believe it."

Bradley went on the attack about crime in a joint appearance on KNXT's *Newsmakers,* which was aired October 24. He charged that Deukmejian's "crime fighter" claims were not supported by an examination of the Attorney General's record. When Deukmejian asked for specifics, Bradley cited Deukmejian's support of a bill allowing certain federal offenders found guilty of minor crimes to once again carry a gun. Bradley asked his opponent how enabling a criminal to once again carry a gun meshed with his campaign claim that he was the "crime fighter"? Deukmejian was clearly shaken and charged that Bradley had distorted the facts, though follow-up study revealed Bradley's claim to be correct.

In the final two weeks, the Deukmejian campaign continued to stress crime as the key issue of the election. In his attempt to actively appeal to conservative voters, Deukmejian stressed his opposition to Proposition 15, the gun registration initiative. The Attorney General told supporters that the initiative would merely add to the bureaucratic glut and would be ineffective. Polls in the early part of the campaign showed voters favoring passage of the proposition, but the efforts of the National Rifle Association and other conservative groups had now put the outcome in doubt.

To Bradley it seemed paradoxical that those most opposed to the measure were the very same voices calling for tougher laws and a statewide crackdown on crime. The gun initiative could help control the proliferation of handguns so often used in criminal acts, and Bradley continued to publicly support the measure.

The candidates' positions on this emotional issue further polarized them in the minds of some voters. Brochures designed for those opposed to gun control offered directives on how Californians should cast their votes in the gubernatorial and senate races. Deukmejian's rhetoric about crime, his comments on the need to change the philosophical makeup of the Supreme Court, and his anti-Proposition 15 stand made for a neat "law-and-order" package. "No" on the gun initiative and "No" on retaining the three justices translated into a "Yes" for "proven crime fighter" George Deukmejian and "Yes" for Pete Wilson in his race against Jerry Brown for U.S. Senate. It was a package that would prove attractive to many Californians on election day.

Deukmejian's campaign rhetoric during the final month dwelled on the crime issue, but sprinkled throughout were references to "welfare" and "social program" themes. The day before his Campaign Manager made his "hidden anti-black" comment, the Attorney General told supporters that the "elimination of welfare fraud" would be high on his agenda as Governor.

In the speech, Deukmejian identified his opponent as part of the problem that wasted millions of taxpayers' hard-earned dollars. He charged that "in Los Angeles alone, there is more than $1 million per month lost in welfare fraud." The allegation was categorically denied by Los Angeles County Director of Social Services, Eddy S. Tanaka, who told reporters, "Los Angeles has the lowest error rate of any major city in the country."

"Welfare fraud" was also a focal point of the second and final televised debate, held one week prior to the election. Addressing the state's impending fiscal crisis, Deukmejian repeated his former allegations of welfare fraud in Los Angeles, and told the audience that he had a plan that would "effectuate tremendous savings in the welfare area."

But this time Bradley was lying in wait for him. In response to the allegation, he turned to his opponent and reminded him that U. S. Congressman Claude Pepper's committee had concluded, in 1980, that Deukmejian's Attorney General's office was "among the four least effective in the entire United States in terms of welfare fraud prosecution." Bradley told viewers that, if Deukmejian was "such a big proponent of cutting the budget by soliciting ways in which welfare fraud is achieved, I think he needs to look at his record."

Despite being confronted with the Pepper criticism, Deukmejian continued to single out welfare, along with taxes and crime, as the dominant themes of his speaking appearances and campaign commercials during the final weekend of the campaign.

During the last weekend of the campaign, the GOP campaign sent a mailer to moderate and conservative Democrats throughout the state. The mailer, described by Bradley as a "late October hit-piece," outlined Deukmejian's opposition to welfare, social programs, higher taxes, and crime, and invited voters to "compare the differences on the issues . . . before you make your choice for Governor."

In anticipation of the standard Deukmejian end-of-campaign mailer tactic, the Bradley campaign had hastily prepared its own postcard, entitled "Don't believe George Deukmejian's last-minute smear campaign on Tom Bradley," which was mailed the same weekend the Deukmejian piece went out. The brochure attempted to set the record straight on issues and in areas where Bradley believed his opponent had misrepresented the facts:

1. George Deukmejian knows Tom Bradley helped create more than two-hundred-thousand private sector jobs. 2. George Deukmejian knows he's never really done anything to help save or to help create jobs in California. 3. George Deukmejian knows Tom Bradley worked twenty-one years as a police officer. 4. George Deukmejian knows Tom Bradley will vigorously and strictly enforce the death penalty. 5. George Deukmejian knows Tom Bradley more than doubled the Los Angeles Police budget and put more police on the street in Los Angeles. 6. George Deukmejian knows the number of crimes committed in California has increased by more than 250,000 since he became Attorney General. 7. George Deukmejian knows that as a state legislator he pushed through the largest tax increase in California's history. 8. George Deukmejian knows Tom Bradley cut property taxes in Los Angeles—even before Proposition 13. 9. George Deukmejian knows Tom Bradley has balanced nine consecutive budgets in Los Angeles with no new taxes. 10. George Deukmejian knows that he supports James Watt's billion-acre off-shore oil drilling plan. ON TUESDAY, REJECT GEORGE DEUKMEJIAN'S NEGATIVE, MISLEADING, DIVISIVE CAMPAIGN, AND VOTE FOR TOM BRADLEY.

The final Field Poll gave some comfort to the Bradley camp. He now held a 49 percent to 42 percent advantage. But, in reporting his final results, Mervin Field explained his findings within a black-white context: "Unless blacks and other minorities turn out in substantial numbers, it is conceivable that Deukmejian could emerge the winner on the basis of white votes."

Bradley knew from experience that the only important poll was the one to be conducted when the voters of California went to vote on Tuesday. His campaign had allotted over one million dollars to the field—"Get Out The Vote (GOTV)"—operation headed by Joe Trippi.

The goal was to have the most extensive and productive get-out-the-vote effort since the 1960s. The final day of the campaign saw Bradley joined by Art Gastelum, George David Kieffer, and others, traveling by chartered plane throughout the state in an effort to personally motivate voters to the polls. After picking up supporters in San Francisco, the Democratic candidate learned from his (as well as independent) pollsters that the exit polls suggested a Bradley victory. Even though it was too early to celebrate, Kieffer remembers, "people were popping champagne as the plane landed in Los Angeles, because the reports were so good." Both Kieffer and Gastelum concurred that even Bradley "seemed to sense the victory within his grasp."

Deukmejian spent the day in Orange County, a bastion of conservative support, reminding older voters at Leisure World that crime would be his top priority as Governor. According to the *Times* final pre-election edition, Deukmejian was counting on "Proposition 15, the handgun initiative, to bring out a large number of 'no' voters, most of whom will be his supporters."

Election day in the Bradley headquarters signaled the end of the long campaign. The once busy offices were, for the most part, vacant. Almost everyone was involved in transporting people to the polls or calling to remind supporters to go vote. The Bradley field operation had rented every available rental car in California to help get voters to the polls. Andy Baron, and Anita Stern talked with deputy issue staffers throughout the state. Wayne Fishman and Alan Tuck told of long lines of voters in San Diego and in the Bay area. It was a good sign. The larger the turnout in the state the better. It was a well-known political fact that, while Democrats outnumbered Republicans in the state, the latter were more apt to cast their ballots. A big turnout was looked upon as an indication that Trippi's troops were getting out the vote.

There were also indications, from field representatives Debbie Bright, Kathy Smith, Trish Long, and Rory Kessler, however, that the Central Valley area, the food basket for the state (and, for that matter, the country), had a large number of voters casting ballots. The area had strongly opposed the gun initiative, and according to press aide Elizabeth Jewel, it looked as though the "no" campaign had touched a responsive chord in the farming area. A large turnout there could prove to be bad news for Bradley. Still, the final tracking polls conducted by the Mayor's organization signaled a Bradley victory. According to Jules Radcliff, the erosion in support that had been noticed two weeks prior seemed to have been checked. And calls by Hank Morris to David Garth in New York elicited the information that network exit polls verified the findings of the final election polls. Bradley would win the election by a comfortable margin of about eight to ten percentage points. Reason would win out over fear and prejudice.

One of the major tasks of the day was to prepare remarks for Bradley to deliver to supporters at the Biltmore Hotel in downtown Los Angeles. The feedback from thoughout the state made the task easier. It was all good news—a confirmation of the eleven-point victory predicted by Bradley's pollster, Hugh Schwartz. Everything pointed to a victory speech. In it Bradley would spell out what the election meant for California. There would, indeed, be a new spirit of leadership in Sacramento. But one of the major themes the Mayor wanted to stress was what the election symbolized to people throughout the state and country.

Bradley wanted the speech to communicate a special message to the state's most precious resource—its children. The draft included a section specifically addressed to them. Bradley looked it over at Getty House prior to leaving for the Biltmore to await the election returns. He decided to ask parents throughout the state to have their children come listen to the message.

What Tom Bradley planned to tell the children was that tonight was a celebration of hopes and dreams now realized:

> What this election means, the message it sends to you, all the children of California when you see me here tonight, is that, if you set your mind to it, develop high goals, and never lose sight of them. . . . If you work hard, if you remain determined, you can do anything that you want. This election sends the message loud and clear that California is still a very special place. A special place where what matters is not your name, not where you live, but what you do. What this election says to the children . . . , what it says to all of us is yes, we

can redeem the California dream. With your help, I'll be
one governor who will make a difference.

He had never liked giving speeches, but this was one he was
looking forward to.

Volunteer organizers Joe Collins, Trish Long, Lee Brown,
and Jimmy Mackey joined thousands of other supporters in
sensing victory in the Bradley for Governor quarters of the
Biltmore, located very appropriately in the midst of the re-
developed downtown area that Tom Bradley had helped bring
about. Ironically, the hotel was also where Jerry Brown's supporters, gathered in another ballroom, would wait to learn how
successful their candidate had been against San Diego Mayor
Pete Wilson in the Senate race, though their hopes were not as
high as the Bradley supporters, as their candidate had been
trailing in the polls.

As the polls closed throughout the state, there was further
reason for celebration at the Biltmore. Television coverage began
immediately, and it was very encouraging. Mervin Field projected Bradley a winner in the Governor's race on CBS' Channel
2 at 7:59 P.M. KABC's pollster Steve Teichner concurred at 8:30
P.M.. The final pre-election editions of the city's major newspapers also projected Bradley as California's next state executive. In the ballroom of the Biltmore, Nelson Rising indicated
to George David Kieffer that the Mayor would be coming down
for a victory speech within the hour. The clock on the wall read
8:15 P.M.

Throngs of supporters continued to flow into the Biltmore.
Then Randy Smith, Jeff Kravetz, and Kent Goss, students who
had given speeches supporting Bradley's candidacy on college
campuses, arrived with some strange news. The national NBC
network had declared Deukmejian the winner. They did not
know what to make of the report, and were happy when Mike
Hird of the speechwriting unit assured them that the local networks, who had declared Bradley the winner, would prove to be
right. After all, according to Hird, Who knew more? Those in the
state or some pollster sequestered in a snow-covered cubbyhole
in Rockefeller Center three-thousand-miles away in New York
City? Let the celebration continue.

Upstairs, the Mayor was only waiting to get additional reports from some key precincts throughout the state from Trippi's Boiler Room Brigade. Then he would go down to greet the crowd. He felt good. He was glad that he had resisted the advice of those who suggested a negative tack, pleased that he had continued to stress positive issues during October and the whole Roberts' mess. Today Californians had proved that they were above the smear and fear tactics of such a strategy. However, Ali Webb, Assistant Press Secretary, noticed the concerned look on Nelson Rising's face as he emerged from the Boiler Room at around 9:35 P.M. He no longer looked as he had only minutes before. As supporter David Voss congratulated him, Rising failed to acknowledge Voss' words. Sam Williams and George David Kieffer, as well as Bee Canterbury Lavery and Fran Savitch, knew something was wrong. But what? What could possibly be wrong on the biggest night of their boss' career?

Gathering them and the other members of Bradley's kitchen cabinet on his way to see Bradley, Rising announced that there were problems with the initial numbers. There were factors that had not been taken into account. The absentee ballot count had been grossly underestimated. There had been perhaps as much as a sixty-percent increase in absentee ballots cast in Los Angeles County alone, and the trend seemed to be statewide. The group started to make its way through the crowd to the Mayor's suite.

Holding his victory speech, Bradley realizes his dream to be Governor is over in the 1982 election. (Courtesy of Rick Browne)

"I HAD A DREAM."

Paul Conrad cartoon that appeared in the Los Angeles Times after Bradley's defeat in 1982. (Courtesy of Los Angeles Times Syndicate)

18

A Taste of Victory and Defeat

"What my victory means tonight for the children of California is that you can not only dream dreams, but through your hard work also realize them."

—Undelivered Bradley
Victory Speech

In the suite with the Mayor and Mrs. Bradley and family were close friends. One of the Bradley inner circle who had felt uneasy all day was Maureen Kindel. Head of the Board of Public Works, Kindel had risen quickly through the ranks to be one of the Mayor's most trusted aides. Even though everyone else was celebrating, Kindel couldn't. There was something that didn't seem right to her.

However, even though she was worried about the outcome and had never really believed that California was ready to elect a black man as Governor in 1982, it was clear from watching Bradley that he felt no doubts. He was mingling comfortably with the crowd, not second-guessing the results.

Close friends of Kindel had often teased her, saying that, while everybody else would be sitting around enjoying themselves at a party, only she and Tom Bradley would choose to "talk about garbage or sewage or some other details of government." Kindel had attributed their similarities to the fact that both were Capricorns—"people who go the long hard way and endure." Tonight, however, Bradley was enjoying himself, leaving her to worry alone.

As the positive reports continued to pour in, scheduler Linda Tibi told Kindel she had a phone call. "How could anyone get in touch with me here?" Kindel wondered. On the phone she spoke with her husband, Stephen Reinhardt, who had been kept from attending the festivities only because he was in the hospital. He told her that his son had called from the East and "was sorry to hear that Mr. Bradley was not going to be Governor."

Distraught over the news, Steve had asked his son where he had heard that, given that the networks in Los Angeles had already predicted a Bradley victory. "ABC in New York has just predicted Deukmejian the winner," was the reply. Kindel dropped the phone just as Fran Savitch, Nelson Rising, Duane Garrett, and Hank Morris walked in the door. She ran up to Hank and told him the ABC prediction. Morris immediately called New York and verified the news. It was 10:00 P.M.

What did it all mean? Tibi and other hopefuls pointed out that the polls had already predicted a Bradley victory—by ten percentage points, according to Mervin Field. Rising cautioned that the preliminary data for the polls might be off.

Issues staffers Patty Brock and Kate Hansen noticed that people were beginning to cry. It became increasingly clear that Proposition 15, the gun initiative, had brought out thousands of voters whom the pollsters had not expected to vote. Furthermore, the minority vote had not measured up to earlier predictions. The data revealed that voter-turnout in South-Central Los Angeles had fallen below even that of the last gubernatorial election. And there was evidence of a large crossover vote among Democrats for Senator and Governor.

The only thing for certain was that the polls in this election were worthless. Rising conferred with Radcliff and then told the gathering that it was going to be a long night. The election was going to be very close. The final outcome might not be known until the reporting of the last precinct.

Downstairs, supporters watched the television monitors and learned what Maureen Kindel had heard only moments before— that ABC in New York had declared Deukmejian the victor. What had happened? Rising went to the podium and told the crowd that Mayor Bradley would not be coming down for awhile. While some continued to celebrate the victory, others like longtime supporter and friend Bill Elkins began to sense its ebb from the Biltmore. At 11:30 P.M., there was still nothing certain.

The events were particularly disturbing to the numerous consular corps members who had come to toast the new Governor. Bee Canterbury Lavery was surprised by the number of Consuls Generals, Chiefs of Posts, and their wives who had shown up for the festivities. It was clear that they had all sensed that this would be an important moment in American history and had wanted to be a part of it. The Consul General from China had flown down from San Francisco for the occasion. Lavery recalls, "They were in my suite until 2:00 A.M., many bursting into tears when they heard we were losing after the television commentator had said we had won." The Chinese officials were completely baffled by the entire situation. So were many Americans.

But there was still credible support for a Bradley victory. On KNXT, Mervin Field continued to insist to anchor Connie Chung that his prediction would hold true in the end, that Tom Bradley would win the election. KABC's Steve Teichner concurred, though pointing out there might be a problem with his poll sample. On KNBC, Jess Marlow told viewers the local affiliate's prediction was directly opposite that reported by the national network. There was a sense of utter shock when David Brinkley announced that NBC had declared "George Deukmejian the winner in the gubernatorial race in California."

Back in one of the staff's suites, friends and aides huddled near the television sets. Rising, Depoian, Radcliff, Morris, and Garrett were on the phones. Depoian and others discussed the new figures that had become available. Kindel sat on the couch with a good view of Bradley, who was sitting in a big easy chair in front of the television screen. She remembers: "I would have loved to have been a sculptor, because I could have captured that moment." She noticed Bradley's face get sadder and sadder in a way that she had never seen before. Kindel expressed a feeling common to the thousands gathered at the hotel that night—"My heart just broke for him."

Bradley remained in the chair, very quiet, until Rising told him that the fire marshall was getting concerned because the crowd was getting out of hand downstairs. The Mayor went down at 1:00 A.M. to tell a crowd of over two thousand supporters that the election "was simply too close to call." He advised everyone to go home and get some rest. It was as if Bradley's appearance, his message, verified the doubts that had seeped into the minds of even the most ardent supporters. UCLA student lobbyist Katie Buckland remembers, "People stood still, many doing or saying nothing." Richard Zaldivar noticed the victory balloons remained in the net overhead the podium on the stage and wondered when, if ever, they would finally be released.

Earlier supporters Ron Hansen, Jonathon Lamal, and Dennis McCarthy wandered out of the ballroom in a daze, where they noticed Jerry Brown talking to his supporters. The voters had turned on the controversial candidate. The two-time Governor had been handily defeated by Pete Wilson for the Senate seat. Brown thanked those present for a valiant effort, but indicated the race was over. As he was leaving, he turned and shouted, "I shall return. . . , but not for awhile." Then he left for Lucy's Cafe, his favorite Mexican restaurant. Bradley staffers, Martin Davis and Peter Eason, remembered the throngs of crowds and the enthusiasm that met him everywhere in his past campaigns. But not in 1984. California had voted Jerry Brown a vacation from the political arena.

Alf Brandt, Chris Wright, J. J. Gertler, and John Cornfield of the issues team listened to Brown's final words, and noticed the tears streaming down the faces of his staff, who had put in grueling hours of work in the attempt to overcome what once seemed like an insurmountable lead. Cornfield thought how Brown had nearly closed the gap, but now it was over. Meanwhile, the votes were still trickling in, and Deukmejian was ahead in the gubernatorial race, though only by a few thousand votes. Perhaps his attempt to associate Bradley and Brown had paid off.

At 3:00 A.M., the Mayor had gone to bed with the election still in doubt. He had done everything he could do. Officer Bobby Adams remembers, "He never lets you know what his feelings are. I think his mother taught all of the children to hold their emotions inside. . . . On that night, where he had been on a rollercoaster first up and then down, he was expressionless, but having known him for all these years, I can tell you that the man was bleeding inside."

The television and radio blared on in Nelson Rising's room down the hall at the Biltmore. There, a small cadre of hangers-on refused to go to bed until they knew the final outcome.

Rising talked with Hank Morris, the two Jeffs from the field organization—Montgomery and Brauckman—and with various reporters from around the state about the returns still coming in.

There was a ray of hope. Bradley was closing the gap, slowly but surely. At one point, at about 3:15 A.M., only 137 votes separated the two candidates out of more than seven million votes cast. The Sacramento Associated Press correspondent Doug Willis told Rising that the final precinct would probably determine the race. There was confusion as to which precinct had not reported. At first, the word was that it was from Orange County. The beach areas and Santa Ana were already in and the rest of the county was heavily GOP. No, it was Alameda County, according to a source in Secretary of State March Fong Eu's office, where the returns were sent. If true, that was good news. Alameda County was heavily Democratic. Tom Sullivan recalls, "There for a moment, I thought we could pull it out, that we could bring it home for the Mayor."

But only for a moment. Rising got the word. It was Orange. And, it was over now. In the closest gubernatorial contest in California since 1902, Tom Bradley had lost by about 53,000 votes out of 7,700,000. (The absentee vote brought the margin up to 93,000.)

In what had seemed like his finest hour, Tom Bradley's dream had proved impossible, at least for the moment. Following a breakfast with his family and closest aides, Bradley met with the press and then told Anton Calleia and other staffers, "I guess we had better get back to our jobs over at City Hall." Maureen Kindel recalls, "That morning I spoke to a United Negro College Fund fundraising breakfast, at a very emotional time for all of us. There wasn't a dry eye in the house."

At City Hall, it was as if everyone was in a daze, "like someone had died," recalls Connie Chappell, a secretary to the Mayor. But Bradley was back at it. As Vicki Pipkin from the campaign press office remembers, "it was like he was trying to cheer us up, it was really a bizarre situation." Mayoral assistant

Brenda Richmond recalls, "He never missed a beat and neither did any of us." Yet it would be several months before the staff's optimism and positive "can-do" attitude returned.

Art Gastelum had been so upset when he heard the news that he and his wife had remained in their room at the Biltmore for the night. The next morning, when he went to work at City Hall and walked into the Mayor's inner office, "He was there looking over some papers."

As Gastelum thought again about the last twenty-four hours and what might have been, he broke down. Bradley came over to comfort him. He looked him in the eye and said, "Art, I am sorry I let people down; that's the worst part of it. But we'll try again."

Given the closeness of the outcome, Bradley was advised by many to seek a recount. The *Times* reported on November 4 that 40,000 to 50,000 ballots still had not been processed for a variety of reasons. Duane Garrett reported alleged irregularities that affected thousands of ballots in San Francisco. But, in the final analysis, Bradley opted against a recount. "There is no effort by the Mayor or his staff to prolong this thing," Tom Sullivan told reporters. It was estimated that a recount could cost as much as $1.5 million.

Once the numbness began to subside, the growing question was, what had gone wrong? It was a question with no clear-cut answers, but a subject of debate and discussion throughout City Hall, Los Angeles, and the state. Some Councilmen, such as Joel Wachs, John Ferraro, and Zev Yaroslavsky, had been so confident of a Bradley win that they had started positioning themselves for an inside track to his seat at City Hall and had donated from their own campaign war-chests to the gubernatorial effort. Why was everybody else on the Democratic ticket for state office elected, with probably the most outstanding candidate going down to defeat?

As staffers sadly packed up mementos from the mid-Wilshire state campaign office throughout the day, the switchboard was jammed. Some people like Esther Long cried and asked for a recount. Others wished the Mayor well. Others were indignant. One woman asked the telephone receptionist, Evelyn Tucker, what had happened? She had gone to bed after hearing Bradley had won and woke up to find out that Deukmejian had "stolen" the election. What was the campaign going to do? She demanded action. She thought it was part of a plot to keep blacks from holding public office, and she planned to call the FBI. Her final words were that she would never vote again. The conspiracy theory was voiced by many callers, who thought the election results had been rigged.

A caller from San Diego wanted it reported to the "proper authorities" that he had seen people stuffing ballot boxes with Republican ballots. Another recalled how hundreds of voters in San Francisco had been told to go to the wrong polling place by an "election official" who called them the day before the election. They had arrived at the location after work, only to be told they were in the wrong polling place. They had been unable to vote for Tom Bradley. A distraught supporter from Laguna Beach recalled how, three nights before the election, he had received a call from someone speaking in "strong black dialect" telling him it was important for blacks to vote for the "brothers,"—Tom Bradley for Governor and Wilson Riles for State Superintendent of Schools. He suspected the call was a plant aimed at courting a backlash vote among the predominantly white Orange County population.

The mood within the black community was best summed up in an interview with State Assemblywoman Maxine Waters in the *Los Angeles Times*. "There's a lot of disillusionment out there today. People who feel that, once again, they have been rejected by America." Waters recapitulated Bradley's qualifications: he had "managed the city well, produced balanced budgets, balanced various interest groups—labor, business, minorities, rich poor. . . . Now if he has that kind of an image and he can't win, do you think that there is one better that they will vote for? He's the best of what a fair society could look for, and they rejected him."

Cleaning out her desk, Meg Gilbert, Cal-Labor representative for the Bradley campaign, glanced at the morning mail. A five-dollar bill fell out of a letter that read:

> To the Bradley campaign: I don't have a lot of money, but please use this as you see fit. I have always

been a supporter of Mayor Bradley and I know he will make a great governor. He was my councilman in Baldwin Hills and helped me with a problem I was having with the Veterans Administration. There aren't many people like him, but I'm glad to share him with the rest of the state. I wish I could send more, but I'm 85 and have to live on social security. Good luck.

It was things like this that made it even more difficult to accept the defeat. Gilbert looked at the *Times* folded over on her desk. There was the touching and emotional Conrad cartoon she had noticed at breakfast. It had been too much for her then, for it was more than just another successful example of the Pulitzer-Prize-winning cartoonist's ability to tap into the public consciousness. It was a tribute to the entire Tom Bradley effort of 1982, in all its valor and nobility.

She glanced down at it now. It showed a tall, Lincolnesque Bradley, holding a card that said "Governor Tom Bradley." The caption read, "I had a dream."

Gilbert remembered Bradley's final words that morning at the Biltmore. The Mayor told supporters, "One thing you all have to always remember is never, never, never, *never* give up." It was a favorite quote of Bradley's that Gregory Peck had sent him the morning after. Winston Churchill had relied on it to get him through some difficult times, and it clearly represented Tom Bradley's philosophy in life.

Gilbert thought of Bradley's campaigns of the past, the special pattern—losing the first time. She sent the $5 to Irene Tritschler in fundraising, with a note saying, "for the '86 gubernatorial campaign. . . . You know, the next one, the one we win!"

Bishop H. H. Brookins, who had helped bring Bradley to the attention of the voters of the Tenth District back in 1961, compared the defeat to a death—"like that of Martin Luther King." Brookins returned from the Biltmore and "just cried my eyes out." Yet, there was no reason for the defeat, according to Brookins, other than the fact that Bradley had been misguided by his media gurus and professional consultants. "He ignored the black community, and they didn't feel the fire for the campaign; consequently they didn't vote." The hopes of the history-making election had been dashed by poor management, Brookins maintained. Bill Robertson agreed, "A lot more could have been done in the black community; the Mayor was not agressive enough— too much media and not enough grassroots."

Phil Depoian and Anton Calleia, both of whom had been with the Mayor since his last defeat in 1969, looked at the vote breakdown in Los Angeles and statewide. Why were the vote totals in Bradley's home county and home district below what they were in the last gubernatorial election, when no one from Los Angeles had been on the ballot? Even in Bradley's home district in South-Central Los Angeles, voter turnout, which was expected to set a record, was lower than it had been in the light mayoral reelection effort of 1981. Where did the political organization break down? Gastelum's numbers showed that, while the Hispanic turnout had been better than expected in San Diego, it was disappointing in Los Angeles. "We didn't deliver our home base, and instead spent all of our time in northern and central California," was Gastelum's analysis. State Assemblyman Richard Alatorre (who, in 1985, would become the first Mexican-American to occupy a City Council seat since Ed Roybal's departure in 1962) identified the election as a classic example of taking the minority and the home-base vote for granted, "There needed to be emphasis on television, yes, but it was also important to emphasize the *Get Out The Vote*."

Alatorre was not the only one to feel that the emphasis on television at the expense of grassroots had been a mistake. As everyone searched for a scapegoat, the television campaign came in for special criticism. Playwright and professor Omar Paxson summarized one line of feeling well when he said, "Tom Bradley leaves a lasting impression that only a grassroots campaign can successfully convey, because the television medium has trouble in conveying genuineness." New York media critic Edwin Diamond concurs: "The television campaign didn't seem to capture Tom Bradley's true image or communicate his integrity." Others criticized the television spots for being too conservative. Lifelong Democrat Pat Powell said, "The problem was there was no creativity, because Garth followed public opinion rather than attempting to shape it; there was no aggressiveness in the paid media campaign."

But, as Phil Depoian recalled, people had charged Bradley with being too aggressive in the first debate when he had jabbed his finger at Deukmejian, and the general feeling about Garth's commercials had been good when the polls predicted victory. Still, in retrospect, it did seem that it would have made sense to spend more time and money getting out the vote in the last three weeks of the campaign. More should probably have been done at the grassroots level, along the lines of the kind of campaign Bradley was famous for. This election had perhaps seen too much emphasis on phone banks and modern technology at the expense of the grassroots approach.

Depoian, who had joined the Mayor's staff in 1969 as a gofer, and later become one of Bradley's most trusted aides, had presided over the 1982 effort as Campaign Manager. As such, he was high up on the list of possible scapegoats. He reflected on the old Chinese proverb, "Victory has a thousand fathers, but defeat is always an orphan," which reminded him of "all those people in 1969 who told the Mayor they had noted for him until finally Bradley said to me, 'Phil, if all of those people voted for me, how come I lost?'"

Depoian himself attributes much of the blame to a hugely successful statewide absentee ballot registration campaign by the GOP. "We won the election on November 2"—and indeed Bradley did get more votes at the polls—"but lost it in June, because of the absentee vote drives. The Republicans exceeded their wildest dreams." Absentee ballots had, in fact, played a surprisingly major role.

According to Jules Radcliff, the absentee drive had been a serendipitous stroke of luck. Radcliff had been told by Deukmejian's chief of staff, Steven Merksamer, that the idea for such a statewide drive was not planned until a supporter opted to channel a contribution toward a statewide absentee drive. And so, at the beginning of the summer, the Republicans had sent out two-and-a-half million applications for absentee ballots, accompanied by stamped return envelopes.

Republican Laurie Hunter, who decided to join her first political campaign as an issues staffer for Tom Bradley, remembers showing Joe Trippi the GOP absentee mailing. Trippi grabbed it, ripped it in two, and threw it in the trashcan, laughing, "Those damn things never mean anything. It's just a waste of their money." But Trippi was not totally aware of the ease of absentee voting in California.

Consequently, absentee ballots in Southern California were up 50 percent over 1978, 63 percent in Los Angeles County. The end result was that a traditionally conservative voting group had, due to a well-run Republican effort, turned out in record numbers and delivered a 57 percent share of the vote to Deukmejian, compared to 37 percent for Bradley—enough, according to pollster Steven Teichner, to have accounted for three percentage points in the overall vote, and more than enough to tip the election to Deukmejian. Radcliff adds, "up until 1982 and that campaign, few strategists thought of the absentee vote in terms of an actual statewide effort."

No speculation on possible causes for Bradley's defeat would be complete without an analysis of the role racism played. State Senator Diane Watson expressed an opinion shared by large numbers of Californians when she said in an interview with *Los Angeles Times* reporter Dick Bergholz, "Deukmejian is a minority too [first generation Armenian], but his skin is white. . . . There's no question that if [Bradley] had been white, he'd be governor today."

One political insider summarized what many others were saying. Identifying Bill Roberts' "unexpectedly candid observations" about hidden racism as the turning point in the election, he maintained in an interview with Bergholz, which ran on November 4, that Roberts' remarks had caused "Bradley's lead to drop in half." Furthermore, the insider concurred with what Bradley supporters throughout the state had suspected since the controversial incident in early October: "Roberts was used by Deukmejian to remind voters of Bradley's race." Bradley's own private polls, according to Radcliff, showed a "collapsing of the Mayor's lead about two weeks out from the election," at the height of the Roberts controversy. But Radcliff continues, "our final polls and, according to Merksamer, even Deukmejian's final tracking polls on the day of the election showed Bradley with a narrow win." By reporting the incident so obsessively, the press had acted as a surrogate voice for the Deukmejian effort, keeping the issue of race at the forefront of the public's consciousness at all times.

Another question on everyone's mind was how could so many polls have been so wrong? How could Mervin Field's ten-point projected victory (to take one example) turn into a defeat?

In total, five polls—Field, the *Los Angeles Times,* Teichner, Schwartz, and Tarrance—had been wrong. All had forecast victory for Bradley. Only the Republicans' poll—Decision Making Information—offered an accurate prediction of the gubernatorial election's final outcome. Based on a random telephone survey of 1,000 voters, conducted the night before the election, DMI forecast that Deukmejian would garner 49.1 percent and Bradley 48.5 percent of the final vote. The final total for the election was 49.0 percent to 48.3 percent.

Bradley's own pollster Hugh Schwartz attributed his error to the large number of the electorate, between 24 percent and 33 percent he estimated, who were influenced in some manner by the racial issue (most of whom, according to Schwartz, ended up voting for Deukmejian) and to the GOP's successful absentee ballot campaign.

Field, who also predicted a win for Jerry Brown in the Senate race, remained insistent on a Bradley victory throughout the night on CBS's KNXT station in Los Angeles. It was only at 1:15 A.M. that the pollster finally conceded there were problems with his polling procedure. He later attributed his error to a disproportionately large sample of minority groups.

The post-election analysis supports arguments that Bradley's defeat was due, at least in part, to racism within the California electorate. A headlined front-page story in the November 7 *Los Angeles Times* echoed the paper's coverage of the much ballyhooed Roberts statement throughout October—"Anti-Black Vote Key In Governor Race." Based on a poll conducted by I. A. Lewis, the *Times* reported that "500,000 Democrats and independents voted for Republican George Deukmejian for Governor not so much because they were for him but because they were against Tom Bradley."

In exploring the very hypothesis advanced by Roberts, the *Times* analysis suggested that, while both candidates commanded almost identical "straight party-line votes," it was the crossover vote that had made the difference. Some of the crossover vote reflected anti-Brown sentiments, which suggested the strategic wisdom of the GOP's attempts to lump Brown and Bradley together. Among those independents and Democrats drawn to the polls chiefly to defeat Brown, Deukmejian was preferred by a two-to-one margin over Bradley. Almost half of the seventeen percent of Democrats and independents who voted for Deukmejian stated that "they felt the government was doing too much for blacks and minorities." This compared to only one-third of the fifteen percent of the Republicans and independents who backed Bradley because "they felt government was giving too little attention to blacks and minorities." The *Times* concluded: "That three percent difference, possibly the difference between pro-black voters and anti-black voters, could account for 200,000 votes, more than enough to reverse the winner and loser."

The gun initiative had been important, too. Of the crossover Democrat and independent voters who had indicated they were motivated more by anti-Bradley than pro-Deukmejian feelings, the *Times* provided the following sketch:

> More male than the electorate as a whole, much more Anglo, more in the income bracket of $25,000 and above than the whole electorate, more from Los Angeles County and from Northern California, excluding the Bay area. . . . Almost half of the 500,000 said they own handguns, whereas only one in three of the total electorate fit that category. . . . 79% of them voted against Proposition 15, the handgun control initiative. . . . almost half of them said their vote on the handgun measure was their most important vote on the entire ballot. . . . and about 50% of them said crime was the most important issue in the race.

The poll also reported that, while the gun initiative was a dominant motivator for over half, or 250,000 of the crucial crossover voters for Deukmejian, only fourteen percent of the general electorate identified the initiative as their main reason for voting.

According to the *Times* poll, as stated in a story it ran on

November 25, the gun-control initiative overshadowed the gubernatorial race in many regions of the state. Noting the heavy turnout in rural counties and the overwhelming defeat of the proposition in such areas, the story reported, "Overall, Proposition 15, which Bradley actively supported, received 4,690,734 'no' votes. That was a higher number of votes than Deukmejian got (3,773,713) to win the governorship."

Contrary to predictions by Labor, many pollsters, and Bradley campaign officials, the actual voter turnout, far from being a record-setter, was actually lower in 1982 than in the 1978 gubernatorial election between Jerry Brown and Evelle Younger, even in the Mayor's traditionally solid areas of Los Angeles. A *Times* analysis concluded that, had the voters of South-Central Los Angeles "merely equaled their average turnout—not broken records as some of Bradley's campaign supporters had theorized they would—the Mayor could have expected to pick up 11,000 additional votes." In response to such claims, Raye Cunningham comments, "Look, with all the chiefs vying for power, we simply didn't do the job in the field, not in the black areas, the Jewish areas, or the Hispanic areas, and that is because of bad management—rather than a reflection of Tom Bradley's real popularity in the state."

The immediate question following the inauguration of Governor Deukmejian in January 1983, was who would be jockeying for position to oppose the incumbent in the 1986 race? Those expected to be in the forefront for their party's nomination four years later were Attorney General John Van De Kamp, Lieutenant Governor Leo McCarthy, and State Senator John Garamendi. There was talk of Treasurer Jess Unruh, Controller Ken Cory, as well as Secretary of State March Fong Eu.

But to those familiar with the Mayor's history—the pattern of a strike-out followed by a home-run—1986 looked like the second game of a double-header. While there were those who dismissed Bradley as a contender because of age, no one could forget that Ronald Reagan had been 65 when he lost to Gerald Ford in 1976. His resounding comeback and victory four years later disproved the value of such conjecture.

One Democrat who saw a silver lining in the entire bizarre

turn of events in 1982 was Ethel Bradley. She had told her husband, his staff, and even a few voters, that regardless of the outcome, she would be "in Los Angeles during the baseball season—Governor or no Governor." For now it was "no Governor," and Ethel would have the increased opportunity to have Tom by her side when she rooted for the Dodgers. But expectations ran high that Bradley would once again make a run for the statehouse.

Mayor Bradley, Mme. Margaret Papandreou, wife of Greece's Prime Minister Andreas Papandreou (left) and Caroline Ahmanson at the World Affairs Council, 1984. (Courtesy of Los Angeles City Hall)

On the campaign-trail with Vice-Presidential candidate Geraldine Ferraro in 1984. (Courtesy of Ellie Peck)

19

The Dream Continues

"Great works are performed not by strength but by perseverance."
—Samuel Johnson

Bradley's defeat in California in 1982 did not seem to dim his national reputation. In May 1983, Bradley was "roasted" at a $500-a-plate dinner in the nation's capitol, with the proceeds going toward a national voter registration program to help minority candidates. Referring to the 1982 campaign effort to "loosen up" the California gubernatorial Democratic candidate, Senator Teddy Kennedy told those present that Tom was "put in a windbreaker to walk the beaches for a political advertisement, and the result was that he looked about as warm and as comfortable as Richard Nixon walking on the beach in his three-piece suit." In attendance were Senator John Glenn, television's "Benson," Robert Guillaume, and many other notable politicians and entertainers.

The special feeling Democrats had for Bradley after the narrow defeat of 1982 was again much in evidence at a fundraiser in October 1983 at the Century Plaza Hotel in Los Angeles, to help erase the $1-million debt incurred by his gubernatorial campaign. While comedienne Joan Rivers chided Bradley and the Democrats on a number of issues, the real talk was of 1986, but most people concurred with Federal Appeals Court Judge Stephen Reinhardt and Nelson Rising that only time would tell how strong an incumbent candidate Deukmejian would be by then.

Also a subject of discussion at the fundraiser and in the weeks ahead would be the endorsement by Bradley of Walter

Mondale's bid for the presidency. It came at a time when California's senior U.S. Senator, Alan Cranston, had already made known his desire to be President, and amid speculation that Civil Rights leader Jesse Jackson would also be making a bid.

Announcing his support of Mondale in Washington in October 1983, Bradley described the Minnesotan as the man who "best exemplifies those characteristics of integrity, experience, of compassion, and a longtime consistent record of fairness." Indicating that Bradley's support was highly valued, Mondale told reporters, "I only hope that I can be as good a President of the United States as Tom has been a Mayor of Los Angeles."

Though endorsing Mondale, Bradley said his support of Mondale should not be looked upon as "denigrating toward Alan Cranston." But he had decided that Fritz Mondale was the most qualified of the possible Democratic Party candidates, and had given him his word that he would support him in his bid for the White House. Asked how he thought his Mondale endorsement might affect Jesse Jackson's political plans, the Los Angeles chief executive replied that the civil rights activist had "every right to run," and certainly did not "need my advice to run or not to run."

When asked about his plans for the future, Mayor Bradley simply said that he had not decided about seeking reelection in 1985, nor would he rule himself out as a gubernatorial candidate in 1986, but that his immediate efforts would be focused on the upcoming Olympic Games, to be held in Los Angeles the summar of 1984. Still, it was obvious that he intended to take on the Deukmejian administration in a very active way, whether as preparation for a rematch in 1986 or not.

Bradley played gadfly to the Deukmejian administration, constantly demanding that the Governor, whom he described as "missing-in-action," face up to the consequences of his ill-advised cost-cutting. Early, Bradley attacked Deukmejian's education budget, which included a plan for the first time ever to charge tuition at the state's community colleges and which was directly counter to the GOP Governor's campaign pledge on the issue. According to press reports, Deukmejian had told college presidents that, if they would support his tuition proposal, he might be more prone to increase their individual budget allocations for the coming year. The Mayor saw this as nothing short of "blackmail," a charge he made with the Chancellor of the Los Angeles Community College District, Leslie Koltai, at his side. The break in California's long-standing tuition-free junior college tradition prompted outcries from many quarters. Critics viewed the decision to be more rooted in budget than the product of philosophy. George David Kieffer, of the Center of Democratic Institutions in Santa Barbara, argued "that it certainly was not helpful to have such a radical change in the seventy-year-old policy simply to balance the budget."

There were signs from Sacramento that the incumbent viewed Bradley as his primary opponent in 1986, and he went on the counteroffensive. After Bradley had criticized the state for failing to clean up cancer-causing agents and hazardous wastes at a site in Los Angeles, Deukmejian shot back a letter that charged the city was at fault, not the state.

Bradley told reporters the state had indeed allocated money for the clean-up, over $1 million. But, he explained, the city's efforts had been limited by the fact that the funds were under the auspices of the state's Department of Health Services. According to the Mayor's office, the primary concern of the Deukmejian administration had been "cutting costs" rather than the safety of the citizens in the area.

On a campaign swing in San Jose in November 1984, to support the national Democratic ticket, Bradley labeled Deukmejian a "modern-day Scrooge." The reference came during a speech to senior citizens, criticizing the Governor's veto of nursing-home reform measures. The Los Angeles Mayor told his audience that Deukmejian had pledged to improve the quality of living for seniors, but when it came to delivering on the promise, he had not done so.

Some saw Bradley's new activist zeal as a clear indication that he was, indeed, running in 1986. Responding to questions about the increasing frequency of his attacks on Deukmejian and what that might indicate about his own political ambitions, Bradley told reporters, "When he was elected, I promised that when I thought he was doing something wrong, I would say so."

Furthermore, if he were to speak out every time he disagreed with the incumbent Governor, "I would be speaking out, every day of the week."

One of those most frequently singled out for putting new fire into Bradley's public pronouncements was Deputy Mayor and Chief of Staff, Tom Houston, who joined the Mayor's staff when Ray Remy left the post to assume the presidency of the Los Angeles Chamber of Commerce in 1984. Houston brought to his job an in-depth experience in state government and a statewide network of political connections.

The previous Chief of Staff, Ray Remy, was a Republican with a keen sense of the micro-dynamics of government. He had been one of the Mayor's key assests in the RTD strike, transporation issues, the Olympics, and the everyday affairs of city government. Remy had a strong base in the business community and was more issue- than politically-oriented. An invaluable ally, Remy preferred to stay above party politics, leaving that area to other members of the Mayor's staff. Upon learning of Remy's resignation to preside over the Los Angeles Area Chamber of Commerce, in the spring of 1984, key Bradley strategists suggested the Mayor consider a different type of person to fill his job. The general recommendation was that the new Deputy Mayor be not only an expert in government, but also aggressive and outspoken in getting the word out about Bradley. The new Deputy Mayor, argued Maureen Kindel, should be a natural activist, someone who would reflect and communicate the zeal that characterized the Mayor's work schedule and approach to government.

The thirty-nine-year-old Houston seemed to combine the best of many worlds. Born and bred in Missouri, he attended Princeton and then Stanford for law school. His politics had evolved over the years, beginning in his youth when he worked for Barry Goldwater. Later he had headed up Jerry Brown's Fair Political Practices Commission. It was his leadership skills that most impressed Kindel and other top Bradley advisers. Houston was known as a "workaholic," with the determination and temperament to rival an old Missouri mule. "He just comes in, and shakes the hell out of you," commented one past employee. "There's no such thing as just treading water with Tom—it's more like being in the rapids, with only the captain knowing for sure where you're going." It was this energetic spirit, the tendency to push rather than punt, that attracted Bradley to his new Deputy Mayor.

Comparing his love of politics to his favorite sport of wrestling, Houston states, "Your best defense is a strong offense, and the confidence in your abilities to win; you never think about the possibilities of defeat." Outspoken and even abrasive, according to some critics, Houston faults the 1982 gubernatorial campaign with being overly cautious: "The slogan that he doesn't say much but gets a lot done is designed to say that, 'okay, Bradley is black but he is safe,' and I don't think we have to be that conservative; his record is outstanding regardless of what color he is."

Another addition to the new City Hall team was Mark Fabiani, the Mayor's in-house counsel. A Harvard Law School graduate, Fabiani has aided in the Mayor's initiation and support of progressive measures, such as the city's divestiture policy regarding South Africa, Councilwoman Joy Picus' equal-pay-for-equal-work legislation, and the ban on AIDS discrimination, all of which serve as landmark policies for urban development in the United States.

One change in the office has been dramatic. With Ali Webb and Houston prodding him, Bradley seems more willing to let the public know of his activities. For years, Bradley's reticence had been a problem that had dogged the efforts of the Bradley team.

Art Gastelum had once described the "frustration" felt by Bradley's staff when faced with the Mayor's natural modesty: "Our hands are tied because . . . he has never let us package him with the pictures or press releases he deserved." Now he finally seems willing to accept the necessity of packaging. However, as Tom Sullivan points out, "This isn't really a new Tom Bradley; the activism in the office is just showing the public a different facet of an extraordinary man." Ethel Bradley concurs, "This new Tom Bradley I read about is just the same Tom Bradley—a workaholic and eclectic—that I've known for over fifty years."

The new activism in the Mayor's office went beyond photo opportunities. In May 1984, Bradley announced a major shake-up in the city government. He requested that all 175 city commissioners tender their resignations. Many would be reappointed,

Sharing a laugh with Her Majesty Queen Elizabeth during her visit to Los Angeles, February 28, 1983. (Courtesy of Rick Browne)

With Dorothy Hamill and Ira Distenfield at the Kickoff event for the Mayor's Corporate Challenge for Youth, 1985.

Tom, Ethel, and long-time friend Bill Elkins, enjoying a hometown football game at UCLA. (Courtesy of Rick Browne)

but Bradley felt the move was necessary in order to reassess the quality of service being provided to the citizens of Los Angeles. The new commissioners, according to the Mayor, "are more representative of the city's diverse constituencies." One-third of the appointees are women. Blacks compose roughly twenty percent, Hispanics fifteen percent, Asians nine percent, and American Indians three percent of the new commission members.

The summer of 1984 brought Bradley another of the firsts that had long characterized his life. As *Los Angeles Times* reporter Bob Drogin noted on June 19 of that year, Mayor Tom Bradley would be "the first black ever interviewed" for the Vice-Presidential nomination. Presidential hopeful Walter Mondale had called the mayor at 7:30 A.M. the day before, to tell him that he wished to consider him as his running mate. The Minnesotan described Bradley as "one of the most respected public servants in our country, an outstanding mayor." Others to be interviewed included Senator Lloyd Bentsen of Texas, Mayor Dianne Feinstein of San Francisco, Representative Geraldine Ferraro of New York, and Mayor Henry Cisneros of San Antonio.

A visibly proud Mayor told reporters that he was "honored and flattered to be selected for the interview." And he added that, regardless of the decision about the Vice-Presidential candidate, he would "do whatever I can to ensure a Democratic victory in November."

The Mayor had known Mondale since 1973. He had, in fact, delivered speeches supporting his candidacy for Vice-President in 1976 in New York, when Jimmy Carter had selected the Minnesota Senator for his running mate, and in New York four years later. Bradley was the first major Democratic leader in the country to endorse Mondale's presidential bid.

Jody Powell wrote in a national column that Tom Bradley would be "as distinguished and presidential as any candidate on any ticket in our history." The Press Secretary to former President Jimmy Carter hailed Bradley's intelligence and praised his "outstanding political and managerial skills in a tough job." According to Powell, Mondale was not likely to "find a better wager than Mayor Tom Bradley of Los Angeles" to help out the Democratic ticket. Given the success of Jesse Jackson's campaign in capturing the attention and interest of millions who felt disenfranchised from the nation's political life, Bradley's name to the ticket could be a great boost to the Democratic bid for national power. Powell wrote that a Bradley vice-presidential nomination could "turn a less-than-invigorating campaign into a crusade, an election of historic moment." It would mean more than "a hundred speeches and a plane-load of issue papers about fairness." The compliment, coming from a Carter aide, was welcome and somewhat of a surprise, given the cool atmosphere that was known to exist between Mondale and the Carter staff.

The next couple of days were "some of the most exciting I have ever had in my life," remarks Ali Webb, the Mayor's twenty-nine-year-old Press Secretary, speaking of the trip when she accompanied Bradley to North Oaks, Minnesota, to meet with Mondale. It was only after hours of persuasion that Bradley agreed for Webb to accompany him on what could be the most important trip in his life. Webb recalls, "As a reflection of his self-sufficient attitude . . . , he had planned to make the trip alone." A graduate of Stanford, who had spent brief periods away from her home-state while working for a small paper in Texas and for Jack Anderson in Washington, Webb had joined the Bradley staff only two years before, after Tom Sullivan had joined the 1982 gubernatorial campaign staff.

Webb noticed that Bradley himself seemed to be in unusually high spirits as they took off for Minnesota on a 5:00 P.M. flight. "It was as if he had just realized the significance of the trip, of what it meant to his career and to millions throughout the country." A door had been pried open in American history that had been locked since the birth of the Republic. And through it came the man who had begun his life in a little cabin in Calvert, Texas, sixty-six years before.

Bradley had a 9:30 A.M. meeting with Mondale the next day, followed by a lunch, at which Mrs. Mondale would also be present. Prior to the 9:30 meeting, there was a coffee with Joyce Hurrier of the Mondale team. Webb was nervous, but across the table, Tom Bradley, on his way to one of the most important interviews of his life, seemed serenely in control.

On the way to the Mondale home, however, it became apparent there had been some mix-up concerning the attire for the occasion. Mondale would be casually dressed, in a plaid shirt, sweater, and slacks. Bradley was in his usual suit. Upset at the lapse in communications between the Mondale and Bradley camps, Webb consoled herself with the reflection that "Tom Bradley in a suit more accurately reflects the formality of his personality and the occasion." Bradley had, as usual, escaped the dictates of his would-be packagers, so that the photos of him with Mondale would show the formality he has always presented in public.

The Mondales greeted Bradley at the end of a long lane, and all three chatted and talked with reporters as they walked back to the house, situated on one of the 10,000 lakes for which Minnesota is famous.

The party then went inside, where Bradley chatted about his philosophy and his record with the Mondales and John Reilly, a key strategy advisor to the presidential hopeful on the choice of the number-two man for the ticket. Meanwhile, Webb met with Mondale Press Secretary Maxine Isaacs, preparatory to a press briefing that Mondale Campaign Chairman Jim Johnson had set up for Webb. Later Webb returned to the Mondale home in time to join the Mondales, John Reilly, and Bradley for lunch, where she was privy to the discussion, which included numerous questions. How long was Bradley with the U.S. Conference of Mayors? The National League of Cities? What problems did Bradley see as most significant to the cities of America in the next decade? Then Mondale and Bradley discussed the statements that would be made to the press after the completion of their own private discussions.

The press conference featuring Bradley and Mondale went very well. The admiration that they felt for each other was evident to the press contingent crowded into the room. Bradley began his statement by noting the historical significance of Mondale's "opening up the political process." Blacks, Hispanics, women, *all* Americans could now reach for what once seemed impossible, and "children all over this nation, of every creed and color, could see that there was still truth to the American dream" for those who aimed high and worked hard. It was an inspirational message from a man whose life stood as testimony to the claims he was making.

Mondale told reporters that Tom Bradley was "one of the nation's most respected public servants . . . , a symbol of hope and justice" to all Americans. And, in a light-hearted moment, he recounted the adventure he and Bradley had had walking through the Minnesota woods around his house during part of their three-hour meeting. They had discovered, at one point, that they had shaken the secret service agents so effectively that they had gotten lost. So they now had a proven record of working together.

There was no doubt to political observers that Tom Bradley carried impressive credentials that could help the Democratic ticket. In comparison to some of the lesser-known candidates, whose names were being discussed as possible vice-presidential nominees, Bradley was well-known throughout the country. He had a prominent and impressive record in both domestic and foreign affairs. As the Mayor of Los Angeles, he had hosted official visits from dignitaries from throughout the world. Because of the city's work in foreign trade, investments, and as a Gateway to the Pacific Rim, Bradley was undoubtedly the second most widely known American (after Reagan) in many countries of Asia.

His political base in Los Angeles was an example of his efforts to work with diverse groups—a public-private partnership with business, government, and labor—to build coalitions and to administrate effectively. As a champion of minority rights and as a feminist, Bradley could be counted upon to bring back to the Democratic fold those factors of the traditional party membership who had stayed home in the 1980 election. And a Tom Bradley vice-presidential nomination would undoubtedly put pressure on Jesse Jackson to be a strong supporter of the Democratic ticket. Some also argued that a Mondale-Bradley ticket could guarantee a strong minority turn-out for the Democratic ticket, which was crucial to any hopes of beating Reagan in November.

Furthermore, Bradley's mediating abilities and past record of accomplishments could help reduce the division between two traditional components of the Democratic Party—Jews and Blacks, many of whom had been stirred up by off-the-record-remarks Jesse Jackson and Louis Farrakhan were said to have made about Jews. Bradley later would find himself embroiled in a controversy precipitated by Farrakhan's religious viewpoints.

Bradley was a hot commodity. News programs throughout the country requested interviews. Following a satellite appearance on the *Today Show,* the Bradley party traveled back to Los Angeles, where the mayor had a full schedule of events the following day. In flight, there were interviews with Bill Boyarsky of the *Los Angeles Times* and Linda Douglas of KCBS.

The following weeks back at City Hall were especially intense. Calls and requests for interviews from press members throughout the country, as well as from foreign correspondents, flooded City Hall. How did Bradley think the interview had gone? Did the Mayor believe he had made a good impression? Had he spoken with Mondale since the trip to Minnesota? Were there any indications that a Mondale decision was imminent?

It was only then, after the initial shock of what had happened, that Bradley recalls the event finally sinking in: "I really sensed that what I had said a long time ago was now finally true . . . a black could be Vice-President." He succinctly described this realization, "It really amounted to goose-bump time!"

A week after the meeting in Minnesota, which had seen Mondale interview a host of other candidates, including Dianne Feinstein, Geraldine Ferraro, and others, the *Times* reported that a secret Mondale memo identified Bradley as the best running-mate. A special computer survey of nominees for the second spot on the ticket had ranked apparent strengths and weaknesses of each of the candidates who had made the journey to Minnesota. Both the *New Republic* and the *Wall Street Journal* supported a Bradley candidacy.

Of particular importance to the Mondale campaign was Bradley's past record attracting Hispanics to the polls. A staff member revealed that the Mayor had been "13 percent more successful among Latino voters than any other Democrat ever" in California. The computerized study also showed that a Bradley candidacy would motivate other minorities to the polls, without driving Southern whites who supported Mondale out of his camp. However, a top party member argued that "A white woman was looked upon as less of a threat to the American populace than a Black male who happened to be Mayor of Los Angeles." And one of Mondale's closest advisors suggested that Bradley's age was an even more significant factor against his selection than his race.

No one doubted the Mayor's qualifications. He probably had the best credentials on the short list of candidates. But the opinion held by many members of the press corps, as well as party leaders, was that, when it came down to the decision, conservative thinking would (some thought should) prevail. Mondale would not chose a black running-mate. America might not be ready for a black Vice-President, even one with the credentials of Tom Bradley, and his appearance on the ticket would only add to the already heavy odds against a Democratic win. Former Senator John Tunney stated, "Mondale needed a bold stroke, because the old tried and true approach simply wouldn't work. It would take tremendous intestinal fortitude to pick a black as Vice-President, because the world would have said, 'wow what's this guy doing!' In the end, Mondale ended up with a dramatic move, but it was a less dramatic stance." Still, there were those who held out hope that such myopic perceptions would give way to a changing reality, as Tom Bradley had caused them to do many times before.

A couple of days later, Jim Johnson, the Campaign Chairman for the Mondale campaign called City Hall for Mayor Bradley. Mr. Mondale wanted to speak to the Mayor about the vice-presidential nomination. It was 4:00 P.M., and unless he had an appointment, Bradley was always at his desk at that hour, poring over his papers at City Hall. Except on this day.

Ali Webb remembers: "It was one of the few instances where neither the press office nor scheduling knew where to contact Bradley." The search was on. Tom Houston had no idea, and Fran Savitch hadn't seen him since the early morning. The same answer came from Phil Depoian, Grace Davis, Wanda Moore, Ela Vallejo, Maria Lopez, and his security officers Larry Kounalis and Louis Trujillo.

Even Mrs. Bradley at Getty House hadn't seen the Mayor. Here was possibly the next President of the United States wanting to talk to Bradley, either to tell him he wanted him to join the ticket or to ask his support of another running-mate, and no one knew where or how to locate the Mayor of Los Angeles.

The staff continued the search. Johnson was told Bradley would return the call shortly. Undoubtedly, he must by now be at Getty House. No, Mrs. Bradley told Webb again, he hadn't come home, nor had she received a call from him. It just wasn't like Bradley to be out of range for so long. Why now?

As the hours passed, it seemed obvious. Undoubtedly, he had received a phone call from Johnson . . . or Mondale himself. And Bradley was on his way to Minnesota to accept the nomination. That had to be it. He was on the plane, or at least the airport.

The euphoria of that moment evaporated for Webb and the other Bradley staffers when they learned that Jim Johnson had finally reached Bradley at Getty House. Johnson announced that Walter Mondale had selected Geraldine Ferraro as his running-mate. The Mayor thanked Johnson for the call, pledged his enthusiastic support, and hung up the phone. Bradley had been visiting Ellis that afternoon, and had stayed longer to tell his brother about his trip to Minnesota. Ellis was very proud and wished their mother had been alive to have witnessed this event. Ethel noted that the disappointing news that Tom had not been Mondale's choice did not seem to faze him at all; he continued, as usual, to go over the myriads of papers in his study and to watch the news on television before going to bed.

The next day, Depoian remembers that Bradley told his staff that he was going to do all he could to see to it that the Mondale-Ferraro ticket was victorious in the fall. "He didn't even seem disappointed," remarks Webb. "He's such a statesman and gentleman . . ." As he had in 1982, he spent the next few weeks trying to cheer up the staff, when not embroiled in the activities of an extremely eventful summer. For this was the summer of the long-planned-for Olympics in Los Angeles. Furthermore, Bradley was to give the nominating speech for Walter Mondale at the Democratic National Convention in a few weeks. Meanwhile there was city business as usual, and all the last-minute preparations for what would be the most successful Olympics in the history of the Games.

The official Los Angeles welcome to the 1984 Olympics—The Heart of the Place (Courtesy of Los Angeles City Hall)

Dedication of the opening of Tom Bradley International Terminal at LAX. (Courtesy of Los Angeles City Hall)

20

The 1984 Los Angeles Olympics

"All men of action are dreamers."
—James G. Huneker

By the summer of 1984, the Olympics seemed clearly destined for success, but up to that time the Games had often threatened and sometimes proved to be a political liability for Tom Bradley. The people of Los Angeles and California had not unequivocally backed the Olympics. A survey as recent as the November 8, 1983 Field Poll showed that one out of every eight citizens statewide thought "it was a bad thing to have the Olympics in California," and one out of five Los Angelenos thought the Olympics a bad idea. Traffic problems, increasing crime and violence, the possibility of higher taxes to pay for the Games, political problems, the ever-present threat of terrorism, and even smog were reasons cited by those who opposed holding the Games in Los Angeles. Bradley's persistence in wooing the Games to Los Angeles had provided political naysayers with ample ammunition to attack him over the years. Some California citizens had even cited his championing of the Olympics as a reason for voting against him in the 1982 gubernatorial election.

The first privately financed Games in the history of the international competition had attracted criticism in the world press, too. The *London Times* featured a page-one story in December 1983, entitled "The Rapacious City that Denies Pleasure to Millions in Europe." The article condemned the "greed of the Olympics' host city of Los Angeles and of the private, commercially-oriented organizing committee." The West German press also lambasted the Los Angeles Games in a *Der Spiegel* article claiming that the palm trees, beaches, and good weather of Southern California merely obscure "an explosive mixture of nationalities and abnormal criminality."

But Bradley never lost faith in his vision of the Olympics. As Harry Usher, General Manager of the Olympics at the LAOOC, recalls, "Bradley's moral support, especially in the early stages before the spirit built in Los Angeles . . . , when the public-opinion polls were against us, kept many of us going full-steam ahead. He was involved in all our negotiations with the city, at most of which he certainly did not have to be present. But his great mediation skills, his sense of fairness for all parties involved, made the dealings with the city go smoothly . . . , particularly at the level of security and financial arrangements."

Even while under attack, Bradley told a group of visitors, "The Olympic spirit, a force of good in this troubled world, is alive and well in Los Angeles. I am confident that Los Angeles will uphold the finest tradition of the Olympic movement. The Games promote friendly relations among nations and permit athletes of our global village to participate in peaceful competition."

Finally, on May 8, 1984, just eighty-two days prior to the largest sporting event ever convened, the Olympic flame—which had itself been a subject of controversy with the Ancient Olympic Council of Greece concerned about commercialization of the torch relay—arrived in New York.

Awaiting the flame's arrival in front of the United Nations, in the pouring rain, were IOC President Juan Antonio Samaranch, IOC Director Madame Monique Berlioux, LAOOC President Peter Ueberroth, Olympian Rafer Johnson, Mayor Ed Koch, and Mayor Tom Bradley. It was a proud moment for Bradley. The flame sparked a surge of excitement for the Games, which were only three months away. Bradley commemorated the Olympic flame's entry into the U.S., by stating, "It is appropriate that the Olympic flame start its journey of 15,000 kilometers here in New York City. It will serve to link the East and West Coast. It is in the best Olympic spirit . . . of people helping people."

Rafer Johnson, a true Olympic hero, rekindled the spirit of the Olympics as the torch began a journey that would take it before some thirty million Americans in over one thousand communities. At the culmination of a moving ceremony, Gina Hemphill, granddaughter of the heroic sprinter Jesse Owens, and Bill Thorpe, grandson of decathalon champion Jim Thorpe, took the torch from Johnson for the first leg of the relay, reminding millions of past moments of athletic glory, and signaling the beginning of the Twenty-third Olympiad. Tom Bradley's dream was at last a reality.

The same day that the Olympic relay began from the United Nations Building in New York, the Soviet Union announced they would not attend the 1984 Olympiad in Los Angeles. Many Americans saw this as a Kremlin decision made on the day, four years before, when President Carter announced our boycott of the Moscow Games to protest the invasion of Afghanistan.

According to Marat Gramov, the Soviet Sports Minister and Olympic chairman, the decision not to go to Los Angeles was due to the discovery of plans to abduct "Soviet people, for compelling them not to return to their motherland, for treating them with special drugs, including psychotropic preparations which destroy the nervous system." If that were not enough, the Soviet representative cited problems with security and the "infiltration of terrorist and extremist elements into the organizing committee of the Olympics." Part of the protest was in response to the "Ban the Soviets Coalition," an Orange County based group that had pledged to demonstrate wherever the Soviet delegation appeared and to provide "safe houses" for defectors.

Many members of the Olympic host city were surprised at the Soviet action. Less than a month before the boycott announcement, Soviet journalists had visited Los Angeles to determine which Olympic events they would cover and where they would be staying. The Soviet Olympic officials had been finalizing plans to fly into Los Angeles in their own planes, to house their athletes in a cruise ship, and to obtain visas for key officials.

Ueberroth and Bradley were outraged by such "insults to the American people." But both publicly stated that they were willing to go to Moscow or wherever was necessary to try to change the mind of the Soviets. But the situation could not be salvaged. One superpower was getting even with another, and both would be losers. Now the focus of the Los Angeles Olympic effort was on checking the tide of withdrawals by Soviet bloc countries pressured to join the Russian boycott.

While the Soviets decided not to bring their delegation to Los Angeles, the Mayor was successful in ensuring that the largest Communist government in the world, China, made its first trip ever to the Olympics. With the help of Armand Hammer, Chairman and Chief Executive Officer of Occidental Petroleum, Caroline Ahmanson, Chairman of the Los Angeles Guangzhou Sister City Association, and Marcia Hobbs, President of the Greater Los Angeles Zoo Association, Bradley was also able to persuade the Chinese government to bring along two pandas to the Los Angeles Zoo for ninety days, funded by a $300,000 grant from Occidental Petroleum and ARCO.

The torch relay continued to excite people throughout the United States to join the Olympic spirit. The flame traveled through forty-one major cities and one thousand small communities. Passing over mountains, through deserts, and across the nation's fertile valleys, the torch seemed an apt symbol of the Olympic perseverance that Bradley and the members of the LAOOC had in common with the athletes. Bradley regards the struggle to bring the Games back to Los Angeles as "the toughest, longest-running battle of my political career, but worth every minute of it." Roy A. Anderson, Chairman of the 2,800-member Los Angeles Area Chamber of Commerce, a long-standing business leader who also serves as Chairman and Chief Executive Officer of Lockheed, identifies the 1984 Games as a "stunning tribute to Tom Bradley's public–private partnership principle."

In the few months prior to the beginning of Olympics, Tom Bradley was involved in endless activities. From playing host with Ethel to over 150 foreign dignitaries who came to the city for the Olympics to anticipating traffic problems that might result, Bradley was in command of every detail of the complex situation.

One month before the Games started, the Mayor presided over the opening ceremonies of the new $123-million Tom Bradley International Terminal at Los Angeles Airport. Initially rejecting the proposal by the airport commission to name the facility in his honor, Bradley eventually acquiesced. The five level, one-million-square-foot terminal is home to twenty-six air carriers from throughout the world, and is the largest international terminal in the United States. To make sure that visitors to the Olympics from abroad were welcomed properly, Bradley suggested "sensitivity training" for Los Angeles International Airport personnel. Travelers would be able to begin their visit to the city on the right foot. The *Times* reported that 248 security officers would receive such instruction.

One moving example of the Mayor's dedication to the Olympic spirit was his support of Israel's wish to commemorate the Israeli athletes murdered by terrorists at the 1972 Munich Games. Israeli Consul General, Jacob Even proposed to Ueberroth that IOC President Samaranch participate in the memorial ceremonies as a means of conferring international recognition upon them. But even the well-known persuasive powers of the LAOOC leader failed to convince the IOC President to cooperate. Even remembers, "We were disappointed that the IOC would not participate, but when Mayor Bradley learned of the situation, he originated a plan that not only honored the athletes in a ceremony at City Hall, but also featured a memorial plaque, with the names of those who died to be permanently affixed to the Coliseum as a reminder of the tragedy to those attending the 1984 Games." Even and Abraham Spiegel were on hand with Mayor Bradley as the international press reported the commemoration. Even concluded, "Bradley made an outstanding speech at the event and gave it the dignity it deserved. He understands the history of the Jewish people, and is loved in Israel. I have only good words to say about Tom Bradley."

Tom Bradley recalls an incident that took place as the torch, carried by O. J. Simpson entered the City of Santa Monica. One man climbed a cactus to get a better view, apparently not even noticing the thorns. Bradley states, "I knew then that the Games were a success."

As opening day neared, people throughout Los Angeles noted a special kind of camaraderie. The city was coming together. The spirit was there and reflected in the pastel banners and flags that seemed to be everywhere. Even the press, which had been skeptical about the advisability of a Los Angeles Olympics, became enthusiastic. The Mayor's party for the International Olympic Committee at City Hall set the tone for the event. Over 1,000 Olympic officials entered City Hall on a red carpet and enjoyed a huge buffet on the south lawn of City Hall. As they passed through City Hall, they viewed a special exhibit of the 1932 Olympic Games, recalling memories for those who had been in Los Angeles for it.

The banquets with officials and dignitaries from throughout the world kept the official host of Los Angeles more than busy. But even more meaningful for Bradley were the meetings with the athletes and visitors who had come to Los Angeles to be part of the great event. Always a workaholic, the Mayor seemed more energized than ever by the excitement in the air. Anton Calleia remembers, "All that period, he seemed to be about three feet off the ground. He was truly proud of the city and how it had come together to greet the world."

The Opening Ceremonies expressed the spirit and vitality of the city and of Southern California. The roar of the Coliseum crowd grew stronger with the appearance of each team as they marched out of the tunnel onto the field. There were warm words of congratulations from President and Nancy Reagan. A special warmth was extended to Rumania and the People's Republic of China, who were given standing ovations. When the U.S. team stepped onto the field, the crowd went wild.

Thousands of doves and streamers, were released in a spectacle orchestrated by David Wolper. Singer Vickie McClure's rendition of "Reach Out and Touch Somebody's Hand" was symbolic of what the Olympics would achieve during two-weeks of events, which were beamed throughout the world. The four-hour opening ceremony was viewed by over 2.5 billion people.

During the Games, Bradley wanted to attend as many of the sporting events as possible. "His schedule was incredible. Cycling events in the morning, swimming in the afternoon, track and field competition at night, and at each one he was mobbed by well-wishers and autograph-seekers," said Craig Lawson, Bradley's Olympic liaison during the Games. He visited almost every Olympic site and both Olympic Villages during the two weeks of the Games.

More athletes from more nations attended the 1984 Games than any other Olympics in history. It was an emotional experience for Tom Bradley, who fifty-two years earlier, as a young boy, had peeked through the fence to see the events of the 1932 Olympiad.

Councilman Howard Finn recalls, "The real credit to Tom Bradley during the Olympics was how efficiently Los Angeles worked and that he stuck by his guns of no costs to the taxpayer. There were no problems, even though some people had predicted chaos. When I think of Tom Bradley, I think of how relatively few problems this city has had in his tenure. He is a real peacemaker, and the Olympics is an example of his style of government. He is dedicated to make this the best city he can."

Los Angeles Times reporter Claudia Luther interviewed a fan at Dodger Stadium, where the first Olympic baseball game was about to begin. The crowd applauded wildly when Bradley was introduced, and the fan stated, "I don't think 55,000 people could have roared any louder than they did." Speculating on the effect the Olympics' success might have on Bradley's expected reelection bid, and a possible rematch with George Deukmejian, the *Times* noted that, while Deukmejian was embroiled in heated debate during the last part of the legislative session in Sacramento, Bradley was the center of worldwide attention at an event that reflected his style of leadership and conviction—the Olympics.

Bradley remembers: "The President of China told me that 200 million Chinese were watching on television. There would have been more, except they didn't have more television sets." What they saw intrigued them—gracious, hospitable people in Los Angeles.

Bradley appeared on national networks and was praised for his leadership abilities in bringing the Games to Los Angeles and America. Even Bradley's staunchest critics, who had fought against bringing the games to Los Angeles, praised him. Among them was longtime critic, Councilman Bernardi: "It was a superbowl of all superbowls. It was a masterpiece. I congratulated the Mayor at the closing ceremonies because I fully recognized that, had it turned into Munich or Montreal, everyone would point their fingers at only one person, that was the Mayor. If he should take all the blame, I believe he deserved the credit."

Councilman Braude, who had cast the swing vote to bring the Olympics to Los Angeles, adds, "The Olympics were a great symbolic party for the city, but it was cream, it was not the essence of running a good city. Mayor Bradley earned my respect and ardent support for the professionalism, accomplishments, and creativity which was merely exemplified during the Olympics."

None of the fears that residents had about hosting the Olympic Games panned out. The freeways were not turned into "parking lots." There was no overcrowding of restaurants, hotels, or the new airport. There were no terrorist attacks, no increases in crime or violence. There would be no new taxes to finance the games. And there was no increase in smog. Instead, the city enjoyed some of the clearest days Los Angeles had ever witnessed. Commenting on the vision and courage that Bradley had displayed throughout the ten-year struggle, Bill Robertson states, "His political future hung on whether or not it was successful. All of the credit he gets for bringing the Olympics here, he deeply deserves."

Economically, the Olympics surpassed the most optimistic estimates of Bradley, Ziffren, and Ueberroth—a $222.7-million surplus. The Olympics were held at no expense to Los Angeles taxpayers. They brought more than $3.3 billion to the local and state economy, and over 74,000 Olympics-related jobs. According to the agreement negotiated with the Los Angeles Olympic Organizing Committee, forty percent of the surplus was allocated to amateur athletics in Southern California. This $90-million share was a most impressive figure to help provide important channels for the city's youth. The remainder of the surplus was scheduled to go to the U.S. Olympic Committee and to U.S. sports federations. LAOOC Chairman Paul Ziffren later announced a one-time allocation of $2 million to inaugurate a biennial Los Angeles cultural festival that would include programs from throughout the world and reflect the Olympic spirit of community. Bradley announced that the first four-week event would begin in September 1987.

Countless groups commended Bradley for his efforts in bringing and instituting the Games in Los Angeles. Among them was the California legislature, which praised Bradley for his "efforts in negotiating to bring the Games of the Twenty-third Olympiad to Los Angeles, for his leadership in organizing local municipal services to aid in the presentation of the Olympics, for his determined efforts to implement innovative methods to provide athletes and visitors to Los Angeles with a memorable, enjoyable, and peaceful experience, and for his unfailing graciousness as the official host of the Olympic Games."

The afterglow of the Olympics continued to light Los Angeles. One year after the Games, Tom Bradley told a crowd of over 20,000 people for the "Olympic Legacy Day" that nostalgia for the Olympics was fine, but "the best days of Los Angeles are still ahead of us." Calling upon the community spirit that had made the Games such a success, Bradley announced a major expansion of the fourteen-year-old Convention Center to begin in 1986, nearly tripling its capacity to allow it to handle the new interest in Los Angeles generated by the Olympics. On another occasion Earl A. Powell II, Director of the Los Angeles Art Museum, credited the Olympics Art Festival as a major impetus for the new interest in the visual arts in Southern California. Powell told a beaming Mayor and the guests at the occasion that the festival had resulted in Los Angeles being "perhaps the most interesting and open city for the arts in the world."

Los Angeles had reaped more specific benefits than just good press and a more accurate image of the city's promise. Pacific Bell announced that the communication system installed within the city for the Olympics was superior to that of any other city in the country. The fiber optic cable network would have a tremendous impact on more than half of the city's workers who were in the information area. It would be another plus for the city in the effort to increase the trading potential of the major port on the promising Pacific rim in Asia.

The night before the Opening Ceremonies for the Olympics, Tom Bradley had declared, "The eyes of the world are upon us and we are ready." During the following fifteen days, the entire world measured the character of the Mayor of Los Angeles by the truth of his message, and in the final outcome, he and his city not only passed the test, but excelled. In Ziffren's evaluation, "It was a fitting tribute to a man whose life is epitomized by the impossible dream." Dr. Norman Miller, Vice-Chancellor Emeritus of UCLA and Director of the UCLA 1984 Olympics office, sums up, "The Olympics represent the essence of Tom Bradley's promise and record of his leadership for Los Angeles and the United States. I have never seen such a spirit of patriotism since World War II."

Testifying before the Transportation Subcommittee on Metro Rail in Washington, D.C., 1985. (Courtesy of Los Angeles City Hall)

Bradley joins his staff for press secretary Ali Webb's surprise birthday party. Clockwide from bottom, Lisa Kwan, Linda Miller, Ali Webb, Rosalie Avery, the Mayor, Ela Vallejo, Gabriel Bustamante, Vicki Pipkin. (Photo by Guy Crowder: Courtesy of Ali Webb)

21

An Unprecedented Fourth
Mayoral Term

*"If I were giving out medals for
leadership, Tom Bradley would get
the Gold."*

—Peter Ueberroth

Bradley formally announced that he was a candidate for an
unprecedented fourth term at a gathering of supporters at the
Century Plaza Hotel in November 1984. As part of his declaration, the Mayor told the group of one thousand people who had
just seen a film of Olympic highlights, "The challenge of turning
our hopes and dreams for the future of Los Angeles into reality
has never been more exciting . . . our vision can become our
children's reality."

In a speech that echoed the lyrics of Randy Newman's song,
"I Love L.A.," the Mayor explained he was seeking reelection to
continue his efforts to "make Los Angeles the greatest city in the
world, the financial and cultural center of the fastest growing
economic region in the world." Bradley also announced that the
1985 effort would be "going back to the traditional Tom Bradley,
grassroots campaign"—a sign that Bradley wanted to cultivate
and invigorate his core constituency of supporters, whom many
thought he had taken too much for granted in the 1982 campaign.
Kerman Maddox came on board to help establish the strong base
in the black community. The appointment of Assemblywoman
Maxine Waters' chief of staff, who had been so critical of the
abandonment of traditional grassroots techniques in the guber-

natorial campaign, seemed to confirm the disappointment many suspected the Mayor felt regarding his field organization in the 1982 gubernatorial race. There had undoubtedly been a break-down in getting out the minority vote then, and he seemed determined not to repeat that mistake in 1985. Maddox recalls: "The Mayor made it clear from day one that grassroots with field offices all over the city would be the priority." Raye Cunningham, Bill Elkins, and Bishop Brookins worked the black community. One example of the type of events that would characterize the mayoral campaign was the breakfast at a restaurant on Olvera Street with prominent individuals from the Latino communites, including Assemblywoman Gloria Molina, Loretta Hernandez, Larry Gonzales, Senator Art Torres, and Assemblyman Richard Alatorre.

The Bradley reelection effort was headed by an entirely new team. Veteran Phil Depoian explained it as a reflection of the Mayor's desire to do this campaign differently. . . . There would be no old-timers and baggage in this effort. David Townsend was brought in to direct the media effort. Mike Gage, a former State Representative and former Chief of Staff for Lieutenant Gover-nor Leo McCarthy, was appointed Bradley Campaign Deputy. In addition to Gage and Townsend, Tom Quinn, head of the City News Service and a former key strategist and presidential cam-paign manager for Jerry Brown, engineered the Bradley strategy for 1985 as its campaign chief. All three were known for their success in organizing strong grassroots campaigns. According to Gage, the effort would be not only "precinct by precinct, but also block by block, if need be to capitalize on the city's universal feeling of pride; to drive home the point that while the politicians and nay-sayers said it couldn't be done—our Mayor's leadership made the difference—Tom Bradley did it." Steve Monteil, the former Assistant Press Secretary for the Los Angeles Olympic Organizing Committee, would serve as the campaign Press Sec-retary.

Although candid about the style of the campaign he intended to mount this time around, the Mayor would not speculate on his plans beyond 1985. Bradley told reporters, "Anybody who makes a pledge about the future makes a serious mistake."

If successful in his later bid for office, Bradley would be Los

Angeles' longest-governing mayor. Only Fletcher Bowron's fifteen-year tenure from 1938 to 1953 would be comparable. But Bowron had not been elected four times; his three elected terms in office resulted from an appointment to serve out the term of Frank Shaw, who had been forced to resign because of a scandal.

One potential candidate for the mayoral election, Police Chief Daryl F. Gates, who enjoyed support among conservative voters, announced that he would not run for the city's top spot, even though he thought he "could beat the two candidates seeking the office." A critic of the Mayor, as well as an object of the chief executive's criticism, Gates had earlier expressed an interest in the contest, vowing that he "would love to debate Bradley." According to Gates, however, his entry into the race could prompt an attempt by a Police Commission, dominated by Bradley supporters, to move to oust him during the campaign, since it was doubtful that he would be granted a leave of absence to make a run for City Hall. Although Police Commission members discounted this as a reason for the Chief's decision, Gates repeated it and chose to stay on as head of the LAPD and sit out the city elections. The Mayor, who had earlier stated that he approved of the way the department was run under the Chief, called upon Gates to join him in supporting a proposition calling for more police officers on the city's beats.

John Ferraro, who was expected to announce his candidacy in the very near future, reintroduced a motion that had been introduced before the Council in 1973 by Councilman Bradley—that mayors should be limited to two terms. Both Ferraro and the city and state newspapers pressed the Mayor to reveal his plans beyond the city elections. Dennis McCarthy of the *Daily News* asked if Bradley "would be around long enough to keep the seat warm," if he were elected. Bradley was quick to point out that, even though his campaign was under the direction of new leadership with statewide experience, it was "idiotic" to view the 1985 city election as what Janet Clayton in the *Times* called "merely a dress rehearsal for another gubernatorial run in 1986."

One of the most difficult tasks facing Councilman John Ferraro, a former insurance executive and Police Commission member, in his attempt to unseat Bradley for a fourth term was to choose an issue that would rally voters to turn out the incumbent. According to Mike Gage, "the Ferraro campaign's strategic mistake was that they never defined John in a positive light and instead went negative against Bradley."

In June 1984, in what seemed like an attempt to draw the lines early for the upcoming 1985 mayoral race, Ferraro had suddenly declared his opposition to the Metro Rail Subway project. According to Ferraro, the $3.3-billion project connecting the downtown area to the San Fernando Valley was "impractical and economically unfeasible." He likened the expenditures to pouring money "down a rathole." The mayoral hopeful recommended that the Council freeze the $69 million allocated for the city to use to begin work on the project.

Ferraro's criticism reflected negative sentiment in the exclusive Hancock Park area of the city and echoed the attacks voiced earlier by U.S. Congresswoman Bobbi Fiedler of the northwest San Fernando Valley. Ferraro announced his opposition to the project from the MacArthur Park area of the city, included as a station on the proposed project, charging that the Mayor's pet project would probably go no further if it were adopted.

Ferraro had backed the project for years. A visibly angered Bradley reacted by charging that Ferraro's statement was, "The most ridiculous, most outrageous statement I have heard in the last six or seven years of Metro Rail debates."

To the Mayor's staff, the statement by Ferraro seemed a cheap shot. It came the day Bradley was preparing to leave to talk to Walter Mondale about possibly joining the ticket as the party's choice for Vice-President. As it turned out, the attack on the Metro Rail project did not broaden the base of support of the nineteen-year veteran of the City Council. There were differences of opinion on the overall cost and feasibility of the project, but, according to Mike Gage, "it was not a gut issue to the voters." Furthermore, there were no apparent fissures in the widespread support Bradley enjoyed among the city's diverse coalitions. The California Poll showed the Mayor to be extremely popular statewide, second only to Peter Ueberroth.

In the announcement of his candidacy in Janaury 1984, Ferraro charged that Bradley had favored one neighborhood at the expense of the other in making political appointments and in transferring police officers, and that he had been unable to deliver on his major promise to the city—providing a comprehensive transit system. The major thrust of the attack was that Bradley had "transferred some police officers from the San Fernando Valley area to South-Central Los Angeles." Reporters were quick to ask the Mayor if his opponent was "using the South-Central example to raise apprehension among the predominantly white Valley residents." Bradley responded that he could not determine if "that's a tactic of pitting racial groups or communities against each other," but added that, if he later concluded that it was deliberate, "I'll respond to it."

The Mayor's response focused on the lack of specifics offered by his opponent, "Will somebody tell me one thing that John Ferraro had done in eighteen years? . . . He didn't have the courage and the guts to list even one accomplishment." He charged that Ferraro's criticism of the Metro Rail project and his proposal for an alternative plan to be constructed on existing freeways revealed only his own limitation, since it would result in even more massive traffic jams and further limit lanes on the crowded freeway system.

As Bill Boyarsky noted in the *Times,* the megalopolis of Los Angeles (or seven suburbs in search of a city) defied any attempt by a candidate to find a common issue with widespread support: "The oil drilling that sends Pacific Palisades residents to a furious protest meeting is of little interest to an Eastside resident worried about forthcoming fare increases on the RTD bus that is his family's main means of transportation."

One of the old themes revived by Ferraro was the quality of the Police Department under Bradley. The Councilman charged that Bradley had been a less than fervent supporter of the department during his eleven years at City Hall. The Councilman told supporters, "Hell, we ought to give the people some kind of protection, because people are afraid to go out of their houses."

However, he opposed the Mayor's support of a property tax increase to put 1,300 more officers on the streets. The Councilman argued that three hundred officers could be added to the force without new tax sources. Ferraro told audiences that "Tom Bradley becomes very pro-police only once every four years." Additionally, Ferraro contended that adding more police to the city's streets could be accomplished by eliminating the Board of Public Works, whose employees for the most part spent their days "doing political work for the Mayor."

Los Angeles County District Attorney Ira Reiner told a television audience, "I want to set the facts straight." He pointed out how Bradley had strengthened the Police Department and tripled its budget. Reiner labeled the LAPD the best in America and warned voters "not to be misled," emphasizing that Bradley was the kind of Mayor the city needed.

Such charges by former Council President Ferraro were attacked not only by Bradley, but also by Councilman Zev Yaroslavsky, who told reporters, "Twenty-three percent of Ferraro's plan is balanced with mirrors, while the other 77 percent is wishful thinking."

Reviving another past theme, Ferraro noted the Bradley years had been marked by appointments of friends and political contributors to city office. The controversial appointment of Ezunial Burts, a former Bradley aide, as head of the Harbor Department was singled out. And hadn't Tom Bradley criticized Sam Yorty for being in office too long? Taking yet another tack, the Councilman charged that much of the progress evident in the nation's second largest city was not due to Bradley's leadership, but to the hard work of the City Council.

Still, the polls tracking voter attitudes revealed little movement in response to Ferraro's various attempts to find a weak spot in the Bradley record.

Though short on substance, one thing that lifelong Democrat Ferraro's campaign had in abundance was Republican money and talent. In an obvious effort to damage future plans by Bradley, especially a rematch with Deukmejian, the GOP poured money into the 1985 campaign. A fundrasier in February—hosted by former California Attorney General and GOP Gubernatorial nominee Evelle Younger, joined by Jay Grodin, Margaret Brock, and Celeste King, all prominent Republicans—had netted the candidate $425,000. His Campaign Manager, Ron Smith, had been associated with many Republican candidates and was known to be an aggressive and attack-oriented leader in his past campaigns. Arnold Steinberg and Joyce Valdez, the pollster and fundraiser for the Councilman, were prominent in the GOP circles.

It was expected that both candidates would spend over $2.5 million in the mayoral contest. Ferraro ended up spending more than twice as much money than Bradley during the first two months of 1985.

According to Irene Tritschler, Bradley's fundraiser for the 1985 campaign and a veteran of his campaigns since 1973, the Mayor would be able to raise "whatever amount is needed." Scheduled were two large affairs, a Western theme barbecue, hosted by honorary Campaign Chairwoman Jane Boeckmann and Robert D. Selleck, and a major dinner organized by honorary Chairwoman Betty Kozasa with the Asian community backers.

With plenty of dollars filling both campaign war-chests, the media campaign was on. In the television wars, David Townsend's spots featured Peter Ueberroth extolling the leadership abilities of the incumbent and urging Los Angelenos to reelect Tom Bradley. Another spot featured the Mayor telling voters, "Most politicians told me I was wasting my time trying to bring the Olympics to Los Angeles. . . . I said we could do it without tax dollars and we did. Together we've made Los Angeles a great city. During the next four years, I'm determined to make it an even better place to live." On the screen, viewers saw a tight shot of Bradley waving an American flag at the opening ceremonies of the Olympic Games. Off camera, an announcer states, "Mayor Bradley, he makes us proud to live in L.A."

A controversial attack ad of the opposition featured children playing in a junkyard with toxic-waste barrels clearly visible to the viewer. As a youngster was shown struggling to breathe, an off-camera announcer told voters that Bradley's Board of Public Works had delayed closing the Capri toxic dump in East Lost Angeles for two years. Mike Gage attacked the Ferraro spot as unfair because it played heavily to the emotions at the expense of the clear-cut facts—the truth being that the state had failed to marshall its forces to aid the city in solving the problem.

Ferraro spent over half a million dollars on television and radio spots that told voters that Los Angeles deserved a chief executive who intended to serve out his full term. Many believed these were intentionally run not to win the upcoming election, but rather to take "pot-shots" at Bradley in the entire Southern California media, extending beyond the Los Angeles electorate.

In early 1985, in response to a revised drilling proposal submitted by the Occidental Petroleum Company, Mayor Bradley reversed his ten-year stand against drilling in the Pacific Palisades. His decision was a difficult one, which came as a surprise even to his closest advisors and strategists. Deputy Mayor Tom Houston had opposed the proposal. But, given Occidental's long history of its application for drilling, Bradley had spent years accumulating first-hand knowledge of the strengths and weaknesses of the various arguments advanced since the first proposal in 1970. Before making his decision, the Mayor made several unannounced visits to local drilling sites and had talked with people in the area about the issue. He visited areas where similar drilling had occurred. He studied Council files on the current proposal and reviewed how it differed from the ones he had earlier opposed.

There were significant differences in the 1985 proposal. His previous concerns had been adequately addressed in the new plan or had been sufficiently altered in Council proceedings. He had decided that he would concur with the Council's recommendation and approve Occidental's drilling proposal. While some thought the issue could be an opening for Ferraro, one political strategist called it "the greatest yawner issue in political history."

However, the Mayor's support of the Occidental Petroleum drilling proposal caused second thoughts in people who had been among his most ardent supporters in the past. Democratic Representatives Henry A. Waxman, Howard L. Berman, and Mel Levine announced they were reluctant to endorse Bradley's fourth-term bid because of his position on the Occidental issue. Their argument was that Bradley "took his political base for granted" and that the oil-drilling approval was nothing more than an attempt by the Mayor to be more politically attractive to conservative Republicans and business interests. Though all three representatives eventually endorsed Bradley for Mayor, they made it clear that they were looking elsewhere for 1986 gubernatorial candidates—specifically forty-one-year old State Senator Gary Hart.

Berman, Waxman, and Levine announced they were serving on a committee to explore the possibility of putting up Hart, a known environmentalist and liberal activist, for the 1986 Democratic gubernatorial nomination. Assemblyman Tom Hayden of Santa Monica had joined the Westside dissidents who urged Hart to make a bid in 1986. John Emerson (state chairman of U.S. Senator Gary Hart's California campaign in 1982) and Hayden told reporters after the first debate between Bradley and Ferraro that the state's "new guard" of Democrats needed a younger candidate to oppose George Deukmejian in 1986. Hayden remarked, "I like Tom Bradley, and I think he'll do a great job as Mayor and should remain there for a full four years with the sweeping mandate he's going to get on April 9."

Hart told *Times* reporter Keith Love that it was "time for some fresh new faces in California politics." Levine said he thought that "having Bradley heading the ticket would be like Mondale heading the ticket." And there were strong indications that another mayor might also be interested in the Democratic gubernatorial nomination—Dianne Feinstein of San Francisco.

It was evident, however, that while some Democrats doubted if Bradley would be the party's standard bearer in the 1986 election, Deukmejian did not. Quick to point out what he saw as an inconsistency, Deukmejian criticized Bradley for his "flip-flop" on the drilling issue. The Governor even scheduled a press conference in Los Angeles and traveled the distance of the state to ensure that the city's constituency heard his charge against Bradley. Addressing reporters, Deukmejian asked how Bradley could approve oil drilling in one instance and be so adamantly opposed to it in the Santa Monica Bay. The question boiled down to Bradley's "sincerity," according to Deukmejian.

Furthermore, Deukmejian told reporters that the Mayor should tell the public of his future plans. At a press conference in Los Angeles, Deukmejian stated, "There is every indication that he plans to run for Governor. If he didn't plan to run, why doesn't he say, 'I'm absolutely not going to run?'"

Bradley's office wasted little time in responding to the Governor's charge, at the same time pointing out that the Republican had opted to be an active member in a "non-partisan Mayor's race by holding a series of unique press conferences in Los Angeles." Deputy Mayor Houston explained Bradley's position succinctly. Yes, the Mayor had written the Governor and opposed Deukmejian's lifting of a moratorium on offshore drilling in the Santa Monica Bay. And the Bradley administration had indeed played a vital role in defeating the Governor's proposal to Congress to lift the moratorium on drilling in the area. The designation of the Bay as a sanctuary had to be maintained. The bottom line, according to the Bradley camp, was that Pacific Palisades and Santa Monica Bay were different, and Bradley would always be against drilling in the Bay as the Governor had proposed.

The Ferraro camp viewed the situation differently. It was not that the Occidental proposal no longer threatened the environment, as the Mayor had publicly stated. The real reason for the change in Bradley's thinking was motivated by the Mayor's desire for Occidental's backing in the 1986 gubernatorial race. He had sold out the interests of the city to increase his own political fortunes. "It indicates he thinks oil companies would be more help statewide than a few homeowners."

Bradley dismissed this as "idiotic and malicious" speculation. He had little difficulty reconciling the apparent inconsistency, explaining the distinction to reporters as follows: "Drilling in the Palisades will be directly into a pool of oil that does not underlie the Santa Monica Bay sanctuary . . . therefore, drilling on land will not trigger drilling in the Bay." His ten-year record of opposing drilling in the Santa Monica Bay sanctuary stood on its own merit and remained unchanged.

Bradley's ability to crisscross the state and country without missing a beat baffled even the oldest members of his staff. Insisting always on taking a "red-eye" flight when he went east so that he could put in a full day's work in Los Angeles, Bradley would work on the plane and sleep a few hours. Upon his arrival, he changed shirts in the men's room, appeared for his appointments, and then jumped on a night flight back to Los Angeles, where he was back at his desk at 8:30 A.M. It was a regimen few aides could understand—and none could duplicate.

Jeff Matsui, Executive Assistant to the Mayor, recalled that, as he and Bradley returned to Los Angeles from the Far East in 1983, the Mayor's attention turned to home and the question of who would play in the Rose Bowl. Matsui was dead tired. Here they were, halfway around the world; they had met with govern- mental leaders and delivered what seemed like hundreds of speeches and position papers; now Tom Bradley was already shifting attention to college football. When the plane stopped over in Hawaii, the Big Ten championship game was on televi- sion.

After speeding through Customs, Bradley sat in the holding area and absorbed the game, while Matsui had trouble staying awake. When the two got back to Los Angeles and were waiting for their baggage, Matsui asked Bradley if he knew who had won the game. Bradley looked puzzled, told Matsui not only that Illinois had beaten Michigan 16 to 6, but went into details on key plays of the game and the reaction of Illinois coach Mike White. He then noted that he and Matsui should be sure to congratulate Fred Schnell, now that his alma mater was Rose Bowl bound. Matsui thought to himself . . . , maybe after politics, Bradley and Brent Musburger might team up as announcers.

In the mayoral race, in response to his old rival's request that he make a statement about his 1986 intentions, Bradley replied by noting that John Ferraro was his opposition in this election. "I'm not running against the Governor. . . ."

Whether or not he would one day run for Governor, Bradley was as concerned as ever about the well-being of his city. During the early months of 1985, Bradley had defied an order by the Justice Department that cities abandon hiring guidelines if mi- norities could not actually prove discrimination. It marked a radical change by the Reagan Administration in ending what had been a successful and workable approach to achieving equal economic opportunities for minorities. The Mayor would have no part of the new order. "The Justice Department is simply dead wrong in its interpretation," Bradley responded. He further indi- cated that the system operating in Los Angeles would continue. "It was worked out with the Justice Department several years ago and it is working." Leadership in opening up such oppor- tunities to all peoples and his impressive record of forty-five years of public service earned Bradley the prestigious Springarn

*At the NAACP Springarn Awards banquet with Dionne War-
wick.* (Photo by Irv Antler: Courtesy of Los Angeles City
Hall

*The prestigious NAACP Springarn Award. Standing, Bishop
H. H. Brookins, Jack Valenti, Brock Peters. Seated, Benjamin
Hooks, 1985 recipient Tom Bradley, Rosa Parks.* (Courtesy
of Los Angeles City Hall)

medal in 1985, given by the NAACP for "highest and noblest achievement."

The Mayor also backed an initiative on the April ballot, Amendment 2, that could create two new seats on the City Council in Hispanic and Asian neighborhoods, starting in 1987. Bradley hoped that the measure would provide more seats for the city's multi-ethnic populations. More specifically, it would mark the end of a twenty-three-year lack of Hispanic representation in a city where one out of every three citizens was of that ethnic background. Although the initiative would fail, Richard Alatorre was elected to the Fourteenth District seat in a special election in December 1985, called to fill the seat vacated by Art Snyder's resignation.

The media campaigns by both candidates intensified. In response to charges made by his opponent, the Mayor characterized Ferraro's approach as "the most malicious, false advertising campaign I have ever experienced." Bradley was particularly incensed by the toxic-waste spot. Ferraro declared that he too thought the campaign had sunk to what he called "sleazy, gutter politics." He was furious at the Mayor's spots questioning the propriety of condominium purchases he and his wife had made and implying that a City Council vote he had cast on behalf of condominium conversion had been affected by the purchase.

In a March 1985 feature story, the *Christian Science Monitor* referred to Bradley as "arguably the most powerful black politician in United States history." Describing the Mayor's personal style as "steady, deliberate, and almost never exciting," Marshall Ingwerson of the *Monitor* pointed out that Bradley's leadership qualities of "jawboning and horsetrading with private industry in pursuit of mutual goals" had not only made the difference in rebuilding the city's urban areas but had also been the chief ingredient in "his most dramatic achievement . . . , bringing the first business-financed Olympic Games to Los Angeles last year."

A March *Times* poll revealed the failure of Ferraro's campaign to catch on. Bradley was leading his opponent by forty percentage points, 62 percent to 22 percent. More important, 40 percent of the city's population did not even know who candidate Ferraro was.

The two candidates agreed to one debate, even though the Ferraro campaign had asked for twelve. According to Bradley, to subject voters to even six debates would be "cruel and unusual punishment." To the Bradley campaign, Bradley's record was visible for everyone. Tom Bradley was the best Mayor in the country. In comparison to other major cities, Los Angeles had been at the forefront. It had worked when others were at their knees. The downtown, the airport, and the harbors had been revitalized. And the Olympics had been an example of how a partnership between business, labor, and government could work.

The debate between the candidates at the Sheraton Universal Hotel on March 15 witnessed several clashes on the major issues of the campaign. Ferraro called for Bradley to "flat out say you are not going to run for Governor" and charged that the city had "drifted over the last four years." Bradley termed the challenge nothing more than a "gimmick" and vowed that "I'm not going to fall prey to it."

In reference to Ferraro's abandonment of the Metro Rail line, the Mayor told voters, "I believe its a mark of leadership that, when the going gets tough, you don't give up like my friend, Mr. Ferraro did last year." Bradley also noted that the City Council and County Transportation Commission had just approved the measure to begin construction in August of the twenty-two-mile light-rail system connecting Los Angeles to Long Beach, and he called for the completion of the entire 152-mile system.

While many voters expressed their disgust at the personal nature of the attacks, Professor Don Brownlee, of Cal State University at Northridge, and Professor Sid Ribeau, of Cal State University at Los Angeles, awarded the Mayor a "win" according to academic debate scoring.

Prior to the major candidate's debates, Eileen Anderson, known as the "singing-dancing candidate," repeated her proposal for large fans and the construction of tunnels in the Santa Monica Mountains to rid the southland of its smog. She also offered her own proposal for mass transit. Anderson told voters to send her to London and she would purchase the famous double-decker buses. As a result, "we can double up on transportation and give people a colorful ride here." Alluding to Anderson's daily dance routines at the City Hall corner, Bradley stated "Eileen has to be in the best shape of any of the candidates running for Mayor."

In early March, Ferraro Campaign Manager Ron Smith announced that the Councilman's campaign would spend about $1 million in media spots and direct-mail advertising during the last four weeks of the campaign. Former Police Chief and now Senator Ed Davis endorsed Ferraro, telling reporters that Bradley had never really shown any appreciation for the police force during his tenure as Mayor.

The reason was simple, according to Davis. Bradley still harbored resentment for the racism that existed in the department when he had been on the force. He had made the statement that he had felt "consigned and confined" while in the department. "He should have overcome that by now," Davis remarked. The charge from an old veteran opponent of the Mayor was "unworthy of comment," according to the Bradley campaign. Nonetheless, Steve Monteil responded that the "brass of any department may not feel loved when their budget gets trimmed, but most don't take it so personally."

The week before the primary, polls showed little progress for Ferraro. He trailed Bradley 69 percent to 22 percent. The Olympics, fairness, leadership, redevelopment, fiscal responsibility, and mass transit were cited as strengths of the Mayor. His perceived weaknesses included his oil-drilling decision, the possibility that he would run for Governor, and his lack of support for the police.

The *Times, Herald Examiner,* and *Daily News* joined numerous neighborhood papers like the *Wave* and *Sentinel* in endorsing Bradley for a fourth term. They cited the Mayor's past accomplishments in unifying the city—the partnership between business, labor, and the city; the success and challenge in redeveloping its neighborhoods; and his pledge to expand international trade for the city.

Noting a "more conservative, fundamental vote emerging out there," Bob Hedrick of the Ferraro campaign predicted the

Councilman could very well force Bradley into a runoff on April 9. The Councilman also enjoyed the endorsement of another age-old foe of Bradley. Sam Yorty pledged his support of John Ferraro, charging, "I resent his (Bradley) being reelected on a big-lie technique."

Democratic Vice-Presidential candidate Geraldine Ferraro cautioned Bradley supporters against taking his victory for granted. Addressing a large crowd, Ferraro described Bradley as "a strong national figure," telling them that the she knew what John Ferraro was thinking: "Those of us on the short side of the polls kind of hope for apathy."

Although he was three thousand miles away in New York, meeting with Mayor Edward Koch to criticize President Reagain's proposed budget's effects on the nation's cities, Bradley made it clear that his status as a national figure could only benefit Los Angeles. Whether it be on ABC's *Good Morning America,* attempting to lure more filming back to Los Angeles,chatting with *Late Night* host David Letterman on the beauty of Southern California beaches or testifying before Congress for a moratorium on oil-drilling off the California coast, it was apparent that Tom Bradley commanded the attention of a wide audience for Los Angeles' concerns. In various state visits to Japan and the Far East, he had been hailed by crowds. He was asked for autographs by pedestrians in Spain and Israel, and was a recognizable hero to many throughout Asia.

The Mayor told voters that Los Angeles deserved more than to rest on its present accomplishments. Yes, he was proud of the over one-billion-dollar modernization and expansion of the airport, the number-one port status of the Los Angeles harbor, and the redevelopment throughout the city. But the city had to be prepared for the challenges of the next century. Airport Commission President Johnnie Cochran, Jr., adds, "The airport expansion is an example of Bradley's ability to pull together the community. We got the new terminal finished for the Olympics only because the various groups cooperated." Praising the Mayor's leadership, Cochran adds, "They have been trying to get the airport expansion completed in San Francisco for the past fifteen years. Los Angeles did it in three."

In a speech he delivered in late March on the subject of Los

Angeles in the year 2000, the Mayor called for a reinforcement and expansion of the partnership evidenced in the city to establish Los Angeles as the financial and commercial capital of the Pacific rim. The theme of the speech—and of the campaign—was summed up in the Mayor's statement: "The Olympic torch showed us that there is no limit to what we can achieve if we have a bold vision—and if we relentlessly pursue that vision with perseverance and enthusiasm."

The Bradley campaign was taking nothing for granted. Get-out-the-vote efforts were planned throughout the city's neighborhoods. Ferraro workers tended to pin their hopes on the San Fernando Valley. Yet, John Marelius reported in the *Daily News* on March 24 that Bradley held a two-to-one edge even in this conservative area.

Another new tack of the Bradley campaign featured the Mayor attacking Ferraro in a spirited commercial that aired in the campaign's final days. It marked a departure from the philosophy that the Mayor avoid a negative approach. The rationale had been that, with a heterogenous constituency, a black candidate risked alienating prospective supporters with a blatant attack on an opposing white. In 1985, there was no such hesitation. Maybe it had to do with the success of Bradley's Olympics or the attention surrounding the Vice-Presidential nomination.

The issues were the focus of the campaign, and race seemed, for the first time, to be of little concern to either the candidates or the voters. The focus would be on the candidates' abilities, their past records, and nothing else.

A mailer by the Ferraro campaign attempted to link the Democratic candidate with two popular Republicans. The message told voters of similarities between Ferraro and President Reagan and George Deukmejian: "Like President Reagan he is tough and decisive. . . . Like Governor Deukmejian, he's tough on crime and frugal with tax money."

The final weekend saw Bradley visiting important communities throughout the city, from the glitzy Westside to Watts. Introduced by some of the biggest names in the entertainment and political arena, the Mayor urged his supporters not to take the big lead for granted. "The only poll that really counts is the vote totals on Tuesday," Bradley told supporters. "We can rejoice today, but then tonight and tomorrow we have to go back out there to work." The Mayor's own philosophy was to keep punching every minute of the day. There was no time for relaxing.

Jermaine Jackson and Jayne Kennedy told a Bradley rally at the Sherman Oaks Galleria to remember to show the same type of enthusiasm on Tuesday. And Assemblywoman Maxine Waters and Raye Cunningham urged a crowded rally in Watts, held in the Martin Luther King Shopping Center (the first new commercial development in an area known in the 1965 disturbances as "Charcoal Alley"), not to let anyone take away Bradley's leadership from City Hall. Similar messages echoed at the Vermont/ Slauson Shopping Center. Vice-President of the American Jewish Committee, Marsha Hoffmann Kwalwasser, also an honorary campaign chairperson, rallied the Jewish community to be all-out for Bradley.

The Bradley campaign hoped that 150 volunteers on phone banks, eight hundred walking the city's precincts, and 168,000 mailgrams would spell an overwhelming victory for the Mayor. He had raised over $1.6 million in two months. The figure was impressive, and one that could not be matched by Hart, Garamendi, or anyone else looking toward 1986.

Conjecture about the primary was focused, not on who would win (it was conceded by almost everyone that Bradley would), but on how large the margin of victory would be. Would it be substantial enough to establish Bradley as the undisputed front-runner for the 1986 gubernatorial nomination, if he decided he wanted it? The betting was that the margin of victory had to be 64 percent or better. It needed to be an improvement over the 1981 total, when Bradley had beaten his old, worn-out rival Sam Yorty by sixty percent. A smaller margin would be an indication of an erosion in support, in his home-base, which would confirm the charges of Waxman and Berman that public support for Bradley had waned. And that could be the end of any dreams of a rematch in 1986.

The Mayor himself attempted to downplay the speculation about whether a large victory might translate into another run for Sacramento in 1986: "I am not planning on running for Governor. I want to make that very clear. I want to be Mayor of Los Angeles."

22

Never Give Up

> *"No question is ever settled until it is settled right."*
>
> —Ella Wheeler Wilcox

To those gathered at the Biltmore Hotel on April 9, there were some memories of 1982. Then, too, everybody had expected a win. The polls had predicted it all along. But the polls proved to be resoundingly true in 1985. Bradley won a smashing reelection victory with 68 percent of the vote cast.

His opponent had spent over $1.3 million to lose in one of the most lopsided victories in the city's history. Not even the fog that grounded the helicopters, and thus delayed the final ballot-count, affected the jubilation of thousands who celebrated the event— Tom Bradley had become the only Los Angeles Mayor elected to four terms. He had learned of the results while watching newscasts and the Dodger game. Ethel had batted .500 that evening: her husband had won, but the Dodgers had gone down to defeat. Lorraine and Phyllis hugged their dad, congratulating him on another history-making event.

It was an especially pleasing evening for the Mayor. Just three years earlier, he had won the battle on election day, only to see his win in the Governor's race slip away when the absentee votes were added. This time, Bradley had even carried the absentee votes. It was his largest margin of victory as Bradley carried every district in the city, enjoyed the strong support of the various ethnic groups, and improved his previous vote records in the San Fernando Valley. He even carried Ferraro's home district. Encino resident and movie producer Max Keller explains,

Los Angeles presents a special award to Nobel winner Bishop Desmond Tutu of South Africa, May 1985. (Courtesy of Los Angeles City Hall)

As a result of losing a bet, the Mayor took a river rapid trip down the Kern River. From left, Doug Willis of Associated Press; *John Schwada,* Los Angeles Herald Examiner; *Janet Clayton,* Los Angeles Times: *Jon Marelius,* Los Angeles Daily News; *Susan Jetton,* San Diego Tribune; *Bradley; press secretary Ali Webb; security guard Jerry Comfort.* (Photo by Denise Knight: Courtesy of Ali Webb)

"Mayor Bradley has made the Valley and Los Angeles a safe and secure place to bring up my family." Valley physician Dr. Jerry Zimmerman adds, "In hosting the most successful Olympics ever without a tax burden—but instead a history-making surplus—Bradley demonstrates his strong principled stands and the true grit of leadership." The Mayor's success in Hispanic areas was particularly pleasing, even with the efforts of top Latino officials in the Deukmejian administration on behalf of Ferraro. Richard Alatorre viewed the Mayor's strong showing as the recognition of a real leader, statesman, and friend of the Hispanic population.

The *Times* reported that the get-out-the-vote effort had paid off. Maddox, Cunningham, Elkins, and others were pleased with their work. In South-Central Los Angeles, the Mayor had racked up impressive margins that exceeded his earlier election totals. In one district, he received 34,832 votes as compared to 833 for Ferraro. To some voters in the area, Ferraro's campaign motivated many minorities to come out and vote for Bradley. According to supporter Caroline O'Connell, "Seeing Ferraro with Sam Yorty just caused many people to remember back to that particular election in 1969. . . . This time, they were at the polls on election day for Tom Bradley."

Even Assemblyman Henry Waxman, who had earlier stated that Bradley should abandon his efforts for higher office in California, seemed to be having second thoughts, stating, "I think everyone who follows politics has to take the Mayor seriously in whatever he chooses to run for. . . . He has put himself back on top of the list of strong Democratic officeholders." Bradley responded to the assessment by saying that he "never thought he was down [on the list]." Mike Gage told supporters that the stunning victory ensured that all of California was "sure today who is the party's top vote-getter."

The possible future significance of the election was clearly on the minds of many political pundits and especially the press. At the press conference the morning after the victory, a reporter referred to Bradley as "Governor." In response to questions about his future plans, the Mayor indicated that he would "not switch gears the morning after the election" and start talking about something like that. However, the Mayor told the press he would "never put myself in the position of saying never," adding, "times change . . . , circumstances change." Yet, the Mayor reiterated that he was not planning on running for Governor.

The Mayor had lost in one respect on election day. He had bet Mike Gage, his campaign manager, on the campaign outcome, losing the bet because he had won the election by over twenty points, "the spread," according to Gage. As a result Los Angeles' Mayor, known for his formality, would.be taking a river rapid trip down the Kern River, which would result in a front-page photo in the *Los Angeles Times* and other papers throughout the country.

It would be one of the most relaxed times many press members had seen the Mayor enjoy. Paddling throughout the day, exchanging jokes at night before turning in under the stars, Bradley seemed entirely different from the formal Mayor of the nation's second largest city. Susan Jetton, who was one of several reporters to accompany the Mayor and staff members on the trip, echoes the theme expressed by people who had the opportunity to really know Bradley beyond the political responsibilities. The "wooden" image did not apply at all. Tom Bradley was a quiet and driven man, but he also possessed a real sense of warmth and sincerity, not the pseudo-telegenic type so often typical of politicians. In Bradley, there was a deep compassion that really touched people.

Jetton knew first-hand that the quiet nature of Bradley should not be misunderstood as a lack of interest in a conversation. In the 1982 campaign, the former North Carolinian was en route to Los Angeles from San Francisco on a plane with Bradley, Dick Bergholz, and Bill Endicott of the *Los Angeles Times,* among other reporters. Tom Sullivan, of the Bradley campaign, began kidding Jetton about her Southern accent. Jetton—sitting one row in front of Bradley, who appeared to be asleep after a long day of campaigning—told Sullivan that Tom Bradley was also from the South, since he had grown up in Texas. Bradley suddenly stood up and laughingly told Jetton, "Ya shut ya mouth!"

The Berman-Waxman Westside organization had suffered some setbacks in the city elections. Lisa Specht and Dan

Shapiro, both supported by the two powerful Democrats, lost to James Kenneth Hahn and Rick Tuttle for City Attorney and Controller, respectively. While pollster Steve Teichner identified weaknesses in the Mayor's ability to attract new residents and Yuppies to the polls, Professor Mark Hann of USC singled out the Bradley campaign's success in putting together an extraordinary grassroots organization as a reason to hope for success in a possible 1986 campaign. One strategy devised by Gage and Quinn, and in line with the Mayor's return to his winning formula, called for the "targeted grassroots" system to be the core of any statewide campaign in 1986.

The prospects for statewide success against an incumbent Governor seemed bleak for the Democratic gubernatorial nominee, given that the GOP, conservative Senator Jesse Helms, and other fringe groups had targeted Alan Cranston's Senate seat in his upcoming reelection bid as one to win for the Republicans. In addition, various Supreme Court justices targeted for defeat by California conservatives, would be on the ballot, including the controversial Chief Justice Rose Bird, opposed by the California District Attorneys Association and the Governor himself.

In April 1985, George Deukmejian had started his attacks on the Chief Justice, criticizing Bird and the California Supreme Court for not deferring "to the wishes of our people" on the death penalty. Ironically, Bill Roberts, Deukmejian's controversial Campaign Manager in 1982, was selected to devise the campaign to defeat Bird in 1985. Polls showed over 85 percent of Californians favoring capital punishment. During the summer months, Bradley publicly declared that he had always been an advocate of such a measure to protect society against heinous criminals who have no compassion for human life. As a former cop, he had recognized that under some circumstances, the death penalty was the only answer to protect society.

There were early indications that many Democrats would seek to avoid any identification with Bird's efforts to be approved for a new twelve-year term. Given the conservative mood of the electorate, few wanted to associate themselves with the liberal Bird record. Yet, Tom Sullivan, on a voluntary leave from the Mayor's office to write and work for Councilman Richard Alatorre, argued that "the Rose Bird issue could be decided in the minds of the public months before the general election." In any case, Sullivan maintained, "Bird will not draw people out to the polls."

Senator Alan Cranston concurred: "Rose Bird will not be a factor on either Tom's or my campaign. Confirmation is well down at the end of the ballot, and people have historically separated political forces from judicial confirmation." Jules Radcliff and others figured differently, pointing out that "Bird will draw a particularly conservative voter who will also vote at least on the top ticket candidates."

Democratic Party officials openly worried about preserving their majorities in both of the state houses, as well as in the United States House of Representatives, given a perceived weakness at the top of the 1986 ticket. Carefully avoiding any direct criticism of Bradley, some Democrats told reporters they were worried that no candidate would be viable in a race against Deukmejian, given his widespread acceptance. Many seemed to be looking beyond 1986, speculating that a new young face "might even gain stature in defeat." Representative Don Edwards of San Jose and Representatives Berman and Waxman voiced the concern once again. Their talk centered on a Hart or Garamendi effort.

Assembly Speaker Willie Brown, who had sounded a similar theme a year earlier, told the *New York Times* that he did not consider the Mayor to be "the liability some believe he will be. . . . That falls in about the same category as the talk we used to hear about the liability Democrats would have with [me] a black Speaker." Brown indicated that it would be impossible for him not to support Bradley. Deputy Mayor Tom Houston predicted that Bradley, if he did decide to run, would beat Hart, Garamendi, or any other candidate in the Democratic primary "in a walk." Furthermore, to nominate the "new face" suggested by some would result in a "megabath" at the polls for the Democrats, according to Reagan advance man Scott Lane.

Deputy Mayor Houston told reporters that his boss might be four years older, "but he's ten years younger in style and vigor. Check his pulse. He's much more energetic. He would be an entirely different candidate this time around."

Gone would be the overly cautious Bradley of 1982. The

failed campaign's slogan had told voters that "Tom Bradley doesn't make a lot of sense, he just gets things done." What was clear was that, since that time, Bradley had been more productive than ever and had gained greatly in both stature and self-confidence. His success in expanding Los Angeles' share of international trade at a rate of $3 billion a week and his role as proud host to the Olympics meant that Tom Bradley was now regarded as a statesman, not only of California, but of America and the world. The new Tom Bradley continued to get things done as effectively as ever—but was now more willing to make some noise about it. "The fact is that George Deukmejian simply hasn't caught on with anyone," argues Tom Quinn. "People everywhere know Tom Bradley now, and they won't be fooled by such deception by Deukmejian in 1986."

In what was undoubtedly a preview of a major theme of the Governor's reelection bid, Deukmejian identified himself as the "leading advocate for crime victims in our state" and re-emphasized that he would support his old Campaign Manager's aim of defeating Rose Bird. By August 1985, over one year before the election, Roberts announced that opponents of Bird had already spent nearly $1 million to defeat the Chief Justice. Deukmejian had also called for her defeat in one of his Sunday morning radio addresses.

Bradley moved to strengthen his support among the state's environmentalists. Testifying before the House Interior Appropriations Subcommittee, Bradley reiterated his stand against offshore oil drilling in California, lobbying for a one-year extension of the drilling moratorium, and attacked the administration's plan (which Deukmejian supported) as unsafe and unsound. The inland oil-drilling proposal approved by the Mayor for the Palisades did not "diminish in any way" the city's opposition to the proposals, Bradley told the legislators.

Within the state, Deukmejian faced questions on a variety of other issues, some of which would be undoubtedly on the 1986 campaign agenda. The Governor defended his administration's position to abolish the California Coastal Commission which had long been supported by Bradley. Deukmejian charged the Commission lacked "common sense" and was against even "prudent reasonable growth and cut its budget and staff by one-third." Coastal Commission member Duane Garrett charged the Governor's attitude was one of "development rather than protection of our state's precious resource—its beaches."

While vowing to farmers in the San Joaquin Valley that his administration would never allow another "Medfly fiasco" such as that which occurred in the Brown administration, The Deukmejian administration seemed to be up to its knees in questions regarding toxic waste, as well as tainted cheese and aldicarb pesticide-contaminated watermelons. He had failed in reapportionment reform, water development, and toxic-waste proposals. Former State Senator John Knox singled out the Governor's "ineptitude on the water issue" as a lightning rod for the Democratic nominee in 1986. Since 1977's drought, Bradley had pushed for resolution of the state's water problem and had called for a blue-ribbon panel of the diverse interests to help resolve the issue. Since his election, Deukmejian had "chosen to turn his back on this vital need of the state," according to Knox.

Bradley increasingly criticized the Governor on these and other issues during the summer of 1985. Speaking to a group from the Mexican-American Political Association in Bakersfield in August, the Los Angeles Mayor portrayed Deukmejian as struggling to stay afloat in a "sea of bureaucracy." Charging that the present Governor was an "inept caretaker," Bradley faulted the Republican administration's handling of the cheese poisoning that had rocked the state and country, killing eighty-five people. How had this happened? Where were the inspectors to ensure plants were up to standards? And why had the Governor not even as much as issued a statement of compassion to the victims and their families?

Charging that Deukmejian had been "missing in inaction" on a number of other similar issues and inept in his management of the California Department of Food and Agriculture, Bradley asked his audience where was the leadership from the Governor's office? The Democratic Mayor likened the victims of toxic waste, under the "don't-give-a-damn" attitude of the Deukmejian administration, to mushrooms—"kept in the dark, watered occasionally, and covered with you know what." The problem wasn't money. It was there. The reason was quite different—the Governor avoided being identified with the numerous "botches" his administration had committed. As a result, during the summer of 1985, the incumbent acquired the name of "Governor Do-Nothing" from Sacramento-based columnist William Kahrl.

Many who heard the Bradley address or read about it in the papers identified the speech as the beginning one-two punch of a rematch for 1986.

Another potential liability for the incumbent Governor among young and activist voters was the report by the *Sacramento Bee* that Deukmejian owned stock in American companies with ties to South Africa. This was an issue that had produced the largest demonstrations since the 1960s at Berkeley and at colleges and universities throughout the world.

The differences between Deukmejian and Bradley continued to occupy the newspaper headlines. While the Governor owned stock connected with South Africa, Bradley pushed through an ordinance requiring the city to divest $600 million of its holdings in companies that did business with the country. He wanted to send the message not only to South Africa, but cities across the globe, that Los Angeles was a city of justice and humanity, that it would not sit idly by and permit the vicious policy of apartheid to continue. Meeting with Bishop Tutu, who had affected him like no other leader since Martin Luther King, Bradley heard the South African minister praise the Mayor's action as "a feather in Tom Bradley's cap" and a beacon for other cities and national governments to follow.

The Los Angeles City Council had agreed to the Mayor's equal-pay-for-equal-work proposal, which Bradley hailed as a "landmark breakthrough" for women in city government, the first major municipality in America to reevaluate salaries through the collective bargaining process. Deukmejian, like his federal counterpart in Washington, was opposed to the concept. There was also Bradley's leadership in passing the nation's first anti-discrimination ordinance for AIDS victims, while in Sacramento Deukmejian faced criticism for not commiting enough state funds to study the dreaded disease.

After taking the oath of office for his fourth term, Bradley was reported throughout the fall and winter to be meeting with key

California leaders on his plans for 1986. Deputy Mayor Tom Houston explained to reporters that the dialogue the Mayor was having with key politicos was not inconsistent with his statements made during the campaign that he "was not running for Governor." According to Ali Webb, the Mayor was merely "listening" to the advice of the people.

Few bought the "listening" line. Those close to Bradley could sense a new vigor within the Mayor. The huge mandate he had received from the citizens of Los Angeles, despite an expenditure of over a million dollars by his opponent, had to be comforting to Bradley. Those mentioned earlier as his chief rivals, Lieutenant Governor Leo McCarthy and Attorney General John Van de Kamp, were convinced that Bradley was leaning toward another bid. To Van de Kamp staffer Dwayne Peterson, with the popularity of Bradley statewide, the nomination seemed like his for the asking.

Bradley's recent two-to-one win at the polls, coupled with the worldwide recognition he had earned, convinced even the skeptics that a 1986 Bradley for Governor campaign would be quite different from the ill-fated race four years before. "Some were ready to write the Mayor off after 1982," remarks David Wolper, "but those people really never knew the man's tenacity." Commenting on the Bradley penchant for rematches, producer Jerry Weintraub states, "I never doubted for one minute after 1982 that Bradley would run again; he just never gives up; that's the Rocky Balboa in him."

The Mayor's growing international reputation was signaled by his invitation to join the Trilateral Commission, the elite group of two hundred leaders in America, Europe, and Japan, dedicated to promoting better understanding among the world's nations. Furthermore, the *Times* reported that, during a fall trip to the Middle East, Bradley "had acted as an emissary between Israeli Prime Minister Shimon Peres and Jordan's King Hussein."

Wherever he went, the Mayor was greeted with warm crowds and supporters. He was mobbed in his fourth trade mission to Israel and gave hundreds of autographs in South America and Asia in the fall of 1985. Answering critics who reminded him of his own remarks about his predecessor's globetrotting, Bradley told reporters that Yorty had often emphasized "a separate foreign policy for the city from the national government on his traveling." The objective was quite different in the Bradley years: "All of my travel has been to expand our trade, and the facts show the success in our making Los Angeles a world leader of Pacific rim commerce." Back at City Hall, he sensed the message of optimism, and began to consider the possibilities of running for Governor again in 1986. Mayoral staff members Lisa Kwan, Michael Broderick, Robert Hartzell, Julie Tugend, Lloyd Raikes, Donna Bojarsky, and Wendy Greuel urged their boss to "go for it." It would be a tough temptation for a determined man to turn down.

Bradley's penchant for diversity was evident in his attendance at the Bruce Springsteen concert in the fall of 1985. Selecting "Born in the U.S.A." as one of his favorites, Bradley told DeeDee Myers of the press office that the experiences amplified in "My Home Town" echoed his own personal life. Yet the Coliseum crowd did not witness Bradley taking a more active role, as he had at the Neil Diamond concert a few years before. During that concert when Diamond had sung the Diana Ross hit, "Reach Out and Touch Somebody's Hand," Bradley actually found himself onstage with Helen Reddy and Henry Winkler, singing the lyrics, "Make this world a better place if you can." Bradley remembers, "That was my first and last attempt at singing onstage!" Yet, on his office wall at City Hall is a signed photo of the event from Diamond, captioned, "If you ever leave politics, you can always sing with me!"

The lingering positive political effects of the Los Angeles Olympics were evident in a special premiere hosted by the Times Mirror Company of Bud Greenspan's documentary *16 Days of Glory,* shown in August 1985. According to *Los Angeles Times* columnist Jody Jacobs, in the midst of the athletes from throughout the world who brought home the Gold was Mayor Tom Bradley, "the man most instrumental in bringing the Games to Los Angeles."

An emerging theme of the incumbent Governor's bid for reelection became increasingly evident in his numerous visits throughout the state on "non-political trips." Deukmejian repeatedly told voters that "I am Governor for all the people of California," a phrase that—at least to Professor Vito Silvestri—was a "wink" at racism.

Susan Jetton, writing for the Copley News Service, reported that the incumbent Governor told an audience in the desolate areas of the state where few Governors had ever gone before, that the state's voters should look at his first term as "an appetizer." Yet, to retired U.S. Treasury Department official Jack Mackenzie who complained of a lack of programs, policies, or leadership from his office, if this were true, "Duke's second term could amount to nothing less than starvation for the entire state."

One area that showed no signs of starvation was the incumbent's growing reelection campaign fund. By mid-March with the election eight months away, Deukmejian raised $7.4 million for the 1986 campaign. In comparison, Mayor Bradley raised $1.4 million.

On the twentieth anniversary of the Watts riots, Bradley acknowledged that the same strife that had sparked the incident still existed in the community. But there had been progress. Calling on the community and private industry to work together to rebuild the promise of the area, Bradley had worked to piece together a commitment from both parties that had resulted in the December 1984 opening of the first new shopping center in the Watts area—the Martin Luther King Shopping Center—since the riots.

There had been a similar effort to preserve the economic potential of the Crenshaw shopping district. Bradley had been responsible for putting together a coalition of private and public interests that resulted in a $50-million development.

Criticism of the Deukmejian administration continued in the media. William Kahrl, writing in the *Times* more than a year before the general election, identified Deukmejian's primary strength to be his understanding of the "virtues of inaction." The writer argued that innovation always tends to offend someone, and offered Jerry Brown's controversial tenure in Sacramento as proof of how new policies often produce dramatic swings in public popularity. Yet, Deukmejian had avoided such pitfalls.

The Deukmejian Administration's spirit of inactivism was

even demonstrated in the Governor's approach to press conferences. Traditionally held to provide the chief executive an opportunity to support a particular policy and generally opening with a strong statement on the issue, the press conference was redefined in the Deukmejian era. Press Secretary Larry Thomas told reporters, "I take the view that a news conference isn't always called for the purpose of making news." William Endicott of the *Times* wrote that the norm for the news conferences was the "now familiar sentence" read by the Governor: "I don't have any opening comments this morning, so I'll be happy to entertain any questions that any of you might have." Deukmejian obviously concurred with his Press Secretary in the opinion that a press conference need not be newsworthy.

It translated into more than what Deukmejian's speechwriter Kenneth Khachigian termed "a lack of the Reagan rhetorical flare." To Californians seeking a more aggressive voice in Sacramento, the Deukmejian era was characterized by what Senator John Tunney described as a "lack of vision and leadership." Political fundraiser and former State Assemblyman Walter Karabian viewed the 1986 gubernatorial contest as "tight and a tough one to predict," but continued, "Deukmejian is vulnerable and fears Tom Bradley more than the Governor will admit."

Hopes for a Bradley bid were strengthened by an August poll that revealed the Mayor leading the incumbent Governor by six percent. But the Deukmejian staff were quick to point out that the polls had been wrong before. As one staff member responded, "didn't Mervin Field also predict we would have Governor Bradley in 1982?"

One candidate who initially had indicated that he would seek the gubernatorial nomination on the Democratic ticket, who had gone so far as to hire political consultant Robert Squire, opted to cancel his plans in light of Bradley's strong support. Senator John Garamendi announced in the fall of 1985 that he would not seek the nomination. According to Jules Radcliff, given Bradley's strength, Garamendi recognized that the "only possible way to win against him would be to wage a hard-hitting negative campaign, something that John's character simply wouldn't allow." Even though he had not declared for the position, Bradley noted

First Day of 1986 campaign for Governor with San Francisco Mayor Diane Feinstein. (Courtesy of Rick Browne)

A rare moment of relaxation at Getty House. (Courtesy of Rick Browne)

that he "accepted John's reasoning and was appreciative of the strong showing of support throughout the state," for his own stands on the issues.

"There has been a lot of second guessing since 1982, among the electorate," argues political strategist and civic leader John Karns, who notes a realization by Bradley that "he needs to be himself this time around—hard hitting and tough on the issues, compassionate with the people." Sensing a change in voter sentiment, entertainer Ben Vereen predicts that "People are ready to say 'no' to a Governor who has done nothing, who has no vision, who has floundered during his first term, and say 'yes' to an extraordinary leader who is nothing short of an American hero."

But while the 1985 polls and the public speculation were encouraging to Bradley, a review of the contemporary political history of the state was not. In the past century, only three Democrats had been elected Governor—one of whom was the only incumbent Governor to have been turned out of office.

There were also strains within the diverse and fragile constituency that Bradley had delicately pieced together. Jewish leaders expressed bitter disappointment over his reluctance to denounce the controversial Nation of Islam leader, Louis Farrakhan, known for his frequent anti-Semitic slurs, who was scheduled to make a speech in Los Angeles in September. On the other hand, the black community was outraged by demands that Bradley repudiate Farrakhan. Both camps predicted political fallout in a statewide race, if he failed to heed their warnings.

The controversy heated up as Bradley's advisors—representing women, blacks, and Jews—were divided on the approach for him to take. Both sides pressed hard for the Mayor to adopt a particular position. But, as always, Tom Bradley would make the final decision. The highly charged atmosphere was not unlike other circumstances Bradley had faced throughout his long career. He would attempt to mollify the situation through negotiation. He would refrain from making any comment until after the address, instead attempting behind the scenes to pressure Farrakhan to avoid divisive name-calling in his Los Angeles visit.

Bradley was able to claim some measure of success. Farrakhan canceled some of his scheduled appearances in Southern California—and with them, his divisive rhetoric. Yet, the minister's negative references to Judaism in his major speech infuriated the Jewish community, right before the Jewish New Year.

Bradley's decision reflected a long-established trait of conflict resolution and a deeply rooted belief in the First Amendment. His career was a lifelong repudiation of racism, hatred, violence, and bigotry, regardless of the race, sex, or religion of its source. There should be no question to the Jewish community or anyone of where he stood on any of those issues; his record and political life spoke for itself.

Following the Farrakhan speech, Bradley denounced the anti-Semitic slurs made by the minister. Defending his position of not denouncing Farrakhan before the address, the Mayor explained that his actions were the product of a long and deliberative look at how he could best calm the explosive situation. He did what he believed was right—the one criteria he was always true to throughout his career. Nonetheless, criticism would continue from Jewish leaders on the Farrakhan issue. It had been a difficult situation for Bradley, but in the final analysis, his solution was based on a strong sense of principle above the political pressure of any given interest group.

Bradley would continue to boast his mayoral accomplishments during his fourth term. In his 1986 State of the Economy speech, delivered at Los Angeles' Produce Mart, he stated: "Los Angeles has created new jobs more than twice as fast as the other major California population centers. . . . Job growth in manufacturing is over four times the national rate. The Los Angeles apparel industry is vibrant and growing, with 30,000 new workers and $2.6 billion in new sales. . . . Los Angeles is the gateway to the Pacific rim—a $3-trillion market that is growing at $3 billion a week. Our airport is the number-two cargo center in the world. And during my overseas travel I have boosted sales of Los Angeles products, from airplanes in Israel to radar systems in South Korea to agricultural products in Japan."

Bradley's increased appearances throughout the state served as evidence to reporters that he was laying the groundwork for another gubernatorial try. However, it was becoming increasingly evident that, while Bradley would again be a candidate, his statewide operation would feature new people. Mary Nichols, a former member of Governor Jerry Brown's cabinet, would be Campaign Manager. Tom Quinn would serve as Campaign Director, operating from an office in Hollywood under the name, "Friends of Tom Bradley."

Within the Democratic Party, those who had criticized the prospects for another gubernatorial bid by Bradley, promoting other candidates, quickly began to reposition themselves as supporters in early 1986. However, there had never been any doubt about his 1986 plans among his close friends and family—Tom Bradley would run again for Governor in 1986. The reason was simple: it was rooted deeply in his character to never give up.

The only situation in which Tom Bradley would ever accept a defeat as final was if he judged his opponent to be better qualified. It was this approach that had enabled him to come back against Hollingsworth in 1963 and Yorty in 1973. And, even though many friends and journalists would disagree with his conclusion, it was the reason Bradley had accepted Walter Mondale's choice of Geraldine Ferraro as his vice-presidential candidate in 1984. Given the timing and the political atmosphere, Bradley had agreed that Mondale would be better served with the New York Representative as his running mate.

But the four-year record of the incumbent Governor was more that of a mid-level bureaucrat or civil servant than the strong, creative leadership that California needed as it approached the twenty-first century. Where was the vision? What were the plans or goals of the Deukmejian administration? Instead of outlining positive programs, Deukmejian concentrated his efforts on attacking Bradley's character and integrity (in an uncharacteristically shrill manner for an incumbent) months away from the election. Bradley summed it up with a favorite phrase— "Words without deeds have no meaning."

Lorraine Bradley had felt sure of the rematch since the 1982 defeat. That had been the lowest she had ever seen her dad. Even though he had continued on what she liked to kid him as "automatic pilot" in public, his true feelings were visible at home. She had noticed it when she came over to pick up some of her mom's plants at Getty House. In his usual manner, he asked her about her class at Hollywood High and what her students were interested in; but for someone who had grown to know him so well over forty years, his eyes said it all. Yes, he had lost, but he could take a defeat. What bothered him was that his loss hadn't been on the basis of his merit or his record.

As she glanced at her father sitting in his chair, attempting to read through the stack of papers he always brought home with him, Lorraine glanced at the photo on the table beside him. It was from his days at UCLA—running the 440-yard dash. It had been a favorite of hers as she was growing up. When she was about ten, she had asked him what he was thinking about that had made him look so determined in the picture. He had told her then, and she remembered it at that moment—"Never give in, never give in, never, never, never—in nothing great or small, large or petty—never give in, except to convictions of honor and good sense."

She knew from that moment that her dad would not be satisfied until he had tried again, this time being sure that he was—as Bishop Brookins described it—"shooting his best shot."

He would not discuss the earlier defeat—nor his pain and sadness—with anyone, not even with his family. He had always been that way. Grandma Crenner had told Lorraine that her Daddy had never done much of that type of talking when he was growing up. That just wasn't his way. Instead he kept it inside. He just worked through the disappointment with the characteristic Bradley perseverance. For the most part, no one ever saw his love, compassion, and determination, except maybe those who knew him best and could understand his silences.

It had been frustrating to her, her sister, and especially to her mother (who certainly wasn't one to hold back on her feelings) not to be able to help out in some way. To Lorraine, it was surprising at times that her parents could be so different and still be able to get along and love each other the way they did. It must have been a special understanding that people acquired after being together for so many years.

That day in 1982, Lorraine had wanted her dad to know that she understood. She had leaned over, kissed him on the cheek, and whispered to him, "I'm sorry for you, daddy. I love you, and know that you will work your way through this." Bradley's eyes had glistened. He had smiled and said, "I know, honey, . . . I am just piecing it all together."

Ethel Bradley also knew intuitively that her husband would try again. One morning at the breakfast table, as she sipped her orange juice, she asked about his plans for Governor in 1986, and got no reply. His silence told her everything. He kept those decisions to himself. But there were subtle nuances to his silence—the extra spark of energy and vigor when he was pedaling his stationary bicycle, while reading the papers before work in the morning. There was also the inflection in his voice when he had spoken to children in the wake of the space-shuttle tragedy in February 1986, advising them to continue to reach for the stars in their goals. It was the theme of the speech he had planned to deliver on election night in 1982.

But there was also something within Ethel Bradley in 1986 that hadn't been there four years before—a good feeling about the future. For the first time in a long time, both of her daughters were happy and moving forward. The family had worked through some very difficult problems. She had never seen Tom happier, more confident, or as determined as he was now.

Bradley announced on February 25, 1986, that he would again seek his party's nomination for Governor of the Golden State, pledging new leadership and a proven partnership for the future. In his speech, he offered vision instead of vacillation, a state government serving as a beacon to the people's aspirations, rather than a barrier. Bradley once again set forth on his "impossible dream." And the indications of support from throughout the state suggested that millions of Californians were committed to "make it happen in 1986."

But whether or not Tom Bradley won the election would not be the man's personal measure of victory or defeat. He was, in his own eyes, already victorious. Failure was only a reluctance to try. His belief has always been that the future does not belong to the fainthearted, to those who are content with the present, but instead to those who dare to dream and believe in the impossible

To the skeptics and believers, his message was consistent and clear: "We have already done so much that people call dynamics, he would not be able to fly. But the bumblebee being unaware of scientific truths, goes ahead and flies anyway. If it is possible, we will do it here."

"Mr. Mayor—If politics get too rough, you can always sing with me. Thanks, Neil Diamond." (Bradley Family Collection)

Afterword

Tom Bradley is a very private man with an enameled determination to succeed. One trait prevalent throughout this book and which runs counter to human nature is Bradley's almost mechanical ability to steel himself from the doubt and depression most people would encounter in what he and his supporters often refer to simply as destiny. This passionate persistence has benefited Tom Bradley as he has progressed from temporary setback to victory. Yet, through the years it has also served to further bolster a seemingly impregnable wall that separates a public persona from the private individual.

This determined attitude has motivated many who have been touched by the man to push on toward their own hopes and dreams. And this fact seems to have even further intensified Bradley's own drive toward success. If he has ever second guessed a decision or temporarily experienced doubt as to his own ability or direction, only one person—Tom Bradley—is aware of it.

In the effort to search for a time in his life when this seemingly iron will was severely tested, hundreds of people were interviewed in the preparation of this book. Countless hours also were spent with the man himself, who, while approving of the project, nonetheless was clearly uneasy in talking about his private life outside the political arena. One obvious conclusion is that, over the years, more and more of Bradley's life has been consumed by his devotion to public service. It is also clear to us that there are many people from all walks of life who believe they have an impact on Tom Bradley—and they do. Yet, even though numerous webs of influence exist, it is, and always has been, Tom Bradley who makes his final decisions.

Bradley has never been one to open up to people—even to his closest friends and family. Yet, literally thousands of people throughout the world have good feelings, a sense of sharing in his successes, and a genuine caring and respect for a man known to have what Irving Stone calls "an annealing influence" on people. This ability to bring people together—to stress commonalities rather than differences—is one reason polls show Tom Bradley to be one of the most respected men in America.

Taking the time to talk about himself simply goes against Tom Bradley's nature, and this is undoubtedly a reason why attempts to do a biography on Bradley have gone awry. Instead of turning his attention to the past, Bradley is literally consumed by the concerns of the present, doing what his past record and history have shown him to do best—performing pragmatically in the political arena, determined to make a difference in policies affecting the general public. Such a commitment has strained his immediate family and affected his private life. But to those who know Tom Bradley, the man views himself as the head of an extended family that reaches far beyond Getty House or the family home on Welland in South Central Los Angeles. Over the years, Ethel and his two daughters have grown to accept this fact, at times with reluctance and at a personal price. Tom Bradley views himself as a public servant dedicated to doing the best job he can do, regardless of the time or the personal costs.

It is apparent, from the hundreds interviewed for the book, that those who have worked with Tom Bradley find his dedication infectious. Most were at a loss in offering a rationale for the countless weekends and holidays they have spent working to help Bradley realize a goal. It is as if underneath his veneer of disciplined composure lies a charismatic quality that has worked well for Bradley from his school days up to the present. A by-product of this shared experience is a special understanding of Bradley's favorite comments—that "deeds more than words carry life's real meaning."

The fact that many people—and especially children—look up to him as a role model serves to fuel Bradley's determined spirit. One notices that, when the topic of youth enters a conversation, Tom Bradley opens up. One gets a rare glance at his innermost feelings. The sparkle in his eye, the proudness that comes over his face as he recounts particular episodes of his own life, suggests that Tom Bradley readily identifies with this very special audience. He places a tremendous faith in a child's potential.

Friends and colleagues vividly recall Bradley's analytical

mind, and his prowess in negotiating to formulate a particular policy or to hammer out a specific solution. Nonetheless, they are hard pressed to recall an instance where Bradley talked freely about his personal feelings, his family, or his days growing up in poverty. In the course of writing this book, such events were difficult for Bradley—a man with an incredible memory—to conjure up in the course of interviews. It was as if Crenner and Lee's son had been programmed to put the painful details of the past behind him and remember only the ever-increasing success that he encountered in school, as a cop, and in politics. Tom Bradley prefers not to dwell on the past, but instead to have a forward focus—almost on an automatic pilot—toward realizing a goal he has earmarked.

Specifically, there is little detail or recall of the key events and circumstances of his early life—his father's departure from the family, possible flirtations with the temptations of youth, and other human aspects of this driven man. Even his closest colleagues of over thirty years were surprised to learn that Bradley has a living brother and that he was a photographer for Jimmy Durante in his youth, along with other stories that many of us might openly share with friends and acquaintances.

Some attribute Bradley's reticence to open up to shyness, a trait referred to in press reports as his tendency to appear "wooden." But to those who have grown to know and love Tom Bradley, there is only a shade of truth to such evaluations. While sometimes short in his words, Tom Bradley prefers that his own actions and deeds tell the story.

We have attempted here to bring together as much detail and perspective as possible in this, the first work on Bradley's life. That many people recognize Tom Bradley as a contemporary American hero testifies to the fact that he is a man of passioned determination. This book is only the first of what we believe will be many about Tom Bradley. During the course of our research, Ethel Bradley indicated that she would write her story. Her addition will bring to the public further insight into this most private yet remarkable man. Even with her contribution, the chronicle is yet to be written that offers important details and experiences from the first person perspective. It is our hope that Tom Bradley will eventually pick up the pen and record his own odyssey in quest of his impossible dream.

INDEX

City Council, Los Angeles, 44, 45, 57, 58, 59, 60, 61, 63, 64, 67, 68, 69, 70, 78, 89, 100, 110, 139, 142, 158, 159, 162, 179, 181, 189, 196, 211, 212, 217, 222, 223, 224, 281, 315, 318, 320, 325, 326, 339
City Development Department, Los Angeles, 167
City Economic Development Office (CEDO), 199
City government, Los Angeles, 210
City Hall, Los Angeles, 35, 60, 63, 65, 67, 70, 74, 78, 82, 84, 85, 87, 89, 92, 93, 99, 108, 110, 111, 112, 115, 116, 119, 129, 131, 135, 136, 137, 138, 139, 140, 141, 142, 147, 150, 151, 156, 160, 161, 164, 165, 167, 169, 176, 177, 189, 193, 199, 201, 206, 231, 233, 251
City Hall Open House, 147
City Loan Development Program, Los Angeles, 230
City News Service, 314
City Youth Advisory Council, Los Angeles, 162
Civic Center, Los Angeles, 98
Civic Center Project, Los Angeles, 81
Civilian Police Commission, 131
Civil War, 3, 109
Clayton, Janet, 315
Cleveland, 96
Cleaver, Eldridge, 104
Coast Guard, 35
Cochran, Johnnie, Jr., 328
Coffee Klatches, 89
Coliseum, Los Angeles Memorial, 1, 2, 25, 46, 212, 213, 214

College of Cardinals, 216
Collins, Eula, 115
Collins, Joe, 270
Colorado Springs, 219, 225
Columbia Pictures, 106
Comfort, Jerry, 165, 182
Commission on the Status of Women, the Mayor's, 160
Committee of Twenty Five, The, 149
Communist(s), 34, 35, 73, 82, 94, 95, 110, 115, 121, 123, 125, 305
Community Development Department, 230
Community Redevelopment Agency, Los Angeles, 141, 167
Conrad, Paul, cartoon, 28
Constitution, the U.S., 82
Consul General, China, 275
Consumer Affairs Bureau, 81
Convention Center, Los Angeles, 80
Cooke, Josephine, 123
coolie workers, 17
Cooper, Jackie, 101
Copley News Service, 342
Corman, James, 88, 91
Cornfield, John, 276
Corwin, Bruce, 117
Cory, Ken, 233, 286
Cosby, Bill, 101, 164
Costello, Dolores, 206
cotton, 2, 3, 4, 7
Count de Beaumont, 225
County Board of Supervisors, Los Angeles, 80, 139
County Federation of Labor, Los Angeles, 231
County Transportation Commission, Los Angeles, 326
Crabbe, Buster, 213
Cranston, Alan, 88, 92, 100, 196, 290, 335, 336
Cremins, Jerry, 196, 231

Crenshaw, 59, 60, 65, 342
Crenshaw Avenue, 67
Crenshaw Democratic Club, 44
Crocker Center, 141
Crowe, Brad, 140, 141
Cunningham, David F., 46, 159
Cunningham, Raye, 58, 68, 70, 71, 102, 118, 119, 148, 241, 245, 286, 314, 330, 333
Curb, Mike, 233, 234, 235
Curtis, Roland "Speedy," 63, 64, 69
Curtis, Tony, 100

Dale, Francis, 206, 261
Dallas, 2, 6
Dart, Justin, 222
David, John, 262
Davis, Ed, 131, 143, 158, 211, 229, 251, 327
Davis, Grace, 300
Davis, Grace Montanez, 192, 242
Davis, Gray, 117, 219
Davis, James, 34, 35, 52
Davis, Martin, 275
Davis, Marvin, 168
Davis, Sammy, Jr., 53, 101
Deghi, Trish, 251
Delta, Utah, 150
Democrat(s), 84, 91, 106, 113, 158, 171, 200, 208, 222, 227, 232, 233, 249, 259, 263, 266, 268, 274, 284, 285, 286, 289, 298, 299, 318, 320, 321, 335, 344
Democratic County Committee, 84
Democratic State Central Committee, California, 84
Democratic Club, 58
Democratic Convention, National, 115, 170, 231, 301
Democratic Gubernatorial nomination, 321, 335